Gareth Jude and Andrew Smith are an extraordinary combination of retail practitioners and have crafted *Retail Innovation Reframed*, a must-read for retailers in this fast-shifting landscape.
Paul Greenberg, Vice Chair, Federation of International Retail Associations

Essential reading for anyone who is frustrated by innovation not moving as fast or delivering as much success as needed. A helpful guide that will aid you in finding what is slowing things down and how to fix it.
Guy Russo, company chairman; former CEO, Kmart, Target and McDonald's Australia, and former President, McDonald's Greater China

If your business needs to change but so far has been unable to do so or if you serve a retail business that is having difficulty with the process of innovation, I commend this book to you.
Paul Zahra, CEO, Australian Retailers Association

Gareth Jude and Andrew Smith guide us on a journey through the art and science of retail reinvention – delivering both insight and application in a thoroughly readable way. If you are a transformation leader, read it.
Richard Umbers, former CEO, Myer

This is a book for all retailers, most especially for these times. What Gareth Jude and Andrew Smith have been able to replicate, quite remarkably, is the benefit of their careers' experience growing businesses, overlaid with in-depth case studies detailing innovation in all its forms and how it is achieved at scale. This is a step-by-step operating guide to introducing innovation as a process that can be enabled by all your company's leaders.
Peter Knock, retail company director

Many industries have been disrupted in recent years and none more so than retail. Businesses in this sector are having to dramatically transform the way they do things if they are to survive. In this groundbreaking book the authors present a practical road map to guide retailers as they seek to make the transition from the business models of the past. This is a plan of action that every retailer could benefit from following.

Martin Christopher, Emeritus Professor of Marketing and Logistics, Cranfield University, UK

Retail will change more in the next 10 years than it has in the last 1,000. *Retail Innovation Reframed* will enable retailers to not only navigate that change but thrive in uncertain times. The authors' extensive knowledge of retail, technology and innovation is brought together in a simple-to-follow model with comprehensive case studies and examples. An absolute must-read for retailers of all sizes.

Kelly Slessor, Founder and CEO, Shop You

As someone who has led retail teams at all levels for nearly three decades, I have often been sceptical of books that claim to have all the answers about how to run a great brick-and-mortar business – until today, that is. Gareth Jude and Andrew Smith have put all their expertise and bold but necessary ideas into this exceptionally well-written and actionable guide to success that will lead us forward into the future of great retail.

Ron Thurston, Vice President of Stores, INTERMIX

A road map to retail innovation success. Read the book, build on your retail business and be prepared for disruption. Of course you don't have to... survival is not mandatory.

Mark Finocchiaro, Managing Partner and Director, MyChemist

Retail Innovation Reframed

*How to transform operations and achieve
purpose-led growth and resilience*

Gareth Jude and Andrew Smith

KoganPage

First published in Great Britain and the United States in 2021 by Kogan Page Limited

2nd Floor, 45 Gee Street	122 W 27th St, 10th Floor	4737/23 Ansari Road
London	New York, NY 10001	Daryaganj
EC1V 3RS	USA	New Delhi 110002
United Kingdom		India
www.koganpage.com		

Kogan Page books are printed on paper from sustainable forests.

© Gareth Jude and Andrew Smith, 2021

The right of Gareth Jude and Andrew Smith to be identified as the authors of this work has been asserted by them in accordance with the Copyright, Designs and Patents Act 1988.

ISBNs
Hardback   978 1 3986 0092 8
Paperback   978 1 3986 0091 1
eBook   978 1 3986 0093 5

British Library Cataloguing-in-Publication Data

A CIP record for this book is available from the British Library.

Library of Congress Cataloging-in-Publication Data

Names: Jude, Gareth, author. | Smith, Andrew, author.
Title: Retail innovation reframed : how to transform operations and achieve
   purpose-led growth and resilience / Gareth Jude and Andrew Smith.
Description: London ; New York, NY : Kogan Page, 2021. | Includes
   bibliographical references and index. |
Identifiers: LCCN 2020051082 (print) | LCCN 2020051083 (ebook) | ISBN
   9781398600911 (paperback) | ISBN 9781398600928 (hardback) | ISBN
   9781398600935 (ebook)
Subjects: LCSH: Retail trade. | Strategic planning. | Organizational
   change.
Classification: LCC HF5429 .J83 2021 (print) | LCC HF5429 (ebook) | DDC
   658.8/7–dc23

Typeset by Integra Software Services, Pondicherry
Print production managed by Jellyfish
Printed and bound by CPI Group (UK) Ltd, Croydon CR0 4YY

CONTENTS

PART THREE
The different paths of innovation 203

10   Urgent innovation 205

11   Innovation in small retail businesses 235

12 Weaving innovation into the operating fabric of your business 263

Conclusion 277

Online resources to accompany this book are detailed in the relevant chapters
and can be accessed at:

www.koganpage.com/RIR

ABOUT THE AUTHORS

GARETH

Gareth got his first job in a retail store long ago in a land faraway from his current home in Sydney, Australia and has experienced retail from a number of perspectives. The last 20 years have been spent in a variety of management and consulting roles, including stints as CEO of an Australian sporting goods retailer and as group-wide Merchandise/Marketing and Store Planning Manager for the DSE division of Woolworth's. In the latter role, he led the launch of Australia's first full-range, fully trading website by a bricks and mortar retailer which facilitated omnichannel shopping before the word was invented.

Gareth is passionate about educating the next generation of retailers and has done so at Sydney, Macquarie, University of Technology Sydney and Shanghai Jiao Tong Universities.

In 2011 Gareth was appointed Retail Industry Executive in Telstra's Industry Development team. Telstra is Australia's largest telecommunications company which also operates the nation's largest network of telecommunications stores. At Telstra Gareth had the job of explaining the disruption of the retail industry both to the business and their many retail customers. He published six research papers into the digital disruption of the industry for Telstra and conceived and staged the annual Retail Innovation Summit in Sydney with partners Adobe, Grant Thornton, Intel, Microsoft and NORA.

In 2019 Gareth co-founded retail innovation agency ThinkUncommon with Andrew and became its Asia Pacific CEO. He is also a PhD candidate at the University of Sydney.

ANDREW

Andrew started his working life as a pilot, but quickly realized that he wanted to spend his time with people, not planes. He fell in love with the retail industry from the moment he started selling phones on the shop floor for Australia's largest telco. His passion for leading people led to management roles in his first year in the industry. Andrew went on to perform several central-support leadership roles from technology, innovation, operations, productivity and workforce management, ultimately becoming the

Head of Retail Operations for Telstra in Australia in 2014 at the age of 30. It was in this role that Andrew led the team that opened Telstra's internationally recognized and award-winning flagship stores, as well as a successful innovation strategy that boosted customer experience, sales performance and productivity and reduced operating costs.

In 2017 Andrew, with his passion and skills for bringing together human behaviour and traditional data to create more human brand experiences, took on a transformation role to create Telstra's customer experience strategy. After moving to the United States in 2018 to help improve and learn from the retail industry there, he co-founded retail innovation agency ThinkUncommon with Gareth, and became its regional leader in North and South America.

FOREWORD

I have been in the retail industry all my life and am passionate about the opportunities it offers. More than 1.3 million working Australians are employed in retail. The sector is Australia's largest employer of young people, and well over half of those employed in retail are women. Retail offers diverse and flexible career opportunities, everything from your first job, to a job in data analytics, merchandising or supply chain and logistics. The 2020 COVID-19 pandemic has reminded us all of how much our society relies on the retail industry to keep us fed, clothed, healthy and safe.

My own retail career began as a casual shop assistant at Target aged 16. I became a store manager at age 22 then went on to senior leadership roles at Target, Officeworks and David Jones where I eventually became CEO. Since then I have been a board member, advisor and now serve as the CEO of the Australian Retailers Association.

In the last twenty years, I have seen first-hand the disruption and transformation of the retail sector as a result of ongoing changes in technology, consumer behaviour, and the increased impact of strong global retail brands expanding into markets around the world. The combined effect has been to create more competition, a new type of shopper empowered by knowledge and choice and new ways for retailers to serve their customers and run their businesses more efficiently.

It is true that some established retailers have had difficulty adjusting to the new retail environment and some have paid the price. The failure of several high-profile retail brands in the last few years has led to a negative narrative around the industry that is unwarranted. Retail is not dying – it's growing. In Australia, up until 2020, retail has had an unbroken 30-year period of growth, a record few other large industries can match. For every high-profile failure there is a lower-profile success. What excites me is the untold story of innovation, whether in store formats, in online marketplaces, or the many small businesses that started life in someone's living room.

The retail industry does need to reframe if it is to meet the challenges of the 21st century. The old paradigms of range, price, service and customer proximity need to be augmented with new paradigms like blending digital and physical experiences, creating purposeful business models and leveraging technology to serve customers better and more efficiently. To do this, retailers need to know how to change.

What excites me about this book is for the first time it provides retailers with a handbook on how to innovate. There is plenty of information available to us all about what innovation is and what retailers should do about it, but this is the first book that shows retailers how to actually do it.

When we learn how to do anything in life, we become confident, optimistic and empowered. When we learn how to innovate, we see disruption in the environment as an opportunity not a threat, and approach the future with optimism not fear. When that happens, we can leave behind the unwarranted negative narrative that surrounds our industry and replace it with one of hope and opportunity.

If your business needs to change but so far has been unable to do so, or if you serve a retail business that is having difficulty with the process of innovation, I commend this book to you.

Paul Zahra
CEO, Australian Retailers Association

ACKNOWLEDGEMENTS

We would like to thank the following people who have provided invaluable guidance, feedback and inspiration to us in the writing of this book:

Charles Bowie

John Chambers

Martin Christopher

Janet Clough

Leon Condon

Zoltan Csaki

Jon Devine

Jacques Dumont

Tom Erskine

Stephen Eyears

Mark Finocchiaro

Jodie Frew

Sina Klug

Peter Knock

Ken Kuperstein

Marcy Larsen

Michael Shafran

Henry Shiner

Kelly Slessor

Matt Spencer

Jon Stine

Ron Thurston

Richard Umbers

Jean-Baptiste Vincent

Kath Walters

Paul Zahra

To the late Jeff Grover, my former boss, who taught me that there are no rewards in life for a bright idea. All the rewards are on execution.
– Gareth

To my mum, Jan, who taught me how to be a good and caring human. To my dad, Mac, who taught me how to be a thoughtful leader with unwavering drive. To Nelia, Dene, Damian and Cara for putting up with my constant need to debate everything. It made me smarter. To my amazing partner, Kirsten, who inspires me every day and who read every word and did every exercise five times because she is annoyingly incredible. My love, my promise to you is that one day I will learn where to put those commas. Finally, to you, the reader. You obviously love retail like we do, which means we are colleagues on this adventure.
– Andrew

Introduction

This is a book for those who love the retail industry but are feeling pain. It's for those who love the pace, excitement and honesty of retail, but are struggling with industry disruption, seeing old ways of doing business become ineffective and the decline and failure of long-established retail brands. Importantly, this book is for those not wanting their business to be next.

If that is you, this book will re-ignite your love of the industry and show you that there *is* a way to deal with the disruption and turn it to your advantage. Above all, this book is for those retail innovation evangelists who can see the opportunities offered by disruption and crises but who so far have only experienced obstacles, limited success and frustration in their attempts to **ReFRAME** their business. This book is your 'how to' guide to getting retail innovation done and done well.

If your business is trying to adapt to the new world of retail but not succeeding, there is no time to lose. Failure to adapt will lead to a loss of customers or loss of margin while you try to hold onto them. You will cut expenses to balance the books then lose more customers or margin as your offer deteriorates. It is the retail death spiral and it's happening to many well-known retailers in plain sight, wherever in the world you are reading this. If you have not already been disrupted by pandemics, new competitors or new business formats, it's only a matter of time. Now is the time to act.

This book will show you how to give your business what has so far been uncommon in the retail industry – the ability to change how your organization thinks and works. It will show you how to make a compelling case to your stakeholders that innovation is the only viable strategic choice in today's retail environment. It will teach you how to implement a programme of retail innovation that sticks and – most importantly – will show you how to transition your business from an occasional implementer of innovative projects to a perpetual retail innovator. You will learn how to weave an innovation culture and processes into the operating fabric of your business so that you are always ready to take advantage of changes in the external environment and will never again become a victim.

If you love retail but feel the pain, we both walk in your shoes. Both authors are retailers and have been in the thick of digital disruption and retail innovation for most of our careers. We have seen innovation work and seen it fail. We have seen retail organizations transform themselves with innovative initiatives only for new leaders to change course and abandon innovation in favour of cost cutting. We have experienced the power of aligned stakeholders backed by resources as well as destructive blocking forces who resist change at all costs. It is our experience as shopkeepers that has led us to conclude that sustainable retail innovation is not achieved by finding inspirational ideas or inspirational leaders, but through implementing processes that are observable and repeatable.

About this book

This book will explain how to embed innovation into your business through our *ReFRAME* process. *ReFRAME* will show you how to build the launch-pad for your quest, how to find the most sustainable innovation ideas in which to invest your resources, how to get ready to take your initiatives to market, the right way to analyse and test, how to design for scale and how to embed innovation as your new normal. Finally, we will explain how to weave innovation into the operating fabric of your business so that innovation becomes perpetual rather than episodic. Along the way, we provide all the evidence and tools you will need to deal with the naysayers and to inspire your colleagues and other stakeholders to join with you in the quest. Let us begin.

Why the retail industry needs to reframe

In Part One we show why the retail industry is highly sensitive to change in the external environment. Failure to adapt to change can have disastrous consequences, but established retailers do not have a good record of being able to innovate.

We then discuss the reasons why retailers find it hard to innovate, which lie partly in the way their businesses operate. The nature of the retail trade means operators value execution over strategy, short-term thinking over long-term planning, and are driven by process. These characteristics can stifle innovation but we argue that they can be turned into an advantage if innovation is conceived as a process. The core proposition of this book is that retail innovation is not attributable to moments of inspiration or super-human leadership but to observable and repeatable processes.

We then provide an overview of our *ReFRAME* process of retail innovation.

01

Why retail needs to be reframed

(GARETH)

Introduction

Throughout history, the retail industry has been defined by disruption and crises in the external environment. Whenever the external environment changes, it presents opportunities for the adaptable and threats for those who cannot or will not change. When the industrial revolution created an urban middle class, it created the opportunity for the department store format and began the long-term decline of urban markets. When post Second World War prosperity allowed families to buy automobiles, it created the opportunity for the supermarket and shopping mall formats and began the long-term decline of strip shopping. When the 2003 SARS epidemic meant many Chinese consumers were forced to try online shopping for the first time, it created the impetus for the growth of Alibaba and JD.com and the transformation of shopping in China forever.[1]

As we enter the 2020s, the retail industry is arguably more disrupted than at any time in its history. Globalization has meant more of the world's best retailers are trading in geographies remote from their home base. Technology has created new ways for customers to shop and for retailers to serve their customers. The COVID-19 pandemic has created a shock to economic and social systems whose long-term effects are only beginning to play out. But the underlying problem facing the industry is not the disruption created by new technology, globalization, new forms of competition or the COVID-19 pandemic. The underlying problem for retailers is developing the organizational capability to innovate and reframe so that, whatever the disruption, it can be approached as an opportunity and not an existential threat.

The retail industry needs to be constantly reframed to be more relevant to its customers. Just like a favourite old family photograph comes alive when it's surrounded by a new, contemporary picture frame, so too the retail industry comes alive when it surrounds itself with what really matters to customers. Retailers who develop the capacity to innovate and reframe will thrive, while those that don't will die. In head-to-head contests, like Walmart vs Sears, Domino's vs Pizza Hut (Australia), Netflix vs Blockbuster or Mecca vs Napoleon Perdis, it will be the retailer who has the ability to innovate and reframe who wins.

In this chapter we will explain why retail is defined by disruption and crisis, why we think reframe is a better word than transformation to describe what the industry needs, why there is a difference between knowing what's going on and understanding how to change and why gaining the organizational ability to innovate is the biggest challenge facing the industry in 2021. Finally, we explain why, far from being risky, innovation is actually retail's new safe place.

Retail is defined by disruption and crisis: Adapt or die

Clayton Christensen in his classic book *The Innovator's Dilemma*[2] distinguishes between different types of disruption. He says that successful companies are generally good at dealing with evolutionary change in the environment ('sustaining innovation') but not at dealing with revolutionary change ('disruptive innovation'). In retail, every disruption in the external environment has the potential to pose an existential threat. The more fundamental the disruption, the more radical the reaction required.

Large disruptions in the external environment create an obvious threat to retailers who do not adapt. Failing retailers often cite economic crises as the reason for poor results, but in reality, these events are rare. Between 1995–2020, until the COVID-19 pandemic, there was only one recession in the USA (2008–9[3]) and some countries like Australia and China avoided recession altogether. When a genuine economic crisis hits it can be very hard to survive, but most of the disruption retailers face comes from factors other than economic crises. Even relatively small changes in the external environment can create an existential threat to retailers if they are unable or chose not to adapt.

Self-service supermarkets first emerged in the USA in the 1930s. By the late 1940s they had reached Britain, and by the 1950s they were seen throughout the western world.[4] The first self-service supermarkets were not the 4,000 square metre, automobile friendly formats that became mainstream in the 1970s, but much smaller 150 to 250 square metre stores which were often re-purposed grocery spaces. The main innovation in early supermarkets was having customers serve themselves rather than be served by a grocer. This made self-service supermarkets much more cost efficient than a traditional grocer and that cost advantage was translated into lower prices.

As a young boy I remember shopping with my mother at a surviving grocer in my hometown. Cheese was cut, weighed and wrapped. Each tin or packet on my mother's list was picked from the shelf by the grocer and eventually packed in her bag and money exchanged. The shopping experience was similar to what you might expect today in a gourmet deli. When self-service came to my town the grocer didn't last long. Even though he was a very experienced operator and offered superior customer service, his offer was no match for the lure of lower prices on everyday items. The grocer chose not to change and it wasn't long before he didn't exist. I seem to remember the space he occupied on the strip was replaced by an electrical store (which also no longer exists!).

Consumers are like heat-seeking missiles for value. When retailers offer better overall value than their competitors consumers flock to it and there is little loyalty to previous shopping habits.

When an industry faces an existential threat, it does not mean the extinction of the entire species. Many businesses are able to reframe for the new environment. Australia's Holden motor company was originally founded in 1856 as a saddlery manufacturer, but successfully adapted to the automobile age by switching to the manufacturing of cars in 1908.[5] Similarly, Japan's Fujifilm, as the name suggests, had a business founded in film technology, but successfully adapted by investing heavily in digital photography and leveraging its knowledge of film technology to diversify into new areas of business (notably medical imaging).[6] Others operating in the same market were not so fortunate. The names of Holden's nineteenth century saddlery competitors who did not adapt are now forgotten, but Fujifilm's arch-rival, Kodak, is remembered as one of the greatest examples in modern business history of a failure to adapt to an existential threat.

Some established retailers adapt to disruption better than others. Large, established retailers such as Walmart, Target (USA), Nike, Inditex and Lush have thrived through the disruption created by globalization and the internet, while their competitors in the same sector struggle. The success of Walmart and Target (USA) contrasts starkly with the struggles of discount department stores, Sears and Kmart. Nike is kicking goals while sports retailers like Sports Authority are on the ropes. Inditex is soaring high compared with fashion retailers like Nine West and Jaeger. And the success of Lush contrasts with the demise of cosmetics retailers like Napoleon Perdis.[7]

Business failure in retail is a natural part of the competitive landscape. When a retail business serves its customers better and operates its business more efficiently than its competition, it will always win customers and be more profitable than its rivals. Eventually it might even close its competition down. This has been happening for thousands of years. However, when there is disruption to the environment, simply doubling down on the old ways of doing business will not work. When disruption comes along, retailers need to reframe their businesses to solve different consumer problems. Throughout this book we will demonstrate that the difference between success and failure in a disrupted environment is not down to the execution of retail basics, but the ability to reframe.

Some retail sectors may seem immune from threats facing the industry, but they are not. It is only a question of degree and time. Supermarkets, for example, still seem to be able to operate successfully under the old range, price and proximity paradigm. But while the internet has yet to take any significant share of traditional supermarket sales, online grocery sales are growing fast and far outpace the growth of sales in bricks and mortar stores. In Australia, for example, online grocery sales grew 24.5 per cent in 2018 and are predicted to experience compound annual growth in revenue (CAGR) of 10 per cent in the five years to 2023.[8] In other countries, like South Korea, with superior internet speeds and last mile delivery infrastructure, online sales of fast-moving consumer goods (FMCG) items already exceed 20 per cent of the total.[9] Those supermarkets that choose to continue to operate under the old paradigm will forgo growth opportunities and may find themselves unprepared to compete when environmental conditions trigger a behavioural shift by consumers in their markets.

The services sector is one area of retail that may be immune from technological threats for now. Many of the established stores that are closing on the high street or in the mall are being replaced by hairdressers, nail bars and spas. These are hands on, pure services that are unlikely to be available online in the foreseeable future. However, even in these cases, the internet has had an influence. 'Do it yourself kits' accompanied by 'how to' YouTube videos[10] are available for a number of retail services like hair styling but – so far – their influence has been minimal. The good news for the industry as a whole is that these pure service-based retailers keep foot traffic in shopping precincts, keep the habit of going out to 'shop' alive and give goods-based retailers with bricks and mortar outlets a chance to attract those shoppers to their stores.

EXERCISE
The impact of disruption

What this is

A self-survey to calculate how affected your business is by disruption in the retail environment.

Instructions

Rate yourself 1–10 on the questions in Table 1.1 then repeat the exercise for a retailer in another sector and compare the results.

TABLE 1.1 The impact of disruption

Question	Your response									
	(scale is referenced in the question)									
1. Does your mix of business consist of services, goods, or is it somewhere in between? (10 = purely of goods, 1 = purely of services)	1	2	3	4	5	6	7	8	9	10
2. Is competition in your sector based on range and price, on other factors, or is it somewhere in between? (10 = purely on range and price, 1 = purely on other factors that are not range and price)	1	2	3	4	5	6	7	8	9	10

(continued)

TABLE 1.1 (Continued)

Question	Your response									
	(scale is referenced in the question)									
3. How vulnerable is your business to online competition? (10 = highly vulnerable, 1 = not vulnerable)	1	2	3	4	5	6	7	8	9	10
4. How successfully did your business deal with the impacts of the COVID-19 epidemic compared to your competitors? (10 = very poorly, 1 = very well)	1	2	3	4	5	6	7	8	9	10
5. Rate your business's capacity to execute significant change (10 = very poor, 1 = excellent)	1	2	3	4	5	6	7	8	9	10
6. Are your sales in decline or on the rise compared with last year? (10 = steeply declining, 1 = steeply rising)	1	2	3	4	5	6	7	8	9	10
7. How would you rate your business's adoption of digital technologies, eg ecommerce, social media, digital marketing? (10 = very poor, 1 = excellent)	1	2	3	4	5	6	7	8	9	10
8. Has your business reviewed and changed its purpose in an effort to be more relevant to its stakeholders? (10 = not changed at all, 1 = completely changed)	1	2	3	4	5	6	7	8	9	10
9. Is your business's reaction to falling sales to try harder using existing techniques or try something new? (10 = try harder, 1 = try new)	1	2	3	4	5	6	7	8	9	10
10. To what extent is the culture of your business proudly traditional or 'old school'? (10 = extremely old school, 1 = completely innovative)	1	2	3	4	5	6	7	8	9	10

Results

- *Score 10–39:* Congratulations! You have recognized changes in the environment and are making appropriate changes to address them. Be vigilant. The new world will be just as competitive as the old world. You need to be prepared for new competition that solves problems even better than you do.

- *Score 40–69:* There are some signs that the business recognizes the importance of adapting to disruption. You probably know what to do. It's time to pick up the pace of doing it.
- *Score 70–100:* Your business is locked into the past and does not take seriously the existential threat posed by disruption and crises. You urgently need to understand the new retail environment and acquire the ability to change.

The biggest barriers to moving ahead with reframing your business are internal and external stakeholders who believe that there are no existential threats and the best way to solve any retail problem is by the better execution of traditional strategies. You may be one of them. If so, we hope this book causes you to question your beliefs, but we're not going to try to persuade you to change them. Instead this book is for retailers and their partners who recognize the need to change, want to change, but need to know how it's done.

What is a retail reframe?

I used to work for a company that manufactured and distributed picture frames to retailers. We also operated a retail outlet that sold our standard frames as well as offering a custom-made service. What I learned while I worked in the business is that the effect of reframing an old picture can be transformative, but only if the right combination of elements is selected. That's quite an art. There's the style of frame to consider. Should it be a decorative Italian style moulding or something more contemporary? What size, colour and style of mat do you want the picture itself to sit on and should the mat be single or double? What style and quality of glass do you want the picture to be displayed under and what style and quality of backing board should be selected? Getting the elements right is the difference between having something that looks great and something very ordinary.

While I worked for the business, I took the opportunity to reframe many of my own pictures. I was lucky to have a lot of help from work colleagues in getting the choices right. The new frames not only enhanced the pictures themselves, but also enhanced the look and feel of our whole home. At the same time, we also bought some new pictures – which of course came with new frames and set the standard for the reframing we had done. That was a while ago. Times have changed. Looking around the house today I think some of those pictures could be due for another reframe!

The established retail industry is like a picture hanging on a wall in a tired old frame. Many people find it unattractive because it is framed by attributes like range, price and proximity that are not quite as important as they once were. It looks especially tired hanging next to new retail pictures framed in all the bright, relevant attributes of the contemporary world like digital/physical integration, experiences and purpose. There is nothing inherently wrong with the old retail frame – in fact, the new retail frame incorporates the same basic attributes, but it is more attractive than the old one that hangs beside it.

We think 'reframe' is a better word to describe what needs to happen to the established retail industry than words other authors have used – think transformation, evolution, revolution and innovation. The word 'transformation' can be used interchangeably with reframe (and we do use it in this book), but it can also be used to describe creating something completely new. We do not believe that is what's required. The old retail foundations of range, price and proximity are no longer enough to win in the new world of retail, but you cannot compete without them. The industry does not need to be transformed.

The word 'evolution' is also somewhat transferable with reframe; however, evolution suggests change through a natural process. As we will see throughout this book, if traditional retailers are to survive it will be as a result of deliberate acts – not as a result of natural selection. In that sense, we are not seeing a retail evolution.

The word 'revolution' suggests that the old order must be thrown out completely, but we argue that there is no evidence that proves this is the case. Retailers like Walmart and IKEA who have reframed have not abandoned their traditional focus on price while Nike has not abandoned its traditional focus on product. Retail does not need a revolution.

The word 'innovation' is more useful to us, but it is a complement to the idea of reframing – not a substitute. While reframe describes an overall outcome, innovation describes the deliberate acts retailers must make to achieve a reframe. Innovation is how you get a reframe done and that is the main focus of this book.

CASE STUDY
Reframing Walmart

The story of Walmart between 2010 and 2020 is a good example of what a retail reframe looks like. In 2002 Walmart surpassed Exxon-Mobil as the largest company in the world by sales.[11] It was already the largest retailer in the world by some margin. Walmart's customer proposition was based on low prices, a wide range of products (more than 20,000 stock keeping units (SKUs) in the average supercentre), and closer proximity to the majority of the US population than its competitors, Target and Kmart.[12] This was all underpinned by an emphasis on efficiency throughout the supply chain that made their cost of doing business lower than their rivals.

By 2009 things were beginning to change. Sales growth had slowed to low single digits, unlike the double-digit growth experienced earlier in the decade[13] and, in the wake of the global financial crisis of 2007–08, Exxon-Mobil had regained their 'biggest company in the world by sales' title. More worryingly, the question was being asked, 'Is Walmart good for America?' This question was the title of a TV documentary first aired in 2004[14] and the subject of a documentary film of the next year.[15] Criticism ranged from suppliers being forced to source non-domestically due to low buy price requirements, high-paying American manufacturing jobs being replaced by low-paying service industry roles, labour union objections, poor working conditions and environmental concerns. This all came despite the fact that Walmart continued to deliver on its core customer promise of lower prices on a large range of everyday goods.

As a consequence Walmart began a journey of adding social purpose and digital capability to their business model. Walmart now has sustainability goals. In 2017 it announced Project Gigaton, which has the aim of taking 1 trillion metric tonnes of carbon out of the system by 2030. Walmart had already taken out over 20 million metric tons in collaboration with suppliers between 2010 and 2015.[16] In addition, Walmart has embarked on a programme to be supplied energy from renewable sources and in some countries has set a zero per cent waste goal.

Walmart has invested in improved pay, conditions and training for associates, gained a digital capability through the acquisition of Jet.com, Bonobos, shoes.com and others, is making investments in technology like AI to improve customer experiences and store efficiency, and continues to foster a culture of change in the business.

In 2018, Walmart reported its best comp store growth[17] for a decade and online sales growth of 40 per cent. Walmart's customer proposition is still based on low prices, a wide range of products, close proximity (now physical and online) to the majority of the US population and is still underpinned by an emphasis on efficiency throughout the supply chain, but things have changed. In addition to those traditional attributes, Walmart now operates in digital as well as physical channels and strives to serve customers who use both. It has incorporated sustainability and ethical sourcing in its supply chain and has improved conditions for its associates. Walmart is still Walmart, but it has been reframed for the 21st century.

Making the case for a reframe

Some established retailers might believe that there is no need to reframe to compete. They look at new entrants to the industry and see operators who often have no retail experience, seem unable to make a profit and are more concerned with attracting investment than the nuts and bolts of running a good retail business. They may feel, as in the past, that as long as they keep doing what they have been doing well, they can see off this new competition. Unfortunately for them, the world has changed. New criteria will determine who wins and, without a reframe, traditional retailers are likely to be the losers.

Other established retailers may recognize what's going on in the industry but feel a lack of competition in their sector protects them from reframing for now. These retailers may have achieved a dominant competitive position through acquisition, by being better than their competition or by operating in such a specialized niche that it is unattractive for others to enter. All these circumstances are temporary because retail is an inherently competitive industry. It has few barriers to entry, consumers regularly switch their spend between retailers and between categories, competition between retailers is normally intense and overall sales are not concentrated in the hands of a small number of players as, say, in the telco, oil or banking industries. In fact, retail fulfils most of the conditions for an intensively competitive market as described by Michael Porter in his famous five forces model.[18] In this environment, monopolies or quasi monopolies will not be tolerated. When Jeff Bezos tells other retailers 'Your margin is my opportunity'[19] he is simply expressing the natural order in a competitive market.

How do you make the case for a reframe in your business? First think about how urgent the need is. Are you behind compared with your competitors or does your position in the market mean you have some time? This will determine if you need to be considered (you have some time) or passionately emotional (the platform's burning) in your approach. Next think about the reasons no action has been taken up to now. Is it symptomatic of an executive team and board who are supremely confident of their ability to handle threats the way they always have, are they unaware of why they need to reframe or are they in denial? Whatever your particular circumstances, research some cases, preferably from your sector and preferably from overseas (less threatening), where reframing has created big benefits or a failure to reframe has led to disaster (examples of both will be coming up later in the book). Wherever you sit in the management hierarchy, well researched and/or passionate exhortations to act are usually regarded as a sign of initiative and ambition and should enhance rather than harm your standing in the business. First prize would be getting to lead the reframing of your own business and how cool would that be! We know because that did in fact happen to one of the authors of this book. More on that later.

The difference between knowing 'what' and knowing 'how'

There has been so much written and said about the disruption of the retail industry that most retailers should understand what is changing in their world. Authors such as Robin Lewis and Michael Dart have explained the forces disrupting the current retail environment and put the whole of modern retail history into context so those waves of change can be understood.[20] Others such as Doug Stephens have explained what they think the future holds for retail.[21] Consulting companies large and small have produced research aimed at explaining the changing retail environment. Vendors to the retail sector including transport and logistics companies, post offices, banks, real estate companies and tech vendors have produced whitepapers on how disruption in the retail sector will affect their customers. Others have produced indexes to track changes in the retail environment on a month-to-month or year-to-year basis.[22] You will find all of the above – and more – speaking about the changing retail environment at retail conferences and, as if that's not enough, it's also possible to attend formal retail study tours to see best practice from around the world for yourself.

While there is no shortage of available knowledge about the disruption of the industry, there has been a shortage of action. This is reflected in the poor representation of retailers in compilations of the world's most innovative companies. In annual lists like Forbes' 'World's most innovative companies', Fast Company's 'World's 50 most innovative companies' and BCG's 'Most innovative companies', retailers make up only 6 to14 per cent of the total when, in fact, they make up a much bigger percentage of total businesses. More importantly, the gap between knowledge and action is reflected in the continuing failure and decline of well-known retail brands in the face of more innovative competition.

Knowing what is going on, but not knowing how to respond, can lead to feelings of helplessness. In the case of retailers who have tried to innovate and failed, it could be argued that they are experiencing feelings of learned helplessness.[23] Learned helplessness is a psychological concept first observed in dogs. It describes a failure to try to perform a task because of a learned, often irrational, fear of negative consequences. Retailers observing the seemingly inexorable rise of new competitors like Amazon, the failure of long-established retail brands, the daily negative media narrative about the retail industry – and conditioned by their own failed attempts at change – can give up trying. The purpose of this book is to give retailers hope. There is a way to compete in the new environment and that is by innovating and reframing your business. We will demonstrate that retail innovation is a process like any other retail process that any business with knowledge of where they want to head can implement.

EXERCISE
Knowledge and action

What this is

Ascertain the size of the gap between knowledge and action in your business.

Instructions

In Table 1.2, for each statement on knowledge, there is a scoring scale. Select the score for each one that is most reflective of you and add your score together. The results index is below the table.

TABLE 1.2 Identify the gap between knowledge and action in your business

Knowledge	Score
1. Have you and your peers read books about how disrupted the retail environment is? (Rate your knowledge gained from books on a scale of 0–10 where 0 = never have read a book on retail disruption and 10 = we have read many books on retail disruption)	
2. Have you read reports or seen presentations from consulting companies or your vendors about how disruption is affecting the retail industry? (Rate your knowledge gained from consultants and vendors on a scale of 0–10 where 0 = never have read or seen a presentation on retail disruption from a consultant or vendor and 10 = we have seen many of these reports and presentations)	
3. Do you attend conferences where aspects of retail disruption are discussed? (Rate your knowledge gained from conferences on a scale of 0–10 where 0 = we never go to conferences where retail disruption is discussed and 10 = we have attended many of these conferences)	
4. Have you taken the opportunity to observe and understand retail best practice, either independently or as part of a study tour? (Rate your knowledge gained from observing and understanding retail best practice on a scale of 0–10 where 0 = we never actively observe or seek to understand best practice and 10 = we regularly seek to observe and understand best practice and participated in study tours)	
Overall score (out of 40)	

Results

- *Score 0–10:* You really should get out more. The world of retail is constantly changing and the first step to competing is understanding those changes.

- *Score 11–20:* You understand at least some of the changes affecting your industry. Maybe you feel you know enough and need to concentrate on action in your business, and, if so, congratulations. Maybe you feel you haven't got time for reading books or reports, attending presentations or conferences or studying best practice. If so, you need to make time. Simply working harder won't be enough because the rules of the game are always changing and you need to learn them.

- *Score 21–30:* You are well informed about the changes in the retail environment. The next step is to turn your knowledge into action.

- *Score 31–40:* Retail disruption black belt! Industry colleagues probably look to you as a source of wisdom on what is happening in the industry. The question is: have you been able to turn your knowledge into action for your own business or just into speaking engagements at conferences?

Whatever your score, it is now time to think about what your business is doing to turn the knowledge you collectively have about the disrupted retail environment into action. Is there a gap between knowledge and action and, if so, how big is it? If there is a gap, what do you believe are the main reasons for it? Has your business tried to implement change but failed? Is there a sense of helplessness about what needs to be done and your ability to do it?

If there is no gap or you are in surplus, it could either mean there's a deficit of knowledge in your business (unlikely) or that you are one of those uncommon retailers who already match knowledge with action. For the rest of us, we can start closing the gap with a few simple steps:

- The next time you read a book or report, listen to a conference presentation or see an example of best practice in action, take the time to write, in your own words, a short reflection on the knowledge you have gained. (We all mean to do this, but how often do we neglect to do it?) The act of writing it down will force you to think through what you just experienced and begin the process of articulating its importance to others in the team. It will also become a knowledge bank you can come back to at a later date. Put these reflections in folders in your computer with headings that mean something to you, such as store operations, merchandising, supply chain, payments, etc.

- Decide what parts of your new knowledge are important enough to be shared with the team. Don't share everything all the time. Your colleagues are busy like you. They will start to avoid you in the corridor if you habitually share absolutely everything you read, hear and see without a filter.

- Set up a time each month, either as part of your regular team meetings or as a separate session, to share knowledge you have all gained from any source in the previous period. Select any pieces of knowledge that, as a group, you feel need to be turned into action.

- Have your manager articulate your knowledge for action ideas in their own management meeting.

The biggest challenge facing the retail industry

The biggest challenge facing the retail industry is not the internet, the economy, COVID-19, globalization, new competition, new technology, government regulations or any other factor in the external environment, but rather acquiring the organizational ability to innovate and reframe. All the external factors ever do is give everybody the same opportunity. When a business gains the organizational ability to innovate, they can reframe to give themselves the best chance of adapting to any changes that may happen externally. Organizational ability to innovate means having embedded processes that ensure innovation can be operationalized quickly and the flow of new initiatives keeps coming. Without these embedded processes, any attempts to reframe are likely to fail. We argue that the inability to reframe is the underlying reason behind many high-profile retail business failures, empty shops and the parade of retail CEOs presenting their latest set of bad results. It's not the external environment that is causing these retailers to struggle because it's the same environment that's allowing other retailers to thrive – it's the lack of embedded innovation processes.

Some believe that innovation is about inspirational ideas and inspirational leaders, and not about organizational ability. There is nothing wrong with inspirational leaders or inspirational ideas, but they are rare. They are also often no match for organizations that simply don't have the ability to innovate. These organizations often have old ways of thinking so embedded in their processes and culture that innovation doesn't stand a chance. Match an inspirational leader and an inspirational idea with embedded processes of innovation and you have an unbeatable combination.

Conclusion

In this chapter we learned that the retail industry faces constant disruption from the external environment and retailers need to learn to adapt or die. Adapting means reframing your business for the new environment. Reframing doesn't mean throwing away traditional retail fundamentals – it means adding new capabilities that respond to the changing environment. Knowing 'what' is happening in the retail environment is much less important than knowing 'how' to change because acquiring the organizational capacity to change is by far the most important challenge facing the industry. Those retailers who have it are thriving while those that don't are failing.

There will be barriers to achieving change from internal and external stakeholders. Some will believe that retail does not need to be reframed, but that doubling down on traditional fundamentals is the way to cope with the disrupted environment. Others will believe that reframing simply means finding the best new ideas in the market or hiring an inspirational leader rather than building an innovation culture and processes in your business. It's time to take on the responsibility of convincing stakeholders that the biggest challenge facing the industry is acquiring the ability to innovate.

In the next chapter we look at why innovation can be particularly hard for retailers, but how the blockers of innovation built into retail operating models can be turned into an advantage in your innovation quest. Innovation is risky and unfamiliar but it is the new safe place for retailers.

Notes

1   Huddelstone Jr, TH (2020) The SARS epidemic threatened Alibaba's survival in 2003 – here's how it made it through to become a $470 billion company, CNBC, 26 March [Online] https://www.cnbc.com/2020/03/26/chinas-2002-2003-sars-outbreak-helped-alibaba-become-e-commerce-giant.html (archived at https://perma.cc/5929-5D2M)

2   Christensen, CM (1997) *The Innovator's Dilemma: When new technologies cause great firms to fail*, Harvard Business School Press, Boston, MA

3   Amaedo, K (2020) US GDP by year compared to recessions and events, The Balance, 13 March [Online] https://www.thebalance.com/us-gdp-by-year-3305543 (archived at https://perma.cc/S262-GJP5)

4   Groceteria (2009) A quick history of the supermarket, 4 July [Online] https://www.groceteria.com/about/a-quick-history-of-the-supermarket/ (archived at https://perma.cc/794Q-FDPB)

5   ABC News (2014) Timeline: Holden's history in Australia, 11 February [Online] https://www.abc.net.au/news/2013-12-11/timeline-holden-history/5150240 (archived at https://perma.cc/Q2JW-WHJR)

6   Inagaki, K and Osawa, J (2012) Fujifilm thrived by changing focus, *Wall Street Journal* [Online] https://www.wsj.com/articles/SB10001424052970203750404577170481473958516 (archived at https://perma.cc/DC59-NRK3)

7 Centre for Retail Research (2019) Who's gone bust in retailing 2010–19? [Online] http://www.retailresearch.org/whosegonebust.php (archived at https://perma.cc/BCD8-KRWZ)

8 Youl, T (2019) *Online Grocery Sales in Australia*, IBIS World Industry Report, OD5527

9 Harris, B (2017) Which countries buy the most groceries online? World Economic Forum, Global Agenda [Online] https://www.weforum.org/agenda/2017/12/south-koreans-buy-the-most-groceries-online-by-far/ (archived at https://perma.cc/V42M-YWTM)

10 Freestyla (2012) How to layer cut and style hair at home with Wahl clippers, YouTube [Online] https://youtu.be/pKEFgZBpsds (archived at https://perma.cc/JF5C-YRLY)

11 Best, D (2002) Wal-Mart is the world's biggest company as Q4 sales overtake Exxon-Mobil, Just-Food [Online] https://www.just-food.com/news/wal-mart-is-the-worlds-biggest-company-as-q4-sales-overtake-exxon-mobil_id73725.aspx (archived at https://perma.cc/ZU4F-9FU7)

12 Fettig, D (2006) Thomas J Holmes on Wal-Mart's location strategy, Fedgazette [Online] http://www.minneapolisfed.org/publications_papers/pub_display.cfm?id=1382 (archived at https://perma.cc/NPW5-UNGM)

13 Walmart annual reports [Online] https://stock.walmart.com/investors/financial-information/annual-reports-and-proxies/default.aspx (archived at https://perma.cc/V6KS-G3PG)

14 PBS Video (2004) Is Wal-Mart good for America? Alexandria, VA, PBS

15 Retail Project LLC (2005) Wal-Mart: The high cost of low price, New York

16 Stevens, P (2019) Behind Walmart's push to eliminate 1 gigaton of greenhouse gases by 2030, Powering the Future, 15 December [Online] https://www.cnbc.com/2019/12/15/walmarts-project-gigaton-is-its-most-ambitious-climate-goal-yet.html (archived at https://perma.cc/3BGN-RK4S)

17 Comp store growth is the sales growth achieved by stores open in the previous corresponding period.

18 Porter, ME (2008) The five competitive forces that shape strategy, *Harvard Business Review*, **86** (1), pp 78–93

19 Lashinsky, A, Burke, D and Mangalindan, JP (2012) Jeff Bezos: The ultimate disrupter, *Fortune*, Meredith Corporation, **166**, p 100

20 Lewis, R and Dart, M (2014) *The New Rules of Retail: Competing in the world's toughest marketplace*, St Martin's Press, New York

21 Stephens, D (2013) *The Retail Revival: Reimagining business for the new age of consumerism*, John Wiley & Sons, Hoboken, NJ

22 NAB online sales index [Online] https://business.nab.com.au/nab-online-retail-sales-index-june-2016-17897/ (archived at https://perma.cc/P5CJ-8VKF)

23 Seligman, ME, Maier, SF and Geer, JH (1968) Alleviation of learned helplessness in the dog, *Journal of Abnormal Psychology*, **73** (3), p 256

02

Why innovation is hard for retailers

(GARETH)

Introduction

Innovation is hard in any industry, but it has an extra degree of difficulty in retail because of the short-term thinking and executional mentality that are embedded in retailer DNA. In this chapter we explain why retailer DNA has historically made innovation difficult but then show how, when applied in the right way, retailer DNA can become innovation's secret sauce. We also show why, despite the risks and unfamiliarity, a strategy based on innovation really is the only viable choice for retailers in a disrupted environment. Innovation is retail's new safe place.

Innovation is hard in any organization

The difficulty of innovating is founded in the way we think, our attitudes toward failure and the very nature of organizations. It is not surprising that innovation often fails. When we fail, it is easy to blame ourselves. This is natural but it doesn't help. Understanding just how difficult innovation is will help you to stay the course, manage failures and avoid accidentally creating a culture of blame and judgement. Here these top three reasons for why innovation is difficult in any organization are expanded upon.

Human thinking

Psychology and neuroscience tell us that human beings are quick, reflexive thinkers. We prefer to solve problems using what we already know rather than taking on the cognitive challenge of thinking things through each time a decision is required.[1] Because *what* we know is so important to our reflexive thinking style, we seek confirmation of our beliefs in our daily interactions. We become blind to disconfirming data and rationalize away information that contradicts our beliefs. We think, 'That works for them because they are a start-up/have deep pockets/are privately owned/are a public company/have different customers to us (add in your own example), but it wouldn't work for us.' Innovation disrupts reflexive thinking because it involves challenging established beliefs. Having our beliefs challenged is psychologically hard work that most of us would rather avoid. Any attempt to innovate in an organization is therefore contrary to the way we think as humans.

Attitudes toward failure

Our attitudes toward failure are conditioned from an early age. We learn through our education and institutions that good performance means avoiding failure. Unfortunately, innovation inevitably involves failure. As Steve Kaufer, founder of Tripadvisor, once said, 'If we're not failing at something on a regular basis, we're just not trying hard enough.'[2] While seasoned entrepreneurs may be good at embracing the prospect of failure, most people react with fear. Fear of failure leads to what has been called 'defensive reasoning'.[3] Defensive reasoning causes people to deny, deflect and defend against new ideas. This creates powerful opposition to innovation in all organizations.

Why organizations exist

Innovation challenges the fundamental reasons why organizations exist. Organizations of all types are designed to perform processes more efficiently than individuals. Forming an organization allows allocation of tasks to experienced specialists, a smooth flow of tasks between these specialists, financial control and accountability as well as benefits from economies of scale. An organization is at its most efficient when it is focused on performing familiar tasks using accepted processes. Variation is the enemy of efficiency, but innovation is formed from variation. This makes innovation the enemy of the efficient organization.

Organizations protect themselves from innovation by attacking it using organizational 'antibodies'[4] in the form of established processes and culture. Approval processes are formal and long, measurement of success is through traditional return on investment (ROI) metrics, failure is not acceptable and the chatter around the building is, 'We just don't do things like that around here.' Unless the organization has developed a solid innovation capability that includes the ability to ward off innovation antibodies the project will die. This means any attempt to innovate in an organization has to contend with the reasons why organizations exist in the first place.

The degree of difficulty involved in achieving organizational innovation is evidenced by the hundreds of books, articles and blog posts devoted to the subject. Many sectors claim that innovation is particularly hard for them because of unique factors that occur only in their industry ecosystem. In researching this chapter, I found articles about why innovation is so hard in information technology, health care, insurance, government and the public sector. I am sure there are more. The degree of difficulty in achieving organizational innovation is also evidenced by well-known examples of organizations like Kodak, Nokia, Xerox and Polaroid, all of whom failed to embrace innovation at key turning points in their history despite being, large, powerful, well capitalized and having a proud heritage of innovation earlier in their history.

EXERCISE
Overcoming innovation blockers

You may have more reasons why innovation is hard in any organization. Now is the time to write those reasons down so you know your enemy. Use examples gained from outside the retail industry as we have a whole section coming up on the specific challenges of innovating in a retail business. Use your list to start a conversation with your colleagues. Their experiences may be different to yours and the list may get longer! Don't worry, this process will not send you all into a funk, instead it will build empathy and resilience for the quest ahead. Empathy is an essential attribute of teams that attempt innovation so now is a good time to start building it. The good news is that none of the reasons you put on your lists will be immutable. Human beings are reflexive thinkers, but they are also great learners. They fear the unknown, but they are also capable of incredible bravery and although organizations can resist change there are many who have woven the capability to change into the operating fabrics of their businesses.

Now try and think of counterpoints to all the reasons on your lists. Some examples are given here.

Reason why innovation is hard in any organization		Counterpoint
Organizations are careful with their budgets. They always prefer guaranteed return from business as usual (BAU) projects rather than risking it on innovation...	BUT	... if money is quarantined in the budget for innovation projects, they don't directly compete for funds against BAU initiatives.
Organizations always think short term. Innovation often requires long-term thinking...	BUT	... giving innovation projects strict timelines and milestones lets the organization see progress or parachute out in a timely fashion.
The pressure is always on to cut costs. Innovation requires investment...	BUT	... putting innovation projects that cut costs at the top of the list builds credibility and provides permission for future innovation.

Feeling better?

Some will say that the way to become innovative is simply to think like a start-up.[5] Start-ups have the reputation of being quicker, smarter and more creative than established businesses. Start-ups typically have non-hierarchical structures, practise test-and-learn development and have a can-do attitude that contrasts with the reality of established organizations. Many established organizations have been so attracted to the idea of acquiring a start-up mentality that they have engineered start-up-like mini organizations within their business or acquired promising start-ups with the hope of grafting an innovation mentality on to their business.

Established organizations have a lot to learn from start-ups, but to suggest that they can take the next step and actually think and operate like a start-up is unrealistic. Every business in the world is, or once was, a start-up. In the start-up phase, businesses search for some unique combination of value that they can deliver more effectively or more efficiently than what is currently available in the market. They do this without the complication of maintaining existing revenue, current assets or dividends to shareholders. An established business must take care of what exists while simultaneously developing the future. It must become Janus-faced, unlike a start-up which only has to keep its one face in the direction of the future.

Many successful retail companies like Walmart, Amazon, and Target (USA) have benefited from creating innovation mini businesses or acquiring start-ups, but there have also been failures. Many tech companies around the world also followed the strategy of buying in to innovative start-ups in areas of strategic importance to them. Unfortunately, when the tech companies change direction these investments are divested, often resulting in large write-downs. The hope that, by grafting on an innovative start-up, the spirit of innovation would be infused into the established corporation often proves to be false. In some cases, the further away the start-ups and the corporation are kept apart the better they both work.

Why retailer DNA can make innovation especially hard

Many industries claim innovation is particularly hard for them because of the special dynamics of their way of doing business. Retail is no exception. In fact, we argue innovation comes with an extra degree of difficulty in our industry because of the short-term thinking and executional mentality that are embedded in retailer DNA. Here are a couple of examples of the way retailers think that makes retail different to other industries.

'You never get today back'

In retail it is said that you never get today back. If you have bad sales on Monday and good sales on Tuesday that does not mean you've caught up – it means you had a bad sales day on Monday. Retailer logic says the dollars spent today are not available again tomorrow. Most other industries don't take this view. In other industries if you have a bad sales day, there is always the rest of the month or the quarter to make up the difference.

On the face of it, retailer logic may seem short-sighted, but economics broadly support the way retailers think. At a macro level, retail spend is very predictable. In the USA in 2018 retail sales were said to be booming with year-on-year growth of around 5 per cent, while in Australia retail sales were said to be sluggish with year-on-year growth of around 3 per cent. That's a 2 per cent delta between terrific and terrible. With overall spend varying in such a narrow band it's not hard to predict the overall size of the market from year to year. It's also not hard to calculate the size of the available market on any given day. If the overall spend on any given day is known, Monday's spend can never be replaced by Tuesday's spend. Retailer logic is economically sound.

Retailer logic is further backed up by the nature of retail spending. Most retail spending comes from discretionary dollars, ie the amount left after you have paid the bills and covered basic needs. Discretionary spend is notoriously fickle. It can switch between retailers or categories based on deals, proximity, mood, who's hot and who's not, or any other whim the consumer may have. Discretionary dollars can also stay in the wallet if none of what's on offer is appealing. If you applied these fickle and whimsical behaviours to a purchase for a business, you would probably lose your job, but for consumers there are generally few negative consequences from any purchase decision apart from the occasional bout of buyer's remorse. With fickle consumers and a finite spend available, retailers know they have to catch the fish today because they might not be back in the river tomorrow!

If you believe that you never get today back, it makes sense to focus on same day last year comparisons. Retailers do this obsessively to the point that it regularly becomes a topic of results presentations. The placement of key selling days around Easter, Christmas and Thanksgiving is often discussed as influencing results both positively and negatively. When you manage that way, success means making incremental improvement on last year on a day-by-day basis. While this is great for maximizing daily opportunity, the flipside is a management culture based on short-term thinking and an incremental rather than transformative approach toward business improvement.

'There are no rewards for a bright idea – all the rewards are on execution'

One of my former bosses used to remind me regularly that there are no rewards in retail for a bright idea, only for execution. Retail is traditionally not a place for dreamy blue-sky ideas. It's a place for plans that are implementable now and can change the daily scorecard tomorrow. In other industries this is not necessarily the case. In other industries it's normal to be developing concepts that may or may not get to market, for a number of years. Some of these ideas may seem bizarre and unmarketable at first but genius level breakthroughs when eventually launched. In 2017 the Brookings Institution conducted a study that found an estimated $80 billion had been invested between August 2014 and June 2017 in the development of autonomous vehicles.[6] These investments had been made without a firm assurance that governments will even allow these vehicles on the road and, by 2020 there was still no prospect of a commercial launch. It would be hard to imagine my old boss approving.

The people and teams who generate and develop dreamy blue-sky ideas are valuable resources in other industries but in retail the most valuable resources are the people and teams who can execute. The people we promote are the ones who get the stock out and ticketed, order enough stock for promotions, get the till to balance, minimize shrink and waste, etc. To coin another retail catchphrase, they are the people who 'do it once and do it right'. The dreamers, who think about the world as it could be, generally stay where they are or leave the industry. The ranks of retail management have historically been stacked with retail grown, execution led executives.

There is absolutely nothing wrong with having a laser-like focus on today and valuing the ability to execute. However, these qualities are not necessarily the ones you need to develop a programme of transformative innovation. Studies of innovation say that to be successful you need to think big, think long term, think different, be prepared to fail and embrace change as part of your culture. This is not the way most traditional retailers think.

Some believe that the case for the inherent difficulty of innovation in retail compared to other industries is overstated. In 2016 I interviewed Paul Coby, then Chief Information Officer of John Lewis, for a whitepaper published by Telstra.[7] John Lewis was at the time acknowledged as one of the most innovative retailers in the world. I asked Paul about the barriers to innovation at John Lewis versus his previous employer British Airways. He strongly believed innovation was easier at John Lewis than at an airline because, 'we can do most things right away. In the airline industry airplane replacement cycles are ten years. Now that's a barrier to innovation!' The long planning cycles involved in capital intensive industries can obviously generate frustration for the people working within them, but they at least provide the requirement to think long term. That requirement is not part of traditional retailers' operating rhythm.

As we will see throughout this book, some retailers have managed to overcome traditional biases in the way retail operates to become successful innovators. Long-established retailers like McDonald's, Starbucks, Walmart, Target (USA) and IKEA are now renowned as much for their constant change as their mastery of traditional retail business disciplines. If these retailers have been able to do it, what can other retailers do to combat their in-built biases against innovation?

The first thing retailers can do is find the dreamers in the business. They are the team members who write emails with detailed plans about what the future could look like when you are busy trying to finalize this month's promotion or who take time on store visits to tell you about all the things the business could do better. One of the authors of this book was one of those dreamers. The retail dreamer's time has come. Great execution is not enough to reframe your business.

The second thing retailers can do is look for the skills that are needed to mount an innovation quest outside of the industry. In retail we prefer to recruit from within because experience has taught us that not many outsiders have the appetite for the relentless routine and pace of the business. However, as we all know, when the world changes we need to change. At the turn of the 21st century we didn't need data scientists, social media experts, digital marketers or even web masters, but these are now mandatory competencies for a serious retailer. In the era of Amazon and Alibaba the ability to develop programmes of transformative innovation is an equally important mandatory competency that traditional retailers need to acquire.

The third and most important thing retailers can do is to turn their executional focus from a disadvantage into an advantage. This is the secret sauce retailers have for their innovation quest.

Turning retailer DNA into innovation's secret sauce

Retailer operational bias towards execution is baked into the DNA of the industry. But what if innovation could be seen as essentially just another process? Retailers love process. It's what keeps large, geographically distributed workforces operating consistently and efficiently. What if retailer DNA became innovation's secret sauce?

Some think of innovation as inspiration, as great ideas spawned by extraordinary individuals, expensive consultants or teams of boffins in laboratories. In reality, generating ideas is the easy part of innovation. In their book *The Other Side of Innovation*[8] Vijay Govindarajan and Chris Trimble explain how innovation has always been, in the words of Edison, 1 per cent inspiration and 99 per cent perspiration. They propose that innovation is not simply ideas, but ideas + execution. 'The real innovation challenge lies beyond the idea. It lies in a long hard journey from imagination to impact.'[9] Innovation is in fact a definable and repeatable process like any of the myriad processes that keep a retail organization operating from day to day.

Retailers excel at executing processes. Every day in the store we execute opening and closing processes, price variations, returns, stock receipts, price changes, purchase price variances, lay-buys, balancing of the till and more. In addition, when a promotion runs, we will be required to execute another set of processes that involve re-merchandising, changing signage and on floor price tickets. Most of the above will need to be repeated for our online assets. Back at support office all the processes that are required in a store and online have companion processes. Stock needs to be sourced, bought and paid for, and inventory moved so that it gets to the right place in the right quantity when it is required. Inventory needs to be managed through stocktake processes and valuation adjustments. The list could go on and what you would have in the end is a retail operations manual.

Retail is not only full of processes, but retailers themselves can get a bit obsessed with testing and improving them. After he retired as president and Chief Operating Officer of Walmart, Jack Shewmaker spent time in Australia as an advisor to Woolworths. I was fortunate to spend a bit of time with him during this period and found his fascination with process second to none. One process that is a continual conundrum for retailers is the opening of new stores. Finding a site and negotiating a lease is one thing, but fitting the store out, filling it with stock and starting to trade is another. Landlords usually grant a rent-free period so that retailers have time to deal with known points of uncertainty like shopfitting schedules, connection of utilities, local council permits and delivery of stock. The rent-free period is free money for a retailer so the earlier trading can begin after a lease commences the better.

We were opening a lot of new stores at the time and Jack stressed to us that getting them open quickly was all a matter of process. He told the story of how he proved his point to the Walmart team by developing a process that meant a store could open in twenty-four hours from lease commencement rather than the weeks it normally took. There was no suggestion that this became standard practice in Walmart but it did have the effect of inspiring the Walmart team to look again at their processes to see how they could better coordinate and plan to open just that little bit quicker than before. Needless to say, it had the same effect on us.

Some will say that innovation cannot be boiled down to a process, that innovation is an act of creativity that can't be constrained by rules or systems, but in our experience that's exactly when it works best. If we think back to the periods of successful innovation in our careers, they are all characterized by well-executed processes. Processes of aligning the team, selecting the best ideas to pursue, empowering cross functional teams to develop the ideas operationally, testing and learning, scaling then embedding the new initiative as business as usual. Innovation isn't a matter of breaking the rules, it's actually a matter of following them. We'll cover the detail in the following chapters. Start-ups may be an exception. They are usually fuelled by a big idea and a vision of what the future could be; however, they still have to execute. If they don't, they will only last as long as their shareholders' funds.

EXERCISE
Reflecting on your innovation history

Think of all the innovative ideas your business has come up with in the last couple of years. Write down as many as you can think of. Is it a short list or a long list? How many have been successfully executed? Is the main innovation issue in your business generating ideas or executing ideas? If you were to sketch an improved process for executing your innovation ideas more successfully what would it look like?

Innovation is retail's new safe place

My grandfather was a coal miner. When he retired, he became a comedian in the clubs of North East England. As a 10-year-old, I was lucky enough to be the sounding board for his new material. Most of it concerned incontinence (which must have resonated with his audience demographic), but it's a story on another topic that has stayed with me. It's about a racehorse trainer who isn't winning many races. He decides on a radical strategy to cut costs by reducing feed to the horses, the number of jockeys on staff and so on. He wins fewer races but, for the first time in many years, the stables are profitable. The next year he doubles down. Costs are reduced again and even though he wins even fewer races, the profit at the stables increases. News of the stable's success gets out and the trainer becomes something of a media celebrity. He is invited to speak at conferences and is the go-to media head for anything to do with horse training. In the third year, the trainer doubles down again but unfortunately, halfway through that year, he has to call a press conference to announce that all the horses are dead!

As retailers, our race is the race for customers. Our job is to win races. When we win races, sales increase, opportunities increase for our team and suppliers, and profits increase as our costs become a smaller proportion of sales. When we lose races, sales decrease, opportunities for our team and suppliers decrease and profit can only be sustained if expense reductions cover reduced sales. If we *continue* to lose races, the cycle repeats. Doubling down on expense reduction will keep the doors open in the short term but will only lead to the death of the business in the long term. How many times have you seen it? I don't need to mention names. It's happening in plain sight right now wherever in the world you're reading this.

Customers are the foundation of every retail business. If we lose them, we must get the ones who remain to spend more or cover their loss with expense savings. It's much better to win customers, but in today's retail market it is definitely getting harder. Competition from international and online operators is intense; and customers, armed with smartphones, are savvier than ever. The retail tactics that once won the race for customers are no longer enough. Some retailers have reacted by attempting to create one-horse races they can't lose. They buy competitors or saturate the market with outlets, but the market doesn't like one-horse races and won't allow them for long. Others have tried to win by discounting, but winning customers this way involves much lower margins and requires a significant rise in sales volumes to be viable. The only sustainable strategy to win the race for customers is to innovate.

Can you imagine a tennis player winning Wimbledon today with a wooden racket? It's a crazy idea, but some retailers believe they can still win the race for customers using last-century tactics. By doing something different that benefits your customers, generates a return for the business and aligns with your purpose, races can be won. Sometimes expectations for financial return and business purpose need to be revised to match the new competitive landscape and new customer values, but this can be and is being done. Even some of the biggest and historically most successful of retail businesses like Walmart, Target (USA), Starbucks, H+M and Inditex have changed the way they compete and are winning customers again.

It is time to get ready to innovate. If the conversation in your business is always focused on profit, try to widen that focus to customer counts. As we have seen, these are the real driver of profitability in your business. Open every meeting on business performance with a discussion about customer counts. Why are they up, why are they down and what is their relationship to basket size and profitability?

Next, if you are in control of an expense budget, allocate funds to innovation projects. You may have no projects to fund yet, but it won't take long and nothing guarantees failure more than lack of resources. A popular way of allocating resources is the so-called 70/20/10 method.[10] This was originally developed for workplace learning, but has been co-opted to innovation budgeting. Retailers such as Yum foods allocate 70 per cent of budgeted expenses to core business, 20 per cent for innovation projects that will launch within the financial year and 10 per cent for longer-term projects. This means innovation starts each year with budgeted resources, but those resources are subject to control just like the rest of the budget. 70/20/10 also ensures that the projects with the most prospect of delivering a yield in the current year get the bulk of the innovation funding.

Innovation is risky and not the first language of a retailer, but the risks of *not* innovating are increasingly becoming potentially terminal and much higher than the risks of doing so. We must win the race for customers or die. Innovation is the new safe place for retailers.

Conclusion

In this chapter we have shown that while innovation is hard in every organization, it is particularly hard for retailers because the way the industry operates encourages short-term planning and values execution over strategy. These attributes are part of retailer DNA and are not normally associated with innovation. However, as Edison said, innovation is 1 per cent innovation and 99 per cent perspiration. Innovative ideas have no value without execution and retailers excel at execution. Applying that skill to innovation is the secret sauce that can turn retailers from innovation laggards to innovation stars. Innovation is risky and unfamiliar, but it is in fact retail's new safe place.

In the next chapter we give an overview of our six-stage, eighteen-step *ReFRAME* process for retail innovation.

Notes

1 Hess, E (2014) Why is innovation so hard? Batten Institute University of Virginia Darden School of Business [Online] http://www.forbes.com/sites/darden/2014/08/04/why-is-innovation-so-hard/ (archived at https://perma.cc/EAJ4-MQSA)

2 Livingstone, J (2008) *Stephen Kaufer: Cofounder, Tripadvisor*, Founders at Work, Apress, Berkeley, CA, pp 361–75

3 Argyris, C (1996) Unlocking defensive reasoning ((Can you teach your people to think smarter?), cover story), *Across the Board*, **33** (3), p 18

4 Degraff, J (2013) Why is innovation so hard? *Fortune*

5 Linkner, J (2012) Think like a start up, 16 April, Forbes [Online] https://www.forbes.com/sites/joshlinkner/2012/04/16/think-like-a-startup/#18ff2da7456c (archived at https://perma.cc/75VA-UANJ)

6 Kerry, C.F and Karsten, J (2017) Gauging investment in self-driving cars, Brookings [Online] https://www.brookings.edu/research/gauging-investment-in-self-driving-cars/ (archived at https://perma.cc/3EZP-2GZE)

7 Jude, G (2016) *Innovation in Retail*, Telstra, Melbourne

8 Govindarajan, V and Trimble, C (2010) *The Other Side of Innovation: Solving the execution challenge*, Harvard Business Press, Cambridge, MA, p 3

9 Govindarajan, V and Trimble, C (2010) *The Other Side of Innovation: Solving the execution challenge*, Harvard Business Press, Cambridge, MA, p 23

10 Lombardo, M and Eichinger, R (1987) The 70/20/10 model, Centre for Creative Leadership, Colorado

03

Retail innovation as a process

(GARETH)

Introduction

The core proposition of this book is that innovation is not attributable to moments of inspiration or superhuman leadership but to an observable and repeatable process. Luckily, retailers thrive on process. It is as much a part of retailer DNA as a focus on the short term and valuing execution above all else. When retailers leverage their skills at executing a process to innovate, they unleash their secret weapon. Nobody is as good at executing a process as a retailer and with the right processes in place nobody is as good at innovation.

This chapter gives an overview of our six-stage, eighteen-step *ReFRAME* process. The *ReFRAME* process shows you how to embed the capacity to innovate into your business. Acquiring the organizational ability to change is the single most important thing retailers can do to survive and thrive with the challenges facing the industry. With it, retailers can compete in a disrupted environment with confidence and success. Without it they will feel helpless and are likely to fail.

Why retail innovation is a repeatable process (and why all the steps are interdependent)

There are six stages and eighteen steps to our *ReFRAME* process. Each one is dependent on the other. You will rarely achieve sustainable success in innovation unless the following criteria are met:

1 The foundations of the business have been re-set to be innovation friendly.

2 A system to filter the best ideas for development has been deployed.

3 You have activated a cross-functional team to lead your initiative with proper sponsorship and resourcing.

4 The initiative or 'thing' is designed based on specifics, evidence and testing.

5 The 'thing' is built as a prototype then refined for scale.

6 You have embedded the 'thing' as the 'new normal' in your business.

If one link in this chain is broken or neglected than it is likely that the whole programme will fail. How many innovation initiatives have you seen fail because although the 'thing' worked technically, it did not deliver a positive effect on customer experience or provide a return to the business (should have been filtered out)? How many innovation initiatives have you seen that provided positive returns but were withdrawn when leadership changed and management alignment was lost (foundations weren't properly set)? How many innovation initiatives have you seen fail because although the 'thing' provided theoretical returns and management was aligned its design meant it didn't scale successfully (design failure)? All the links in the chain need to be secure for an innovation process to succeed.

Retail innovation as a process: Case studies

The best retail innovators embrace innovation as a process. Here are three examples that illustrate the point.

CASE STUDY
Amazon

Amazon was founded in 1994 and since then has been the single most disruptive retail force in the world.[1] Amazon is more than a retailer; it operates large cloud services and media businesses, but retail (product sales and marketplace commissions) still makes up approximately 85 per cent of its revenue. Amazon has been a perpetual innovator since its inception. It has led the way in customer reviews, buying suggestions, rapid delivery, parcel lockers, voice recognition, drones and robotics. Innovation has helped fuel growth and value for the business. In the decade between 2008 and 2018 total revenues grew from US$ 19.2 billion to US$ 232.9 billion, representing CAGR of over 28 per cent[2] and the market capitalization of the company rose from US$ 23.2 billion to US$ 773.52 billion.[3] During 2019 Amazon joined Apple and Microsoft in the US$ 1 trillion market capitalization club. Most significantly, Amazon has taken a big share of retail growth over the last decade. According to Marketplace Pulse,[4] sales made online with Amazon directly and through their marketplaces accounted for 69 per cent of online sales growth and 18 per cent of total retail sales growth during the decade. In 2019 it is estimated that Amazon was responsible for 36.9 per cent of all US ecommerce.[5]

Amazon is generally a secretive organization, but they have occasionally talked publicly about their process of innovation and it has become quite famous.

Amazon's process starts with an innovation culture embedded in the company based on four principles:

- customer obsession;
- long-term thinking;
- willingness to fail;
- willingness to be misunderstood.

These cultural foundations protect Amazon from the organizational innovation antibodies that we discussed in Chapter 2.

Every innovation initiative follows a process that works backwards from the customer. To be considered, an idea must first be written up in a six-page narrative memo.[6] Amazon favours the narrative memo approach because it forces ideas to be thought through carefully in advance. There are a number of elements to the memo:

- The first element is a press release that should read as if the initiative had already been launched. The press release should contain not only a description of the hypothetical service but how customers would react to it. This is to ensure that the initiative is customer-focused (or 'customer-obsessed' in Amazon speak).

- The second element is a series of frequently asked questions (FAQs) anticipating the concerns of customers and internal stakeholders. This forces the proposer of the new initiative to think through stakeholder implications.

- The third element is to define the customer interaction and write the manual so that the operational implications are also thought through.

Next, the memo is shared with colleagues for about a week until as many issues as possible are thought about.

Only then is a meeting called to discuss the idea. Attendance is limited to roughly the number of people who can share two pizzas. The 'two-pizza rule' keeps meetings small and focused. The meeting begins with 30–60 minutes' reading time for the attendees to digest the narrative memo. If the idea survives discussion, follow-up meetings are used to hone the details.

Winning ideas are deployed quickly by 'two-pizza' sized, properly resourced, cross-functional teams. The 'Prime Now' service took only 111 days to go from idea on a piece of paper to a limited launch in Manhattan.[7] By launching quickly to paying customers, Amazon avoids wasting years developing things that don't really serve customer needs.

CASE STUDY
Starbucks

Starbucks was founded in 1971 and has become renowned as one of the retail food service industry's foremost innovators. Starbucks has been a pioneer in digital technologies, menu choices, store formats, customer experience, partner (team member) benefits and social responsibility. Innovation has helped fuel growth and value for the business. In the decade between 2008 and 2018 revenues grew from US$ 10.2 billion to US$ 25.5 billion, representing a CAGR of over 9 per cent, and the value of the company rose from US$ 6.97 billion to US$ 78.78 billion.[8]

The process of innovation at Starbucks has a few notable features. Current CEO, Kevin Johnstone, articulated a few of these features at the opening of Starbucks innovation lab in Seattle:[9]

- Innovation ideas come from anywhere in the Starbucks ecosystem, not just from the management team. 'Great ideas come from our Starbucks partners, they come from our customers, they come from outside of Starbucks.... We have to continually have our listening systems on.'

- Innovation ideas generated internally are supplemented by investments in promising start-ups in the retail food and beverage space.

- Innovation is focused on customer and business outcomes and is not innovation for innovation's sake. 'We are embracing new ideas and innovating in ways that are relevant to our customers, inspiring to our partners (team members), and meaningful to our business.'

- Once ideas are selected for testing, they are deployed by empowered cross-functional teams, who include store partners.

- Ideas are trialled in stores with real customers.

- Data science and machine learning is used to inform product and process development.

- Development cycles are short. Idea to action target is 100 days. Consequently, when Starbucks fails, it is fast but also safe.

CASE STUDY
Walmart

Walmart was founded in 1962 and has been the largest company in the world by sales revenue for most of the 21st century. In recent years, Walmart has been notable as an example of an established retailer that has reframed its business and continued to prosper while other large established retailers, like Sears, JC Penny, K Mart and others, have struggled. Among established retailers, Walmart has been a pioneer in warehouse automation, supply chain collaboration, click-and-collect, same-day home delivery, third-party returns, in-store robotics, associate (team member) education and sustainability.

Innovation has helped fuel growth and value for the business. In the decade between 2008 and 2018 net sales revenues grew from US$ 373.8 billion to US$ 495.76 billion, representing a CAGR of 3 per cent and the market capitalization of the company rose from US$ 225.23 billion to US$ 269.85 billion. Walmart's market capitalization stood at US$ 337.86 billion at the end of 2019.[10] These numbers may appear modest in comparison to Amazon and Starbucks, but Walmart's sheer size makes comparisons difficult. In pure dollar terms, Walmart's growth in the period (US$ 120 billion) is equal to the total annual revenue of a Home Depot or a Kroger. Online, while Amazon is growing roughly at the rate of the market, Walmart is growing at over 35 per cent pa and now ranks third in USA ecommerce sales.[11]

The process of innovation at Walmart goes back to Sam Walton's days but has evolved in the 21st century:

- Sam Walton always advocated getting ideas from all levels of the company. That has now evolved into a formal innovation community of 1,600 associates in eight countries.[12]

- Innovation ideas generated internally have been supplemented by significant acquisitions of online companies with special skill sets, eg Jet.com, Bonobos and Moosejaw, as well as the establishment of Walmart Labs and Store No. 8 to incubate new ideas.

- Innovation is focused around solving customer problems. In the innovation community the process of testing ideas is:

   o What is the problem?

   o What is its impact?

   o How can it be solved (all the options)?

- o   Why is this idea the best?

- o   What is the return for the business?

- Once ideas are selected for testing, they are first trialled in Lab stores with real customers and associates[13] then gradually scaled up across the business.

The six stages of a retail *ReFRAME*

What follows is an overview of our *ReFRAME* process for achieving the organizational ability to innovate. It is based on the innovation processes used by the world's most successful retail innovators as well as our own experiences of trying, succeeding and sometimes failing in retail innovation. Each stage has a full chapter devoted to it later in the book that explains the details step by step and gives you all the tools, case study evidence and practical hints to make it work.

Stage 1: Reset the foundation (build a launchpad)

Innovation needs a launchpad, which has got to be capable of withstanding the blast forces of change that will engulf your organization. We have identified three essential elements of that launchpad. All three elements must be in place for your organization to consider beginning a *ReFRAME*.

STEP 1: PURPOSE

Some retailers think their purpose is making a profit, but profit is only a permission slip from the market to be in business for another year. Purpose is deeper than that. It's the reason why you exist. In the end, retailers only exist because in some way the world is better off with your retail offering than without it. Purpose can be a variety of things but increasingly team members, customers and other stakeholders prefer a purpose that goes beyond return to shareholders. Whatever your purpose, it must be clearly articulated and resonate with stakeholders to be effective.

STEP 2: INNOVATION CULTURE

Retailers must embrace an innovation culture, starting with the executive team. An innovation culture embraces ambiguity, empowers the team to take risks and frames failure as a learning experience. This is not traditional retail culture (see Chapter 2). Traditional retail culture is results driven, rules based, hierarchical and punishes failure. Traditional retail culture is incompatible

FIGURE 3.1 The *ReFRAME* model

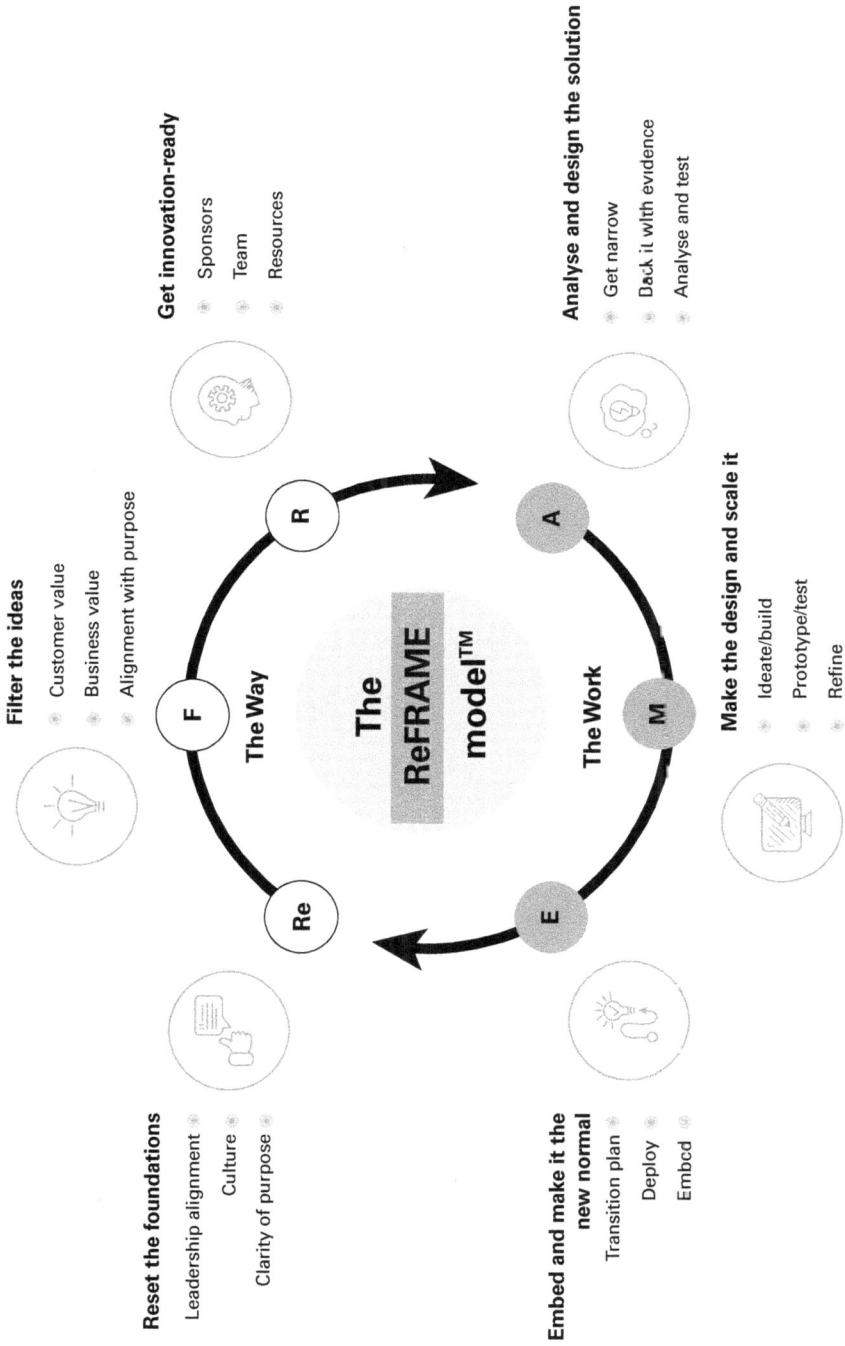

Reset the foundations
- Leadership alignment
- Culture
- Clarity of purpose

Filter the ideas
- Customer value
- Business value
- Alignment with purpose

Get innovation-ready
- Sponsors
- Team
- Resources

Analyse and design the solution
- Get narrow
- Back it with evidence
- Analyse and test

Make the design and scale it
- Ideate/build
- Prototype/test
- Refine

Embed and make it the new normal
- Transition plan
- Deploy
- Embed

The Way

The Work

The ReFRAME model™

Re F R A M E

with innovation. Most importantly, the new innovation culture must be seen to be led from the very top.

STEP 3: ALIGNMENT

Retail executive teams must align on purpose and innovation culture. If the executive team is not aligned, the broader team will become confused and cynical, while traditionalists in the business will sense weakness and infer permission to block innovation projects. This does not mean an end to competitive tension between senior managers or an end to challenge and dissent, but without alignment on purpose and innovation culture an executive team will not be able to deliver a programme of innovation.

Stage 2: Filter the ideas

Innovation ideas are normally abundant in retail organizations, but the big fear retail leaders have is choosing the wrong idea to pursue. This is a good fear, because failed innovation programmes plague the industry and are a waste of resources, opportunities and careers. The wrong idea is often selected because senior managers have pet projects or because innovation is mistaken for its three common impersonators: technology, design and cost cutting. These impersonators are often good facilitators of innovation, but are not innovation itself.

To choose the ideas with the best chance of sustainable success, retailers must test them against the golden rule. The golden rule has three components. All conditions must be met for an idea to be selected to progress to the next stage of development.

STEP 1: SOLVE A CUSTOMER PROBLEM

As retailers, we serve customers every day, so solving their problems is a good place to find opportunities for retail innovation.

STEP 2: DO SOMETHING POSITIVE FOR THE BUSINESS

There must be a return for the business on the money and time invested. This return typically is sales increases or expense reduction, but other positive outcomes could include improvements in brand image or customer engagement. Each assessment of worth will be dependent on the situation of the business.

STEP 3: ALIGN WITH YOUR PURPOSE
Whatever your purpose for being in business, the more closely aligned your innovation ideas are with that purpose, the better their chances of success.

Stage 3: Get innovation-ready

Any quest without the right team, resources and guidance is bound to be unsuccessful. Innovation is no different, especially in retail where the margins are tighter, and the pace is quicker.

STEP 1: CREATE THE RIGHT TEAMS
Innovation teams should be cross-functional and may need to be supplemented with new skills that do not exist within the business – such as behavioural design, collaborative project styles (agile is one example) and data science.

STEP 2: GET THE RIGHT SPONSORSHIP
We identify three types of sponsor. The right sponsor for a retail innovation project is the 'innovation legend' who sees their role as working for the team, giving them everything they need to be successful, creating boundaries and knowing when to get out of the way. Unfortunately, rank is also important, so generally the more senior the sponsor the better.

STEP 3: SECURE ADEQUATE RESOURCES
Innovation teams must be given all the space they need to be successful in delivering innovation. We define space as the resources (financial and non-financial) required to be successful. These resources are time, investment, processes and governance.

Stage 4: Analyse and design the solution

Once we have a set of great ideas or 'things' to do, and the teams are innovation-ready, it's time to start analysing and designing our ideas. This stage is often missed in the excitement of the quest. It is tempting just to launch full-steam ahead. Unfortunately, doing so risks embarking on a poorly designed project that has a high chance of failure or becomes expensive to fix further down the line.

STEP 1: NARROW DOWN TO SPECIFICS

To truly understand the 'thing' you want to create and how it delivers on the outcomes you want, build a framework for the idea that covers the specifics of how it will be experienced by your team and customers, and how it will change your current state.

STEP 2: COLLECT EVIDENCE

Collect evidence, both data and behavioural, about the environment surrounding the 'thing' you want to implement. Proper evidence collection is objective, thorough, and covers a breadth of potential environments in which your 'thing' will be required to perform.

STEP 3: ANALYSE AND TEST THE IDEA

Analyse and test the 'thing' against evidence to assess whether it is likely to deliver on the outcomes you want in the way you expect them to be delivered. This can be done through a set of activities that help decide whether to move on to making your design or to parachute out. 'Parachuting out' means leaving a project when it becomes apparent that your 'thing' is not going to fly (more detail later in the book).

Stage 5: Make the design and scale it

Your 'thing' must be capable of scaling if it is to be deployed across the business. Making your design and scaling it is an iterative process of learning and refinement through various levels of maturity requiring a 'measured and driven' mindset. This stage of the process is unique in that, as each level of maturity is reached, the three steps of the process are repeated. At each level of maturity, a decision must be made whether to continue to refine the 'thing', pivot, or parachute out.

STEP 1: IDEATE/BUILD

Ideate and building your 'thing' should be based on evidence you have gathered at each level of maturity.

STEP 2: PROTOTYPE/TEST

Testing of the prototype should take place, if at all possible, in the real world so that environmental issues can be considered. Testing should consider human interaction, what stories came out of the test and what new things were learned.

STEP 3: REFINE

If the results of the testing step are positive, then the solution should be refined and developed to the next level of maturity.

Stage 6: Embed it and make it the new normal

An innovation project might work at scale, but to have a lasting effect on the business it must embed itself as the new normal. The project has not been a success if it needs perpetual early life support, people have to be forced to use it or errors in use need constant management and correction. There are three steps to embedding your 'thing'.

STEP 1: TRANSITION PLAN AND TEST

In this step the support ecosystem and communication for the transition needs to be planned and tested.

STEP 2 TRANSITION

The transition itself must be done in manageable chunks and its performance measured. There is still time to test and learn and improve as the transition progresses.

STEP 3: EMBED

Embedding is complete when all the short-term mechanisms designed to support the transition are removed and your 'thing' is standing on its own two feet. Embedding may be fast or slow but if your 'thing' does not transition successfully there is still time to parachute out.

Conclusion

In this chapter we explained why retail innovation is a process and why that makes it something retailers can excel at. Retailers like Amazon, Starbucks and Walmart who have been able to continually innovate over many years have clear and repeatable processes of innovation underlying their success. Our own **ReFRAME** process is based not only on observing best practice but also on our own successes and failures as retail operators. There are six stages and eighteen steps, which are interdependent. One break in the chain and the whole process can fail.

We are now ready to go into the detail. In the next chapter we look at the first stage of the *ReFRAME* process and explain how to re-set the foundations of your business so they can become a launchpad for your innovation quest.

Notes

1 Galloway, S (2017) *The Four: The hidden DNA of Amazon, Apple, Facebook and Google*, Random House, New York

2 SEC annual 10K filings, 2009 and 2019

3 Retrieved 1 November 2019 from https://www.macrotrends.net/stocks/charts/ AMZN/amazon/market-cap (archived at https://perma.cc/B722-GABC)

4 Retrieved 1 November 2019 from https://www.marketplacepulse.com/stats/ us-ecommerce/us-e-commerce-sales-22 (archived at https://perma.cc/ S2TF-J9PZ)

5 Young, J (2020) US ecommerce sales grow by 14.9% in 2019, Digital Commerce 360 [Online] https://www.digitalcommerce360.com/article/ us-ecommerce-sales/ (archived at https://perma.cc/Y7PX-69EB)

6 SEC annual 10k filing 2018, exhibit 99.1

7 Satell, G (2018) *How Amazon Innovates*, Inc.com (archived at https://perma. cc/3UKF-5RSF)

8 Retrieved 30 October 2019 from https://www.macrotrends.net/stocks/charts/ SBUX/starbucks/market-cap (archived at https://perma.cc/Y8CN-6JHV)

9 Warnick, J (2019) Inside the Tryer Center, the Starbucks lab where anything is possible, Starbucks Stories and News, 11 June [Online] https://stories. starbucks.com/stories/2019/inside-the-tryer-center-the-starbucks-lab-where-anything-is-possible/ (archived at https://perma.cc/X7KA-XLDW)

10 Retrieved 3 November 2019 from https://www.macrotrends.net/stocks/charts/ WMT/walmart/market-cap (archived at https://perma.cc/D3RY-SAEF)

11 Marketing Charts (2019) Top 10 ecommerce retailers in the US [Online] https://www.marketingcharts.com/charts/top-10-e-commerce-retailers-us-2019/ attachment/emarketer-top-10-e-commerce-retailers-in-the-us-mar2019 (archived at https://perma.cc/45DN-KP5X)

12 Mallis, A (2019) How Walmart allows all its employees to contribute to innovation culture, Which-50 [Online] https://which-50.com/how-walmart-allows-all-its-employees-to-contribute-to-innovation-culture/ (archived at https://perma.cc/SY85-FKKD)

13 Perez, S (2019) Walmart unveils an AI-powered store of the future, now open to the public, Tech Crunch [Online] https://techcrunch.com/2019/04/25/ walmart-unveils-an-a-i-powered-store-of-the-future-now-open-to-the-public/ (archived at https://perma.cc/335G-TAYC)

Your innovation quest

In Part Two we look at the detail of how to launch and conduct an innovation quest in a retail business. This part of the book shows you not only how to navigate your innovation quest but also how to sail the ship through whatever conditions you face. There is a lot of detail to follow so we have added a 'how to' guide to this part of the book below.

How to use Part Two

After reading this section and working through the exercises, you will be equipped to lead an innovation project in your own retail business. The process we present is not intended to replace existing methodologies like Agile and Human Centred Design. In fact you will see that *ReFRAME* incorporates elements from many methodologies. What is unique about *ReFRAME* is that it has been designed specifically to be applied in a retail environment.

In Part Two there is a lot of operational detail, which will be invaluable for some but less relevant for others. In order to help you get to the most relevant sections we have developed recommended reading for eight different situations. See which one best matches your own and plan your reading accordingly.

TABLE P2.1 Planning your reading

Your group	Your situation	Our recommendations
Retailers	I've just been handed the job of running a major innovation project in our retail business. I'm looking for some guidance on how to make it successful.	It's your lucky day. Everything in this part of the book is going to be useful and you may also wish to follow the links to some of the online resources that are available.
	I'm unlikely to get involved in the day-to-day running of an innovation project but I'm interested to know how I can support our team to be successful.	Gain a detailed understanding of the parts of ReFRAME you can influence directly by reading Chapters 4, 5 and 6 in full.
		Gain a general understanding of the remaining elements of the process by reading the case studies in Chapters 4–9, Chapter 7 Innovation biases, heuristics, and Chapter 9 conclusion.
	We have a poor record of actually executing innovation in our business. I need to convince the executive team that we need to change the way we do things or face the consequences.	Part 1 should have helped you to begin building your case.
		To build your proposal for action read Chapters 4 and 5 and the case studies in Chapters 4–9.
	I am not on the executive team, but I can see our business desperately needs to innovate. How do I convince management that it's time to take action?	Part 1 should have helped you to begin building your case.
		Identify whether it is feasible to implement innovation as a process in your business at this time by reading Chapter 4 (it may not be).
		If innovation is feasible, design a pitch for a single project to prove the value of innovation as a process using Chapters 5–9.

(continued)

TABLE P2.1 (Continued)

Your group	Your situation	Our recommendations
Retail suppliers	I can see great opportunities for some of my retail customers to innovate but they don't seem to think it's important. I would like to know how I can help them.	To identify your best potential retail partners read Chapter 4.
		To understand how you might be able to help in kicking an innovation process off read Chapter 5 and the case studies in Chapters 4–9.
	I have trialled innovative ideas with a number of my retail customers but only a low percentage have been fully deployed. I'd like to increase my deployment percentage.	Identify whether your customers have the right foundations to execute a programme of innovation by reading Chapter 4.
		Determine whether the ideas they have chosen to pursue are viable in their context by reading Chapter 5.
		Understand whether your customers are set up to deploy innovation projects properly by reading Chapter 6.
		Determine whether you customers have proper embedding processes by reading Chapter 9.
		Gain some useful anecdotes by reading the case studies in Chapters 4–9.
Industry outsiders	I've just been handed the job of running a major innovation project in our non-retail organisation. I'm looking for some guidance on how to make it successful.	You need to be clear on how similar your organization's environment is to a retail environment (re-read Chapter 2). Even if your environment is very different, most of this part of the book is going to be useful. You may also wish to follow the links to some of the online resources that are available.
	I'm really interested in the process of innovation. I want to see what lessons can be taken from the ReFRAME process and applied to other contexts.	If you have a personal interest in innovation read Chapters 4–6.
		If you have a professional interest in innovation as a process read Chapters 4–9.

04

Stage 1: Resetting the foundations and building an innovation launchpad

(GARETH)

Introduction

Retail organizations, like most companies, have their foundations in structure, process and resources. Foundations ensure that an organization can carry the daily weight of customers, transactions, team members and expectations. Foundations need checking from time to time but they are generally taken for granted as they are so inextricably linked with the routine running of the business.

Beginning a **ReFRAME** is not routine. It requires that foundations be re-set to become launchpads for innovation. If the quest is successful, your organization will be transported to a new way of operating. Launchpads are different to foundations and need to be built properly.

When NASA built launchpads for its missions to the moon and later for space shuttles there were a number of components to their construction.[1] First was a concrete hardstand measuring about 130 metres by 110 metres capable of withstanding the blast of the flames at launch, carrying the weight of the rocket itself and the infrastructure surrounding it. Next was the launch platform, whose job was to physically support the rocket and accommodate a service structure so that fuel, electrical power and communications infrastructure could be connected, and the astronauts could board. Finally, access platforms were needed to allow assembly, inspection and maintenance in the weeks and months before take-off. The launchpad as a whole needed to be capable of holding the rocket while the engines built up to full thrust. Only when the rocket was stable and ready to fly would the hold-down arms be released, and the take-off commence. NASA would not have contemplated launching a rocket into space without a properly built launch-pad, and neither should retailers consider beginning their innovation quest without one.

Like a NASA launchpad, a retail innovation launchpad has a number of components. First there must be a clear definition of business purpose. All stakeholders must be clear why the world is better off with your business and why your quest is important. Next there must be the establishment of an innovation culture that embraces ambiguity, empowers the team to take risks, frames failure as a learning experience and is seen to be led from the

FIGURE 4.1   The 'reset the foundations' process

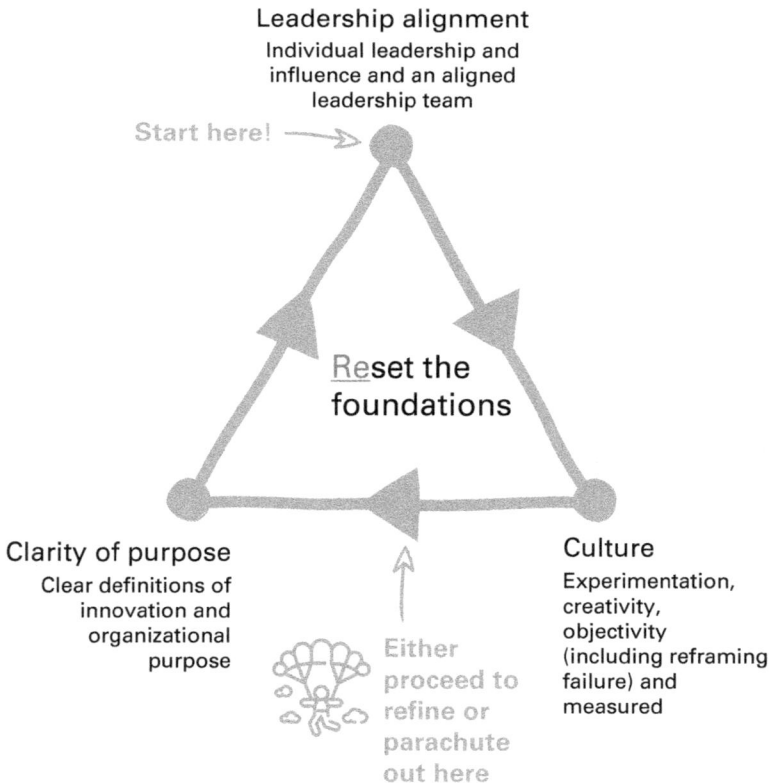

Leadership alignment
Individual leadership and influence and an aligned leadership team

Start here!

Reset the foundations

Clarity of purpose
Clear definitions of innovation and organizational purpose

Either proceed to refine or parachute out here

Culture
Experimentation, creativity, objectivity (including reframing failure) and measured

very top of the organization. This is the hard stand of retail innovation, which must be capable of withstanding the blasts of organizational change you are about to experience. Finally, there must be alignment among the executive management team. There will always be disagreements between executives around details, but without alignment on purpose and innovation culture the quest cannot begin.

Unlike a NASA launchpad, a retail launchpad can't be built by ordinary team members. This is a job for the executive management team with the approval of the board, which means the chief executive officer (CEO) must lead.

Purpose

Purpose is the reason why an organization exists. Some retailers think purpose means making a profit, but profit is only a permission slip from the market to be in business for another year. Purpose is why the world is better off with your business than without it. As we will see, retailers have many different purposes, but increasingly team members, customers and other stakeholders prefer a purpose that goes beyond 'return to shareholders'. Whatever the purpose, it must be clearly articulated and resonate with stakeholders to be effective.

Finding a purpose is especially important for established retailers at this point in their history. For thousands of years retail's purpose was clear. It was to bring products to customers at prices they were willing to pay. The emergence of the internet has changed that. The internet means we all have more than enough access to products, they can be delivered to our door and the best prices are always available. Established retailers need to find a new purpose if they are to thrive in the modern era of retailing.

From 2010 onwards, many of the biggest and most successful established retailers have adjusted their purpose to take account of the new environment. In most cases this has meant evolution rather than revolution. IKEA, like other price-based retailers, has traditionally had a purpose of creating a better life for people through lower prices. IKEA's classic vision statement is:

> At IKEA our vision is to create a better everyday life for the many people. Our business idea supports this vision by offering a wide range of well-designed, functional home furnishing products at prices so low that as many people as possible will be able to afford them.

Now, this classic vision statement has an addendum emphasizing the importance of environmental impacts and fair trade:

> Our vision also goes beyond home furnishing. We want to create a better every day for all people impacted by our business.[2]

Nike's classic mission 'To bring inspiration and innovation to every athlete in the world' is based on emotion and product innovation. It remains, but is now supplemented by a purpose statement that incorporates social responsibility: 'Our purpose is to unite the world through sport to create a healthy planet, active communities and an equal playing field for all.'[3]

Having a modern retail purpose that goes beyond range, price and proximity is an essential foundation for retail innovation. An article 'Getting uncomfortable on purpose' by the Boston Consulting Group explains the reasons why purpose is important to businesses generally.[4] I would now like to translate the reasons described in that article to a retail context and an innovation quest.

Alignment

Purpose helps build organizational alignment. (We will deal specifically with executive management and board alignment later.) Alignment is essential if you are embarking on a retail innovation quest. If the team doesn't have a clear articulation of where they are headed, how can they be expected to all move in the same direction? Alignment around purpose will also help when the time comes to make key innovation decisions like which technologies to adopt and which ones to filter out. Part of the Body Shop's purpose is to 'Enrich not exploit', which means their sourcing strategies are designed to support communities in poorer countries. Body Shop's decision to deploy a digital media network in their stores was taken, in part, to tell customers the story of the products on range made by African communities supported because of Body Shop's purpose.

Without the chance to align around a clear purpose, sceptics have a chance to opt out and do things the way they have always done them, potentially killing your innovation quest before it even gets started.

Innovative thinking

Purpose can, and should, be a stimulus for innovative thinking. A purpose statement should cause the team to think about the difference between how things are today and how they could be tomorrow. IKEA's modified purpose of creating 'a better every day for all people impacted by our business' has led to many innovative changes in their business. One of the most recent initiatives is a trial of renting products rather than selling them.[5] This programme not only gives customers a lower acquisition cost (part of IKEA's traditional purpose) but also extends the life of products, reduces waste and moves IKEA towards a circular business model. Similarly, H&M's revised purpose of 'leading the change towards a circular and renewable fashion industry' has created many innovative initiatives. Recently, H+M has implemented used clothing collection in-store, had designers trained in circular practices, and set a target that 35 per cent of its materials be sourced from recycled materials. It has also signed up to a number of global agreements with other fashion industry players to minimize environmental impacts and ensure ethical sourcing.[6]

Resilience

Purpose creates resilience. We have seen that innovation is particularly hard for retailers. When the going gets tough, a clear purpose reminds everybody of the big game and that this will be worth it in the end.

Inspiration

Inspiration is particularly important to retailers because customers and team members have plenty of choice of where to shop and where to work. An inspiring purpose can make the difference. Doug McMillon has spoken about the positive effect of Walmart's environmental and fair-trade purpose on customers: '(they) expect us to make decisions that are good for the planet and good for the people that make the products in our supply chain.... And the companies that provide it better than others will win.'[7] For retail team members, an inspiring purpose can be the difference between joining and not joining, staying and leaving, or giving 100 per cent or just enough. At '@Pizza' stores in the USA, the purpose statement is more prominent than the menu. The team member 'tribe' are so inspired by it they are likely to have '@Pizza' tattooed on their arm. Wouldn't we all like to have team members who are that engaged when starting an innovation quest!

Stakeholders will not be inspired without a purpose that resonates with them. A 2019 study by Parmar, Keevil and Wicks showed team members are between 17 per cent and 33 per cent more motivated when a business purpose de-prioritizes corporate profits.[8]

Financial performance

Some retailers will say that purpose is just middle-class fluff and that it is no substitute for great products and great prices. While great range and great prices are still vital, they are no longer enough on their own to win. Finding the right purpose and articulating it clearly will make team members feel good about working for you and customers feel good about shopping with you. You will harness what has been called their 'discretionary effort', which means they will go above and beyond to support your brand.

If that's not enough, then there are the financial rewards. A 2019 study by Gartenberg, Prat and Serafeim shows that purpose-driven companies outperform their peers both in financial results and stock market performance.[9]

EXERCISE
How to find your purpose

If your retail business does not have a purpose beyond creating economic value, how can it be created? We will start with what not to do. Do not go to one of the consulting companies that tell you they 'did' the purpose for other retailers. Although you may need some coaching, purpose is something you must find for yourself. It is a job for the executive management team and board led by the CEO. If you are not in that group, you might be entitled to nudge them on the benefits of purpose, but you will not be able to get it done. For those of you that are in that group, aspire to be there or are just curious about process, try the following exercise. This exercise is based on an excellent *Harvard Business Review* article, 'Creating a purpose-driven organization', by Robert E Quinn and Anjan V Thakor.[10] Included in the article is an eight-step guide to creating a purpose-driven organization. The following exercise relates to the first three steps, which are concerned with developing the message. We have adapted it for a retail context.

Step 1: Look for excellence and examine the purpose that drives the excellence

Retail is not the highest paying occupation. Many of your team could make more money working in another industry, but chose to stay in retail and with your company. Some are just marking time, others do it because it's convenient, but some are superstars. The superstars are those team members who consistently do an incredible job no matter what part of the business they work in and whatever they are getting paid to do it. Why do they perform so well? It would be easier for them to just turn up and put in an average performance, but they do not. The difference is that they have an underlying purpose motivating the way they work.

Some time ago, when video stores were still abundant and Netflix was still a mail order business, I worked for Video Ezy, a large Australian chain that was trying to lift its retail game. Each year, Video Ezy ran a movie knowledge quiz that was open to every team member. The grand final took place at our support office with the executive management team, CEO, chairman and some of the board in attendance. The grand final happened to take place not long after I joined. What I saw on the night of the grand final was the purpose that drove the excellence of the finalists. They were all motivated by their love of movies and loved working for a business where they could watch movies and share their love with their customers.

Action

Talk to some of your best performing team members. What is the purpose that drives them to produce excellence?

Step 2: Discover the purpose, don't make it

Your purpose cannot be manufactured, but the good news is it is already in your organization waiting to be discovered. Organizations that try to manufacture a purpose and only involve the executive management team (with the help of consultants) to do so will end up with a box ticked but most likely a collection of platitudes. Retail is a unique industry in that the majority of its employees have direct contact with the customer every day. They know why your business has value in the world better than anybody else. In our experience the answer to every problem in retail is waiting to be found if you only listen carefully enough.

Action

Go out (yourself) and talk to as many people as you can about what your business means to the world now, and what it should mean in the future. You will be surprised at the number of gold nuggets and the level of consensus you will find.

Step 3: Be authentic

Creating a purpose statement that is inauthentic will generate cynicism in the team and an expectation gap with customers. Being inauthentic is worse than not having a purpose statement at all. Have you ever worked for a company that says it cares about customers but at the same time is knowingly collecting unnecessary fees and charges, sometimes for offering no service at all? That's what happened in the banking industry in Australia and led to a Royal Commission.[11] There is also the famous case of Cadbury, whose purpose, 'to shine a light on the kindness and generosity that we see in society,' was somewhat contradicted by its failure to pay UK Corporation Tax for six years.[12]

There is some evidence that corporate inauthenticity does not significantly change purchase behaviour. An IPSOS study[13] showed millennials prefer brands with purpose but only 12 per cent have chosen a brand because of its responsible behaviour and only 16 per cent have boycotted one. However, if your employees think you are inauthentic, they will give less than their best and may start looking for somewhere else to spend their days where their work will mean more.

Action

Now look at the gold nuggets you gathered in step two and see which ones you are ready to live by today and which ones you are prepared to aspire to live by tomorrow. Once you have done that you are ready to write your purpose statement.

Culture

Organizational culture has been described as an organization's 'personality – sometimes overt but often unstated – that guides the decision-making process at all levels of an organization'.[14] In the retail world it is 'the way we do things around here'. Culture is the most powerful force in a business. It is capable of propelling an innovation quest into orbit or sabotaging it before take-off.

An innovation culture is different to a traditional retail culture. While traditional retail culture values execution, short-term results and control, an innovation culture embraces ambiguity, sees failure as a learning experience and empowers the team to take risks. Deploying an innovation culture requires leadership from the very top. The first step towards developing an innovation culture is having the executive management team embrace it.

Ambiguity

The world of retail is normally one of certainty. To operate a retail business successfully there need to be strict policies around stock management, staff management and operational procedures. Part of being a successful member of a retail team is being comfortable with living in a business environment bound by strict rules. In contrast, the world of innovation is one of uncertainty and ambiguity. There is no rule book. One of the challenges of innovation is to write the rules as you go. Retailers must recognize the dichotomy and that culture needs to accommodate ambiguity if innovation is to thrive.

Failure is a learning experience

Innovation must be supported by a business culture that sees failure as a learning experience, not something to be punished. In my first role running a retail buying office I had a CEO who actively encouraged my team to fail. His philosophy was if the buying office isn't making a few mistakes then they are not trying hard enough. He knew that sales growth came when our buyers took risks, not when they played it safe. All he asked was that we get it right at least 51 per cent of the time.

When the CEO retired, his replacement had exactly the opposite philosophy. A bad buy was punished and, at worst, deemed as grounds for dismissal. Needless to say, the culture in the group changed almost overnight. Risk taking was out, playing it safe was in.

Motivating through threats of punishment can be effective in some circumstances but an innovation quest is not one of them.

Empowerment

A retail business runs on strict authority levels. When you go to a retail store for a refund or exchange, a manager usually has to authorize it. The same will apply if there is a problem scanning the purchase price, or stock needs to be transferred from another location to satisfy your request. Hierarchical authority levels in retail operations are considered necessary to protect thin operating margins.

The application of hierarchical authority levels is less effective when dealing with innovation. I once talked to a prominent retail chief information officer (CIO) in a large, established retail organization about the difficulties multiple levels of approval caused him in delivering innovation for his organization:

> We have a business case process that you go through where you get sign-off from all the various stakeholders, do the due diligence around the numbers, create a net present value (NPV) and create a statement of business benefits

and quantify those. Then it goes up through four gates – and where it's a big amount, it goes up to a fifth stage. You do that with innovation and you've probably lost three or four months and by that time you should already have seed-funded a piece of work, got it to at least an idea/concept stage [where you can] evaluate it to see if it smells good and give it a bit more funding.[15]

Innovation can't wait that long. Teams running innovation projects must be empowered to get on with it.

Leadership

Culture change must come from the top. Team members must be able to see the executive management team living the 'new way we do things around here'. An inauthentic change in culture is just as bad as an inauthentic purpose. Certain actions in a business must still attract punishment, but a failed innovation project can no longer be one of them.

Incoming CEOs often find established business cultures difficult to change. That's because the various elements of a business culture interlock and are mutually re-enforcing.[16] But once team members see the executive team comfortable with the ambiguity of innovation, empowering the teams who are tasked with producing it and nurturing innovation not punishing failure they gain the authority to begin the innovation quest.

EXERCISE
How innovation-ready is your business culture?

Instructions

Rate yourself 1–10 on the questions in Table 4.1, then repeat the exercise for a retailer you know in another sector and compare the results.

Results

- *Score 70–100:* Congratulations! Your business culture is innovation-ready. Time to start the quest

- *Score 40–69:* There are some positive signs of an innovation culture emerging in the business. Isolate the remaining issues and deal with them before you begin the quest.

TABLE 4.1 Ratings comparison

Question	Score									
1. Does your business tend to reward compliance more than initiative (Yes = 1, No = 10) or is it somewhere in between?	1	2	3	4	5	6	7	8	9	10
2. Are reporting lines always rigid (score 1), always fluid (10) or somewhere in between?	1	2	3	4	5	6	7	8	9	10
3. How hierarchical is your business? (1 = very hierarchical, 10 = not hierarchical) or somewhere in between?	1	2	3	4	5	6	7	8	9	10
4. In general, are arguments decided based on the relative rank of the protagonists (= 1), by who has the best idea (= 10), or somewhere in between?	1	2	3	4	5	6	7	8	9	10
5. Are the approval processes for innovation projects the same as (= 1) or different from (= 10) other projects in the business?	1	2	3	4	5	6	7	8	9	10
6. Are the people that thrive in your business risk takers (= 10) or risk avoiders (= 1)?	1	2	3	4	5	6	7	8	9	10
7. Are the people that thrive in your organization compliant (= 1) or disruptive (= 10)?	1	2	3	4	5	6	7	8	9	10
8. Generally speaking, is failure in a project seen as something to be punished (= 1) or a learning experience (= 10)?	1	2	3	4	5	6	7	8	9	10
9. Do you feel that failure in an innovation project would be detrimental to your career even if you had performed strongly in every other aspect of your job (= 1) or would the experience be seen as a positive for your chances of promotion (= 10)?	1	2	3	4	5	6	7	8	9	10
10. When your CEO interacts with the team, do they talk more about the importance of generating innovation (= 10) or the importance of compliance (=1)?	1	2	3	4	5	6	7	8	9	10

- *Score 10–39:* You have a long way to go. The culture in your business has probably served you well for a long period of time, but now it's the problem. Unless you adopt a culture that's supportive of innovation you will not be able to make the changes you need to adapt to the new environment. Call for help!

The biggest barrier to developing an innovation culture is tradition and a history of success. Businesses will keep doing things the way they have always done them if they have a proud heritage of positive results. Unfortunately, if that culture values execution, short-term results and control above all else then it is incompatible with an innovation quest. Some will not be convinced that their culture needs to change. This book is not for them. For those that do recognize the need for change we will show how accepting ambiguity, relinquishing control and embracing failure as learning can be de-risked and provide the culture you need to begin the quest.

Leadership alignment

Once your purpose has been articulated and an innovation culture has been established, the management team must align. If the management team is not aligned, the broader team will be confused and cynical while traditionalists will sense weakness and infer permission to block innovation projects. This will make it impossible to deliver a reframe.

A few years ago, I was asked to run a retail innovation workshop with the executive management team of a large Australian public company. The opportunity had come about because of a meeting between our CEO and the CEO of the customer. The customer CEO had said that the key to their success in the future would be their retail offer but that they needed to transform what they were doing to be successful. He was also unhappy with the rate of transformation up to that point. Having been on our own journey of retail transformation, the customer was eager to learn from our experience. It was agreed that there would be three workshops that would include all the customer CEO's direct reports. This was a golden opportunity for us, so we prepared well. We hired a professional facilitator and assistance from a big 4 consulting firm with building and validating the process and methodology.

The day of the first workshop arrived and the customer executive management team gathered in one of the boardrooms. One conspicuous non-attendee was the CEO himself. We started to go through our material, but it was hard going. Rather than being aligned on purpose and innovation culture, the executive management team were at each other's throats and attempted to score points off each other at every opportunity. We limped to the end of the workshop and agreed a date for the second session.

The second session was predictably worse than the first. The CEO was a no-show again, and this time some of the executives had excused themselves as well. We got to the end and agreed a date for the final workshop, which was to be the one where actions were agreed. In the end the final workshop never happened. A long-term supply deal was done between our two companies in the interim, which took the urgency out of the project from our side. I think this was a relief for the customer executive management team, who were glad to see us go away.

In the years that followed, not much changed. Innovation at the customer continued in fits and starts but it was not coordinated and not transformative. Most of the executives we met in the workshop left the business, but the frustrated CEO remained.

CASE STUDY
Digital transformation at 7-Eleven
by Stephen Eyears, Head of Strategy, Innovation and Business Development

In our business (just like many, I guess), we had been thinking long and hard about how we best meet the needs of our customers in terms of digital engagement. Early efforts had turned out to be more successful with customers than expected and we were looking to take some incremental steps to capitalize on that. We are fortunate that we have a board that constantly pushes us to think big, and we were reminded of that when our first set of plans were put forward. So incremental steps turned into a long-term plan and an audacious digital ambition or North Star. The plan was backed by a road map for 'no regrets' technology and people capability coupled with near term substantial upgrades to our customers' digital experience to put us among the leaders in our space. But the foundations we sought to lay out and the investment required also needed a belief in the long-term horizon. In that respect, we were looking at scenarios for the end of the decade where we could never be so specific in relation to customer needs and supporting technology.

So how do you get everybody to the point of aligning on the scale of investment, the priority and the inevitable offset around the things we are not going to do as a consequence? I would never underestimate the value of a 'go see'. Of course you need to do the work on the business case, have the debates around the conference table and lean in to the detail, but seeing things in action, hearing perspectives from experts and getting some glimpse of the future (perhaps outside your market or immediate industry) as a group will always accelerate your path forward.

'Go sees' are normally quite small-scale affairs involving the managers most directly affected by the innovation. Fortunately, in this case the business was prepared to think big. A proposal for an intensive week-long overseas 'go see' trip with a large number of executives and board members was approved. It was a substantial investment of resources and time but considered necessary by key stakeholders given the ambitious scale of the plans.

The trip was planned meticulously based on very specific business drivers and everyone worked really hard from breakfast to bedtime. We varied the experiences from start-ups to some of the world's leading technology companies and store visits in and outside the convenience sector. We encouraged the team to ask a lot of questions even if they considered them dumb (they rarely are). Who doesn't value a global expert giving you a really super practical explanation as to what blockchain really is and how it may benefit your business?

Even with our tight schedule there was still plenty of time around the dinner table, on the bus or at the airport lounge to talk about what we were seeing and what it means. These are very powerful moments for a board and executive to share and can compress months of discussion into a few days.

Is alignment really possible or desirable?

Some CEOs believe that they need challenge and dissent within their management team to make sure that the best ideas come to the fore. A range of perspectives in the room is always more likely to result in good decision-making. In rugby, the halfback is the player who feeds the scrum, takes the ball from lineouts and feeds the ball to the backline from the break down so they can attack. It is a key role, but one with very specific skills. A good rugby team needs to blend a range of specialist skills to be successful. One of my old bosses used to say, 'We don't want a team of halfbacks.' He meant we would always be better off embracing a range of perspectives as well as challenge and dissent as part of our culture of innovation. As a management team, you should be aligned on that. On the other hand, there is room for debate but not dissent on purpose and culture. Purpose is an expression of a set of guiding principles for the business and, once agreed, should be championed by all. Culture is an expression of the way things are done and it has to be constructed to support innovation. There will still be competitiveness and disagreements among executives, but those that are not aligned on purpose and culture are not buying in to the fundamental reasons why the company is in business and the way it operates. They should consider finding a business that aligns more with their view of the world.

A lack of alignment among the executive team and between the board and the CEO can create danger for the CEO in two ways. The first source of danger is executives that say one thing in executive meetings and another when they interact with their own team. The two-faced executive is not a rare species. I have observed them in the wild on a number of occasions. One of these sightings was when a new CEO took charge at a publicly listed retailer. The new CEO was a long-term employee and had a tough task ahead of him given a number of years of inaction and deteriorating results from his predecessor. As a long-termer, the new CEO had faith in the organization and conducted a series of internal meetings to share with the team the challenges faced by the business and his ambitions. He ended by saying that his door was always open if there was something they could see needed to change. After one of these meetings an executive manager thanked him warmly for taking the time to address the team and escorted the new CEO from the room. The executive then addressed his team. Worried about his reputation and his personal channel of communication to the CEO, he told the group, 'We heard what was said, but we know how we do things around here. Any communication with the CEO must go through me.' The new CEO didn't last long. His message of change was undermined by his own executives.

Another source of danger for CEOs is boards. Boards are constituted to represent the interests of shareholders. For some that means maximizing return. This is especially true if the board contains members from the venture capital community who have invested in the business and are looking for their minimum 20 per cent return on invested capital each year. We have already referenced studies that show purpose-led businesses outperform non-purpose-led businesses both in income and capital growth, but that may not be enough for your board. Your innovation quest may require investment before the financial results of being purpose-led and changing business culture can be delivered. The unfortunate truth is that most CEOs only get eighteen months to deliver. I once asked one of the most innovative retail CEOs in Australia how he managed to get so many projects funded by the board. He said to me, 'The only reason I get permission is that I've got the next two years' results in the bag. Without that it would stop.' Eventually the results dipped, the board lost their nerve and innovation faltered.

If you are a CEO, one of your most important jobs is to align your executive team and board around purpose and innovation culture. Any innovation quest is likely to be sabotaged by your own team unless you do.

Launching your quest without a launchpad

Finding your purpose, creating an innovation culture, and aligning the management team and board are not trivial tasks that can be achieved overnight. Some would say that if you wait for all those things to happen you would never get around to achieving any actual innovation. Wouldn't it be better to just launch your *ReFRAME* anyway and use the momentum of the project to pull the organization along with you? What's certain is that the result will always be better if you have built the launchpad. If there is a reasonable prospect of that being achievable it should always be your first option. As we have seen, innovation can be doomed before it starts if the platform is not in place at launch. However, in some circumstances launching your quest without a launchpad might be the right strategy but those circumstances are limited and come with risk.

The first circumstance under which you may consider launching your quest without a launchpad is when the project is relatively small. NASA's launchpads were constructed to blast rockets to the moon, but maybe your ambitions are a little more modest. If you are building a model rocket sometimes all you need as a launchpad is an empty matchbox. According to the Digital Trends website,[17] if you have a match, a bamboo skewer, some aluminium foil tape, and a candle or lighter, you're ready for launch! Your rocket isn't going to go on a spectacular mile-high flight, as the match rocket can only fly up to about 40 feet on a single head, but that may be all you want in the first instance.

The second circumstance under which you may consider launching without a solid launchpad is when you have CEO sponsorship. CEOs have the special power of being able to construct temporary launchpads. They can use this power to force the organization to align around an explicit purpose and culture of innovation and that is usually enough to get your project on its way. If you have a reasonably ambitious project and an organization not quite ready for innovation this may be your best option. We talk in Chapter 6 about the pros and cons of CEO sponsorship generally.

It goes without saying that relying on CEO sponsorship is risky. If the project fails, you may survive but will be wounded. It could also mean that the cause of innovation in the business is set back for a while. Even if you are successful, don't forget that a CEO's tenure is short. According to a study by PwC,[18] the average tenure of a CEO in 2018 was only five years. Once the CEO moves on, their temporary powers to build launchpads moves with them.

The third circumstance under which you may consider launching without a launchpad is when the need to innovate is genuinely urgent. These are the times when your business is faced with an immediate and compelling opportunity or threat. Under these circumstances you cannot afford to spend 90–100 days or more carefully running through the stages of a *ReFRAME*, you must implement change in a month, a week or even a day. Urgent innovation is rare but vital to get right. We cover it in detail in Chapter 10.

If your project is neither urgent nor small, and doesn't come with CEO sponsorship, then you need to make a valued judgement on whether the risks of launching the quest without a launchpad are worth it.

Conclusion

In this chapter we have learned that the foundations of a retail business need to be re-set to become launchpads before your innovation quest can begin. Without a properly built launchpad the innovation quest will be unable to take off, most likely sabotaged by the team that built it. Building the launchpad is the job of the executive management team led by the CEO. Its key elements are alignment around business purpose and innovation culture. In addition, the CEO must make sure that the board is aligned during the build, as the process may detract from financial results in the short term.

Tradition and historical success are the major barriers to building the innovation launchpad. Members of the board, shareholders and executive management are entitled to feel that the business practices that brought success in the past will bring success again. To overcome this the CEO needs to be able to demonstrate the superior performance of purpose-led businesses and the effectiveness of an innovation culture in achieving change. The CEO also needs to protect the business from the risks of innovation by ensuring projects are carefully selected and tested before rolling out at scale. We will cover the de-risking of retail innovation in subsequent chapters.

If you are a CEO, and you don't have the launchpad for an innovation quest in place, book a management retreat to begin the process of reviewing your business's purpose, identify cultural barriers to change and align the group. Clearly communicate the results of your retreat to the board and get their approval to build the launchpad. If you are a member of the executive management team, persuade your CEO to do the above. If you are a team member and the executive management team is not building a launchpad it's unlikely much is going to change where you work. Unfortunately, there is not much you can do. The executive management team are the only ones that can do this job. If you want to work at a retail company on an innovation quest, look for one who has a launchpad, or at least has one in construction.

Notes

1   Pearlman, RZ (2017) The milestone space missions launched from NASA's historic Pad 39A, 17 February [Online] https://www.space.com/35736-nasa-greatest-space-launches-from-pad-39a.html (archived at https://perma.cc/5SVL-ZUB7)

2   IKEA (2019) IKEA vision, culture and values [Online] https://ikea.jobs.cz/en/vision-culture-and-values/ (archived at https://perma.cc/RD7P-4ZEZ)

3   Nike (2019) Purpose moves us [Online] https://purpose.nike.com/ (archived at https://perma.cc/8VR3-JRFZ)

4   Grice, A, Reeves, M and Fuller, J (2019) Getting uncomfortable on purpose, The BCG Henderson Institute, BCG [Online] https://www.bcg.com/en-au/publications/2019/getting-uncomfortable-on-purpose.aspx (archived at https://perma.cc/E5WG-X3UD)

5   Thomasson, E (2019) Rent a Billy: Ikea to test furniture rental in 30 countries, *Sydney Morning Herald* [Online] https://www.smh.com.au/business/companies/rent-a-billy-ikea-to-test-furniture-rental-in-30-countries-20190404-p51amk.html (archived at https://perma.cc/USE3-LJRE)

6   Wightman-Stone, D (2019) H&M reports 'strong progress' towards sustainability, FashionUnited [Online] https://fashionunited.uk/news/business/h-m-reports-strong-progress-towards-sustainability/2019040242499 (archived at https://perma.cc/4T8Y-YNCW)

7   Ignatius, A (2017) We need people to lean into the future, *Harvard Business Review*, 95 (2), pp 94–100

8   Parmar, B, Keevil, A and Wicks. A (2019) People and profits: The impact of corporate objectives on employees' need satisfaction at work, *Journal of Business Ethics*, 154 (1), pp 13–33

9   Gartenberg, C, Prat, A and Serafeim, G (2019) Corporate purpose and financial performance, *Organization Science*, **30** (1), p 1

10 Quinn, RE and Thakor, AV (2018) Creating a purpose-driven organization, cover story, *Harvard Business Review*, **96** (4), pp 78–85

11 Wright, S (2019) The banking royal commission final report at a glance, *Sydney Morning Herald* [Online] https://www.smh.com.au/business/banking-and-finance/the-banking-royal-commission-final-report-at-a-glance-20190203-p50vg2.html (archived at https://perma.cc/S46L-Z9E3)

12 Osborne, H (2015). Cadbury owner paid no UK Corporation Tax last year, *Guardian* [Online] https://www.theguardian.com/business/2015/dec/06/cadburys-owner-paid-no-uk-tax-last-year (archived at https://perma.cc/S46L-Z9E3)

13 Duffy, B, Shrimpton, H and Clemence, M (2017) *Millennial Myths and Realities*, Ipsos MORI, London

14 The Hon Justice C Owen (2003) *The Failure of HIH Insurance: A corporate collapse and its lessons*, vol 1, Commonwealth of Australia, p 13

15 Jude, G (2016) *Innovation in Retail*, Telstra, Melbourne, p 41

16 Denning , S (2011) How do you change an organizational culture? Forbes, 23 July [Online] https://www.forbes.com/sites/stevedenning/2011/07/23/how-do-you-change-an-organizational-culture/#1909601939dc (archived at https://perma.cc/XL3B-CYQT)

17 Adams, D (2016) Up, up, and away: 4 high-flying rockets you can build at home, Emerging Tech, 8 September [Online] https://www.digitaltrends.com/cool-tech/how-to-build-a-rocket/ (archived at https://perma.cc/8YWY-LENR)

18 Per-Ola Karlsson, MT and Gassmann, P (2019) Succeeding the long-serving legend in the corner office, Leadership (95) [Online] https://www.strategy-business.com/article/Succeeding-the-long-serving-legend-in-the-corner-office?gko=90171 (archived at https://perma.cc/EDP5-QFYT)

05

Stage 2: Filter the right ideas using the golden rule

(GARETH)

Introduction

One of the big fears retail leaders have is choosing the wrong innovation idea to pursue. This is a good fear to have. Pursuing the wrong idea can be expensive, time consuming and drain the organization of the will to try again. The retail industry is littered with examples of well-intentioned initiatives gone wrong. In this chapter we introduce the golden rule and demonstrate how to use it to select the best and most sustainable innovation ideas to pursue. We also show how the golden rule can be used to distinguish true innovation from its impersonators. Finally, we show how to run an idea treasure hunt using the golden rule so that only the ideas with the best chance of sustainable success move forward.

The golden rule

The golden rule of retail innovation is:

> An initiative is only sustainable when it solves a customer problem, does something positive for the business and aligns with your purpose.

Retail innovation projects are like a three-legged stool. If all three legs are not securely in place it will inevitably collapse in use. The golden rule sounds

FIGURE 5.1 The 'filter your ideas' process

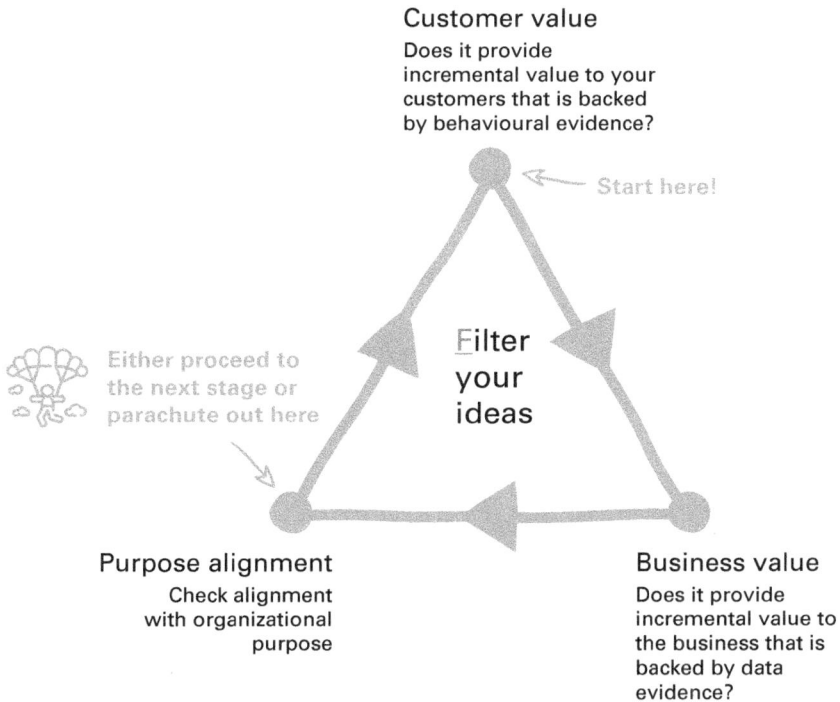

Customer value
Does it provide
incremental value to your
customers that is backed
by behavioural evidence?

Start here!

Filter
your
ideas

Either proceed to
the next stage or
parachute out here

Purpose alignment
Check alignment
with organizational
purpose

Business value
Does it provide
incremental value to
the business that is
backed by data
evidence?

simple but, in my career, I have seen retail innovation collapse many times. Failed innovation programmes plague the industry and are a waste of resources, opportunity and careers. Let us talk a bit more about the three legs and why you need them all in place to succeed.

Solving customer problems

As retailers, we serve customers every day so solving their problems is a good place to find opportunities for retail innovation. A common customer problem is that the way we serve them today is often no longer the way they want to be served. The digital world has changed shopping forever, and while customers may still be buying the products and services we sell, they might not be buying in the way we are set up to serve them. Solving customer problems is undoubtedly a worthy goal, but solving customer problems is only one leg of the stool. If the programme you put in place does not do something for the business or align with your purpose it will not stand up.

It is hard to imagine solving a customer problem not fitting a retailer's business purpose, but it does happen. Imagine you are running a chain of restaurants. Your research tells you a big customer problem is the lack of choice and options in your menu. You implement a radical programme that dramatically increases menu options and even allows customers to assemble meals to their own preferences from a range of options. Unfortunately, the programme fails because it does not align with your purpose. Your core purpose is to serve good food quickly and the extra menu options slow you down. Customers who love options love the programme but others who were attracted by your core purpose of good food served fast, drift away. Even worse the results are bad for the business. The extra options decrease efficiency and increase costs and your service quality surveys show satisfaction decreasing due to longer wait times. This example is not so imaginary. It is the dilemma being faced by the quick service restaurant (QSR) sector worldwide. Solving a customer problem is only one leg of the innovation stool. Solving a customer problem is not enough in itself to sustain a programme of retail innovation.

Doing something positive for the business

Retail innovation that does something positive for the business is also worthy, but pursuing this goal alone can easily conflict with customer outcomes and business purpose. Imagine you are running a chain of service-based retail outlets. More and more customers are doing their basic business online and you are receiving less and less traffic to your stores. You decide to radically reduce the store footprint and increase the services available to customers online. You begin to close stores, but new business falls almost in direct proportion to the number of stores you close. The upturn in online transactions is not enough to make up for the lack of new customer recruitment the store closure programme is causing. The programme is unsuccessful, because while there were obvious cost benefits to the business it did not offer enough positives to the customer and it undermined your purpose of being a trusted community advisor. This example is also not so imaginary. It is the dilemma being faced by service-based retailers worldwide. Doing something positive for the business is only one leg of the innovation stool. If the programme you put in place does not also solve a customer problem or align with your purpose it will not succeed.

Aligning with purpose: The golden rule in action

If we think back to some of the famous examples of retail innovation from 2000 to 2019, they all followed the golden rule. When Apple decided to open a chain of their own stores, they gave customers an experience they couldn't get in a regular retailer or dealer, they drove dramatically increased sales and margin for their business and created a retail space which embodied their purpose which was to educate and serve. When Starbucks introduced free Wi-Fi and mobile apps they created a digital haven and quicker transactions for customers, a decade of growth for their business and alignment with Starbucks' purpose of creating a 'third place' for its customers. When Nike decided to introduce customer co-creation to their stores, they enhanced customer experience and connection with the brand, delivered positive financial and customer engagement results for their business and alignment with Nike's purpose of providing innovation and inspiration to every athlete they serve.

Some retailers may feel that there are exceptions to the golden rule. They may look at their online competition and think while some online innovation is solving customer problems and probably aligns with purpose, it cannot possibly be delivering a return to the business given the lack of profits delivered by many online businesses. Essentially, those retailers say these online-only competitors cannot be following the golden rule because only two of the three legs of the stool are in place. This is not the case.

There are many legitimate measures of a return to a business, of which profitability is only one. What constitutes a return to your business is completely dependent on the context in which you operate. In the case of online retailers many have been primarily concerned with building economies of scale and logistical superiority. If an innovation initiative delivers these things for them then it is delivering a positive return to their business. If the initiative promises to also deliver a financial return in the form of increased market capitalization rather than positive cash flow or profit, then that too is legitimate. In his chapter on Amazon in his book *The Four*,[1] Scott Galloway demonstrates that while Amazon delivered virtually no profit from its retail operations between 2006–16 its market capitalization increased by 1910 per cent. During the same period, the market capitalization of other (mainly profitable) retailers declined. Online retailers like Amazon still need to follow the golden rule if they want to find the most sustainable and successful innovation initiatives to pursue. It is just that their idea of a return to the business might be different to yours.

EXERCISE

Your innovation health

Think of two recent innovation initiatives in your business – one that worked, one that did not.

- Do you know what the selection process was that got each of them resourced?
- To what extent does each initiative measure up against the golden rule?
- How could the innovation project selection project process be improved in your business?

Barriers

One of the enemies of the golden rule is the pet project. Pet projects are usually driven by senior managers or board members who have seen something or heard something and are sure this initiative will be a game changer for the business. Because of their rank and power, senior managers and board members can often get their project resourced without anything like due process. Some will work and some will fail, but if they fail it will not be before the organization doubles down on resourcing the project in an attempt to save the face or career of the sponsor.

The golden rule can help save pet projects and their sponsors. By running them through the process it will ensure only the most viable and sustainable proceed to resourcing. This protects all stakeholders. The best ideas still get through, meaning the business gains the benefits and the sponsors gain the kudos. The weaker ideas are filtered out, protecting the business from a waste of time and resources and the sponsors from loss of face and potentially loss of career.

How to distinguish real innovation from fakes

Do you ever get mistaken for somebody that is not you? It used to happen to me a lot. One day, when I was much younger, I was at Leeds railway station in England waiting for a connection. A very attractive Spanish lady kept looking at me. Normally I would have been flattered, but these looks were not endearing. In fact, if looks could kill I would not be writing this now. After a while she came up to me and gave me what they call in the

North East of England, a 'gobful'. I only understand a few words of Spanish, but I got the drift, and the drift was 'how dare I not speak to her after all we had been through together'. I replied, in English, that I was sorry but could not speak her language. Her face dropped and went from red and fiery to white and deathly. She had clearly mistaken me for somebody she knew well. She stared at me again, then apologized in English and went back to her place on the platform, occasionally giving me a double take as if she still couldn't believe what she had just seen.

Retail innovation often gets mistaken for things that it is not. Technology, design and cost cutting are often mistaken for innovation when at best they are facilitators and at worst expensive distractions from real innovation. Innovation is only real when it follows the golden rule, ie it solves a customer problem, does something positive for the business and aligns with your purpose. The shock of recognition when retailers realize what they thought was innovation is in fact just something that looks like innovation is just as bad for them as it was for that Spanish lady on the railway platform all those years ago. Why do we have so many cases of mistaken identity in retail innovation, and how can we guard against it?

Technology

The National Retail Federation (NRF) Big Show takes place in New York each January and is a great place to see the best retail technology the world has to offer. Just about every serious retail tech vendor in the world is there with their latest and greatest on an expo floor that covers 27,000 square metres. Imagine you have just come back from the Big Show, where you've seen some digital technology that's going to transform the way you communicate with customers in store and at the same time gather valuable data that will help you serve them better in all channels. You conduct a trial and the technology works beautifully, customers react positively, and it aligns with your purpose of offering customers a blended digital and physical experience. You think you have just found retail innovation, but you soon find it was a case of mistaken identity. The trial is unsuccessful because the resources required to keep developing content, analysing results and developing new campaigns after the trial is over are not available internally and are prohibitively costly if sourced externally. This should have been known before the trial started, but too much time was spent on the amazing technology and not enough time on what outcomes it could deliver for the business.

Trials of innovative technology that work technically but do not roll out plague our industry. I know of one company in Australia who deployed over 50 trials of a very impressive technology but failed to gain a single full-chain roll-out. This is a tremendous waste of resource and opportunity for both tech company and retailer. The most common problem is that trials tend to be sold on the features of the technology, not the benefits to the business. When business issues arise mid-trial, it looks like bad management not to have considered them earlier. Unsuccessful trials therefore become too embarrassing for many retail managers to re-visit.

Technology can be a marvellous facilitator of retail innovation, as we have seen over the last couple of decades. At Walmart, radio frequency identification (RFID) has facilitated higher rates of products being in stock for customers, lower inventory costs for the business, which in turn has allowed Walmart to support its purpose of low prices for its customers. At McDonald's, free Wi-Fi has provided customers with an extra reason to visit the store, increased dwell time, and created a new customer communication channel for the business, and alignment with McDonald's purpose of being their customers' favourite place and way to eat and drink. The internet itself has facilitated perhaps the greatest changes to retail we have ever seen making infinite amounts of product and services available to customers anywhere, anytime, allowing retailers to reach customers outside of their physical footprint and trading hours as well as allowing a host of new formats to develop. With mass adoption of smartphones, IOT, AI, block-chain and much more efficient ways to store and manage data, we may be living in the most exciting era ever for retail technology. But technology is still just a facilitator; it is not innovation in itself.

To ensure we do not mistake technology for innovation we should always apply the golden rule upfront by asking: Does the technology solve a customer problem? Does it do something positive for the business? Does it align with our purpose? If these three questions are answered positively then many more technology trials will be successful.

Store design

Being involved in the design of a new store is one of the most exciting things you can do as a retailer. Usually, the marketing/design agency will be called in to present a view of macro trends, how they affect consumer behaviour and how they relate to your brand personality and customer journey. Ultimately, a design will be presented that looks so good (they never look bad) that it could easily be mistaken for retail innovation. It will tick all the boxes from the research. It will include some greenery because your customers are environmentally conscious (which is also part of your purpose) and feel more comfortable in spaces that include plants. It will include places for customers to sit so that they feel happy spending more time in your store. It will include digital technology like screens, assistance kiosks and maybe Wi-Fi because contemporary customers value blending the physical and digital in their shopping experience.

You roll out the first stores in the new design and they look great. Unfortunately, the impact on sales is not what you had expected. In addition, when you walk the shopping centre you see a lot of other new stores looking very much like yours (lots of greenery, lots of places to sit, digital screens, free Wi-Fi, etc). The new design did not work because too much time was spent on making the store look good and not enough on solving core customer problems like long waiting times, complicated payment systems and poor omnichannel integration. The store looks so good that the fact that it is still really hard for customers to do business with you irritates them more than it did before.

Retail design that is based on looks rather than facilitating customer and business outcomes is common in our industry. When a new design fails to deliver, retailers often try to solve the problem by hiring another designer and going through the whole process again. When a design follows the golden rule, it does not need to change that much from year to year. Apple is a great example. I have pictures from my first visit to an Apple store more than a decade ago and while some things have changed the look and feel is still very recognizable. The design has substantially survived because it followed the golden rule. It still offers customers a better shopping environment than is available in other stores, it still allows Apple to convey its value propositions more effectively than it could in another environment, and it still helps facilitate Apple's original purpose for building its own retail channel, which was to educate and serve.

Cost cutting

Cost cutting is a good and necessary part of running a retail organization, but it should not be confused with innovation. Fortunately, this impersonation is easier to identify. Cost cutting's disguise is on par with a joke store moustache, glasses and a funny voice. You would have to be pretty naïve to mistake it for innovation. Management know this and tend to dress cost cutting up with futuristic sounding names or even just a date that's about five years away. When cynicism sets in, it is re-launched with another futuristic name or even just a new date. Cost cutting can facilitate innovation, especially in improving return to the business, but it should not be confused with real innovation.

Adapting to the golden rule

Retail is very competitive. As a retail leader, it is natural to want to go to trade shows, look at the latest designs and go to strategy conferences to get an edge on your competition. It is also natural to want to take action and deploy what you saw or heard in your own business as quickly as possible. Of course, it is important to keep up with what is going on in the world, but just because an initiative works in another market or in another company it doesn't mean it will work for you. Take the extra step of testing the initiative against the golden rule to see if it will provide a benefit for your customers and a return to your business, and aligns with your purpose. The golden rule will also help you work out whether there are better ideas already waiting in your business to be actioned.

Barriers

Tech companies, store designers and cost-cutting consultants are powerful influencers in the retail market and are sure to have strong connections into your business. They would not be doing their job if they did not try to convince you that what they have to offer is the most compelling investment you could make for your business. They will feel threatened by their ideas being subjected to the rigorous internal scrutiny that the golden rule implies.

On the other hand, tech companies, store designers and cost-cutting consultants can add great value to an innovation programme if they are involved when the time is right. All can provide insight from their wider experience of the retail world as to what ideas you should consider for your pipeline. Once an idea has been selected, they can become vital partners in the execution phase. The key to controlling their involvement is to make sure you use the golden rule as a filter between filling up the pipeline and selecting projects to pursue.

Tech companies, store designers and cost-cutting consultants may feel they stand to lose when you start using the golden rule, but rather than being a threat, the golden rule works to the benefit of all parties. Tech companies, store designers and cost-cutting consultants will be able to assist you more effectively when they understand how each specific initiative fits into your innovation programme as a whole. Furthermore, they have no more to gain from a failed initiative than you do. The golden rule can help preserve reputations and careers internally, but it can do the same for your external partners. For any external partner there is nothing more damaging than a negative reference site.

CASE STUDY
Domino's vs Pizza Hut 2013–18

In this chapter we have looked at how technology can, in some instances, be a marvellous facilitator of innovation while in others it can be merely an impersonator. Domino's Pizza Enterprises (DMP) from 2013 to 2018 provided an exemplar of how to deploy technology to facilitate true innovation. The technology deployed did not impersonate innovation – it facilitated it. What's more, the innovation deployed during this period clearly satisfies the golden rule. From 2013–18 DMP:

- increased sales and profits, and earned a share price multiple more like a tech stock than a retail stock;
- provided incremental value to customers through quicker and more assured delivery, easier ordering, new delivery options and co-creation opportunities;
- delivered on its purpose of 'bringing people closer, connecting them through the world's best bonding food: pizza'.[2]

Furthermore, the story of Domino's during this period also demonstrates how innovation is the only viable strategic choice for a retailer in a changing world. In head-to-head contests, traditional retail tactics like price reductions, cost cutting and increased marketing are no match for true retail innovation. We will also see in this case how a lack of stakeholder alignment (Stage 1 of **ReFRAME**) can stop innovation before it starts.

Domino's and Pizza Hut were the two leading retail pizza chains in Australia and New Zealand (ANZ) during the period 2013–18. Domino's ANZ is part of Australian Stock Exchange listed DMP, while Pizza Hut was operated by the local subsidiary of Yum foods for most of the period. DMP operates restaurants in Australia, New Zealand, Belgium, France, the Netherlands, Japan and Germany primarily through a franchised business model. DMP itself is a master franchisee of Domino's Pizza Inc, based in the USA. Yum is famous internationally for restaurant brands such as KFC and Taco Bell. Like Domino's, Pizza Hut operates its business predominantly through a franchised model. In 2017 Pizza Hut ANZ was sold to local private equity company Allegro, which has maintained the franchise model.

Detailed data to compare Domino's and Pizza Hut is difficult to obtain for two reasons. First, while both are part of publicly listed companies, results for the ANZ market are only partially revealed in company reporting. Second, where sales revenue to end consumers is reported, it is only for company-owned outlets. Most of the sales revenue for both brands is generated by franchisee outlets, but these are not reported at a corporate level. Instead, the fee income generated from the franchise agreement is reported. The analysis that follows is therefore based predominantly on estimates contained in industry research reports, company releases and press articles from the period.

Domino's

During the period 2013–18 Domino's reframed its business through technology. It became known and valued by the market as a technology company rather than a pizza company. Its share price peaked on 12 August 2016 at $A 76.91, valuing the company at a tech stock like multiple of more than 50x earnings. Major initiatives were announced in each year of the period (Table 5.1).

TABLE 5.1 Major Domino's initiatives, 2013–18

Year	Initiative
2013	World's first Facebook ordering app.
2014	iPad ordering app.
	Pizza Mogul: A co-creation programme in which customers designed their own pizza using Domino's ingredients, promoted it on their personal social media then were rewarded up to $4.50 for each pizza sold by Domino's online.[1]
2015	Smartwatch ordering.
	20-minute ordering guarantee.
	GPS Driver Tracker initial launch. Allows customers to track progress of their pizza delivery and for drivers to see the actual location of the customer. GPS Driver Tracker offered customers improved assurance that their order was on its way and created logistic and safety benefits for Domino's and their drivers.
2016	Domino's Robotic Unit (DRU) established. The main objective of the DRU was to improve customer experience and competitiveness through AI and robotics in the growing online ordering and delivery market. Domino's trademarked the phrase 'Internet of Food' to describe this segment.
	Project 3–10. The deployment of high-speed ovens that cook a pizza in 3 minutes, allowing delivery to a customer's home within 10.

(continued)

TABLE 5.1 (Continued)

Year	Initiative
2017	Domino's Anywhere. Facilitates delivery to a location without a street address, eg a beach or a park, using GPS technology.
	Social Logins: Direct login to Domino's online from social media accounts.
	Pay Pal bill share: Bill splitting for Pay Pal payments.
2018	New Cloud platform for ordering.
	Voice ordering via Alexa.
	Domino's Pizza Checker AI monitoring of pizza assembly to ensure correct toppings and product consistency, addressing the number one source of customer complaint from Domino's customers.

SOURCE Company announcements and industry reports
NOTE (1) Ross, K (2015) Crowdsourcing helps Domino's Pizza serve up rise in profit: Mobile application Pizza Mogul allows customers in Australia to design their own pizzas, *Wall Street Journal*, New York

While some of the Domino's management team were personal technology enthusiasts, these initiatives were far from technology for its own sake. Cumulatively the initiatives had the effect of improving customer experience (ordering, delivery, quality, payment) and creating a competitive advantage for Domino's. The financial results estimated by IBIS world were an estimated compound annual growth in revenue (CAGR) of 12 per cent (see Table 5.2),[3] growth in earnings before interest, taxes, depreciation, and amortization (EBITDA) from A$ 30.4 million to A$ 118 million, and growth in customer visits from 1.8 million per annum to 2.3 million per annum.[4]

TABLE 5.2 Domino's estimated sales revenue and growth, 2013–18

Year	Estimated revenue (AUD$m)[1]	Growth %
2012–13	485.5	N/A
2013–14	561	15.6%
2014–15	623	11.1%
2015–16	775.9	24.5%
2016–17	894.4	15.3%
2017–18	996.5	11.4%

SOURCE Vuong (2018)
NOTE (1) Includes estimate of sales revenue from franchised outlets.

Pizza Hut

At Pizza Hut, the focus was on generating growth through more traditional retail tactics, ie lower prices, efficiency improvements and marketing. In 2014 the Value Strategy (VS) was announced to franchisees. The VS required franchisees to reduce the ranges of pizza offered to customers, from four to two, leaving only 'Classics' and 'Favourites'. It also required that the price of 'Classics' pizzas would be reduced from A\$9.95 to A\$4.95, and for 'Favourites' from A\$11.95 to A\$8.50.[5] It was intended that the VS be part of an integrated marketing programme that included simplified menus and being first to market with a '\$4.95 Pizza all day every day'. The VS was tested in the Australian Capital Territory (ACT) and New Zealand. Pizza Hut claimed that these trials demonstrated a 48 per cent increase in sales for most franchisees.

The roll out of VS met resistance from franchisees. Franchisees considered the new low price-points uneconomic and the majority of them joined a court challenge against Pizza Hut to stop its deployment. Meanwhile, Domino's blunted the marketing impact of the VS by simply launching their own '\$4.95 pizza all day every day.' The court action by the franchisees was unsuccessful and was settled in Pizza Hut's favour in 2016.

The financial results Pizza Hut achieved during this period were less impressive than Domino's (see Table 5.3).[6] Although sales increased, Pizza Hut's CAGR is estimated to have been less than 3 per cent and most of this came from the acquisition of rival chain Eagle Boys in 2016. In addition, during the period 2012–16 a Roy Morgan research report shows customer visitation actually declined from 1 million per annum to 750,000 per annum.[7] EBITDA figures are not publicly available.

In late 2016 Yum sold Pizza Hut to Australian venture capital company Allegro[8] for an undisclosed sum, at about the same time as DMP shares peaked at \$A76.91. The DMP story shows that while technology can sometimes be an impersonator of innovation, it can also be a marvellous facilitator of genuine customer, business and purpose enhancing innovation.

TABLE 5.3 Pizza Hut estimated sales revenue and growth, 2013–18

Year	Estimated Revenue (AUD\$m)[(1)]	Growth %
2013	156.5	N/A
2014	158	1.0%
2015	170.1	7.7%
2016	174.6	2.6%
2017	240.4	37.7%
2018	240.5	0.0%

SOURCE Vuong (2018)
NOTE (1) Includes estimate of sales revenue from franchised outlets.

How to run an idea treasure hunt using the golden rule

If you are like most retail companies, you are sitting on a mountain of ideas. We know that those ideas must be filtered using the golden rule, but what is the best way to actually do that? The traditional approach is to have executive management filter the list and allocate resources as they see fit. This is slow and applies only the perspective of the senior management team to selecting which projects to pursue. Amazon favours devolving the filtering process in the organization. Initiatives are proposed on a 'narrative memo' then discussed in a 'two-pizza' sized meeting among a small number of stakeholders before moving on to the next stage or being rejected. Other organizations like Starbucks have dedicated innovation hubs that do the filtering. Retailers like Amazon and Starbucks are very successful innovators who already have innovation woven into the operating fabric of their businesses. Most retailers do not. We believe a different approach is required for retailers at the beginning of their innovation quest.

For retailers at the beginning of their innovation quest we recommend a more holistic approach to idea filtering. We call our process the 'idea treasure hunt'. It is designed to motivate the organization to take on the innovation quest and facilitate the transition to an innovation culture. The process involves representatives of all internal and key external stakeholders, is founded on regular face-to-face workshops led by the CEO, requires that 50 per cent of the attendees be customer-facing team members, is based on consensus but relies on management to make the final decision on which projects progress. The next sections describe the details of the process and provide tips on how you can justify it to management.

Where?

The best place to conduct an innovation idea treasure hunt is in a room, face to face. This presents a challenge for all retailers with operations in different towns, cities, states and countries and in periods where face-to-face meetings are not possible. Face-to-face meetings take a long time to organize and are expensive and difficult to justify when compared to quicker and cheaper alternatives. We have seen time and again that face-to-face meetings produce better innovation outcomes than the alternatives. If you have had the same experience but are having problems justifying the expense of bringing the team together in one place, especially after the boom in virtual meetings during COVID-19, the next few paragraphs should help.

ELECTRONIC SURVEYS

One alternative to the face-to-face meeting is the electronic survey. Surveys are quick and easy to administer and are inexpensive. Some are sophisticated and carefully present choices available to the stakeholders while others simply state, 'This is what we have decided to do – we're interested in getting your feedback before we do it.' Whatever the level of sophistication, surveys have a number of disadvantages.

The first disadvantage is that a survey will generate guarded responses. Written communication in a business is a big deal. Every organization has rules about what can and can't be said and employees know intuitively that once something is written, in the words of the arresting officer, 'it may be used in evidence against you'. There is a place for guarded responses in a business but deciding which ideas to bet your future on is not one of them.

The second disadvantage is that the survey approach misses the opportunity for interaction between the team members. Groups are pretty good at recognizing good ideas and working together to build on them. It's what separates humans from most other species. A group can also bring different perspectives to an issue that may help overcome a deployment concern or identify a risk that others hadn't thought of.

TELECONFERENCE/VIDEO CONFERENCE

Another alternative to the face-to-face meeting is the teleconference or video conference. They became the new normal during the period of COVID-19 social distancing restrictions. Teleconferences and video conferences are a little harder to organize and a little more expensive than surveys, but they have the advantage of being quicker and less expensive than face-to-face meetings. They also allow a degree of interaction between the team, which a survey can't provide. However, they do have number of disadvantages.

Since COVID-19 we are all a lot more experienced and skilled in the use of teleconference/video conferences, but they are still subject to technology and related user problems. Most conference calls are conducted on voice over internet protocol (VOIP) technology. This makes the calls cheap but the bandwidth supporting it thin. Calls often drop out and the quality can be poor. The teleconference/video conference is also reliant on the quality of the technology held by each user. If the camera or microphone on a device is inadequate, or the Wi-Fi connection available on the day is not good enough, the result will be a poor conversation. In addition, users unfamiliar with your particular conference call application may not leave enough time to load it on their device, meaning they join late or not at all. Some software has rules about the number of attendees that can join a call, which can mean that even experienced users can find themselves excluded if they join after the cut-off point.

The second disadvantage of the teleconference/video conference is the 'busy' executive. Many executives use the 'mute' button as an opportunity to catch up with email or even catch up with colleagues in the office during the call. If this is what happens in your business, then the teleconference/video conference is worse than a survey.

For international businesses, the third disadvantage of the teleconference/video conference is time zones. Time zone differences exist within many countries but are generally manageable. When the difference goes intercontinental, it means some people will be attending when they are barely awake or ready to go to sleep. Some international businesses are proud of their 24/7, anywhere, anytime culture but it's unrealistic to expect engaged interaction on a topic such as which innovation initiative to bet the company on from people attending meetings way before their day has started or way after it has ended.

I have attended some video conferences where it was as if we were in the same room as the people on the other end of the line. This type of video conference is much closer to the face-to-face meeting. However, they can only be conducted in dedicated facilities equipped with the right technology at each point of the call. If you have access to these facilities then videoconferencing becomes a more viable option. The costs are high compared to any VOIP system but very low compared to the cost of flights and accommodation to bring the team to one place. Even so, there are still some disadvantages.

The high-quality video conference cannot deliver the informal chat in the coffee break, at breakfast or the unguarded moment at the team dinner before or after the session. One of my old bosses used to say, 'We all do our best work when nobody is looking.' As far as innovation is concerned, the best contributions often come when we are unguarded and in informal situations. In other words, when the cameras are off. We also need these moments to build relationships, because when we build relationships, we build trust. Trust is the most precious commodity in an innovation quest because it facilitates the speed and agility required to get things done.

FACE TO FACE

Face-to-face meetings have further advantages when compared to any other way of conducting your idea-filtering session. The first is that it will give you full access to non-verbal communications between attendees. The often-quoted assertions that 93 per cent of all communications are non-verbal or that the impact of a communication is determined 7 per cent by the words used, 38 per cent by voice quality, and 55 per cent by the non-verbal communication have largely been debunked. However, in their book *Nonverbal Communication*, Burgoon, Guerrero and Floyd[9] show that, regardless of the actual percentage, there is plenty of evidence to suggest that people rely on non-verbal cues both to express themselves and to interpret what others say. They also cite research that shows when verbal messages contradict non-verbal ones, adults usually believe the non-verbal messages over the verbal ones and rely on non-verbal behaviour to judge another's attitudes and feelings (For example, 'We heard what they said but we know what they really meant'). High-quality video conferences come close to delivering this but can't quite replace the visceral experience of being in a room with other people.

The other unique advantage of bringing a team together is its motivational effect. Being picked for any team can give all of us a lift, but being part of this team is special. Our business lives are often lonely, especially if you are trying to promote real change. Being part of the team that is deciding which innovation initiatives to pursue will make your attendees feel they are part of something bigger. This feeling will be enhanced when they see that others in the group are real people not just names on an email or faces on a screen. The attendees will also appreciate the investment the company has made in them to attend the meeting and be motivated by the opportunity to have their say in a major company forum.

Who should be there?

The idea treasure hunt is a team game. It is not a job that can be done solely by the management team or dedicated innovation groups. A broad cross-section of stakeholders, including representatives from the board and all functional areas of the business, need to be involved. The CEO is the captain of the team and must attend. If you work in a very large organization or one where retail is only part of the portfolio then it should be the functional head of retail that leads. In the previous chapter we showed why leadership is so important to an innovation quest. It would not make sense for the captain to abandon the bridge so early.

INVOLVING THE CUSTOMER-FACING TEAM

The team that serve your customers every day will always be in the best position to judge what changes are needed to improve your business. They need to make up at least half the numbers at the meeting. Your customer-facing team are not burdened by what they have seen at a trade show or study tour or heard at a conference or from a partner. Instead their ideas will come from first-hand experience of what is required to serve your customers better than they are being served now.

Customer-facing team members also have inbuilt 'BS' filters and will call an idea out if it does not work logistically or practically, or would require a significant change to current systems to be implemented. I once asked a team member at an international cosmetics retailer if the new technology management had introduced to facilitate virtualization of the in-store experience was working. They confided a flat 'No' because the key to selling cosmetics in store is making a physical connection with the customer either by applying product or assisting in the cleaning process. In this instance the management mandated technology was an inhibitor, not a facilitator, of a better shopping experience and business outcome. This innovation failure could have been prevented if the customer-facing team had been involved in idea filtering.

It is important to carefully select which team members are invited to attend. Not all team members are equal. Some are motivated superstars who always give extra, whatever their role or pay scale, while others merely do the job. It is of course the first group and not the second that you should invite to your filtering session. The first group are problem solvers, can work within constraints and are purpose driven. Your company is where they want to work. They are invested in your future. The second group will tend to tell you everything that is wrong with the business and why you should do everything that your competition does. (Maybe that's where they really want to work.)

EXTERNAL STAKEHOLDERS

External stakeholders often try to take control of the innovation agenda. That is why they invite you to expensive paid study tours, trade shows, or learned presentations from international strategists. External stakeholders have a vital role to play in exposing you to broader perspectives of what is happening in the world and in generating ideas for the innovation pot but under no circumstances should they take control of the idea treasure hunt. Having said that, as long as the business is firmly in control, external stakeholders can add significant value.

Key service providers like your marketing agency, long-term tech partner or your legal counsel are especially valuable in providing an important perspective on many issues that's not available internally. Ideally, only service providers who have legal and ethical agreements on non-disclosure should be considered. It is obviously not appropriate to invite service providers whose future is put in doubt by the initiatives you are going to discuss.

One external stakeholder that will be important to making the meeting a success is a facilitator. Facilitators have the experience to keep moving things along, have tricks to keep everybody engaged and are also not hampered by ingrained opinions about what needs to change. The facilitator's job is to simply help draw out the value that already exists in the room.

HOW MANY?

The group you assemble needs to be big enough to provide a perspective from all parts of the company and comprise at least 50 per cent customer-facing team members. There will be group work involved, so four to six groups of four to six people are optimal to keep things interesting. This means there should be no less than about sixteen people in attendance and no more than about thirty-six. Thirty-six may seem like a lot, but as a percentage of your workforce it is not many at all if you are a large company with thousands of employees.

When?

Retail is a fast-paced business. You always need to be able to respond to opportunities and competitive threats as quickly as possible. Retailers are generally good at this, and whatever mechanisms are in place to generate these tactical responses should remain. Innovation is different. It is about changing the way business is done and does not and cannot run at the same pace. Even nimble and experienced retail innovators like Amazon and Starbucks need more than a hundred days to deploy an innovation trial and the initiative may have waited for some time before that to be selected.

It would be great to run a CEO-led idea filtering session every month, but that is not practical and doesn't reflect the time it takes to actually develop an idea to test stage. Remember, in most retail businesses idea generation is not a big problem. There are always likely to be a backlog of ideas to act upon. The problem, and the motivation for writing this book, is execution is often falling short. The purpose of the treasure hunt is simply to select the best and most sustainable ideas to move on to the first stage of development. That being the case, three to four sessions per year should suffice. The cadence of meetings to manage the progress of projects once they have been selected will be discussed in subsequent chapters.

Preparing the treasure hunt workshop

There are any number of books and articles that can help you structure an innovation workshop. We particularly like the techniques described in the books by Alex Osterwalder, Yves Pignuer *et al* on *Business Model Generation*[10] and *Value Proposition Design*.[11] There is no need to go into detail here about every aspect of how an innovation workshop should be conducted. That is the artistic part, and something you should lean very heavily on your facilitator to provide. Instead we will look at some of the key design elements that have made workshops we have been involved in over the last few years successful.

Set your goals and define success

You have got approval to run this workshop, but it's a lot of work and it's expensive. It is important that it yields actionable outcomes. Remember that this group has never been together before and, if you have done your groundwork right it includes the CEO and members of the board. The stakes are high. Everybody will want to see results. It is fine to have soft goals like team building and collaboration between stakeholders, but that is not enough. Success should include recommending a number (you decide how many) of innovation projects to the executive management team for resourcing. One of your goals should be to attach enough information to each recommendation so it can be considered properly. Do not worry about detailed financial information, other than perhaps your estimate of sales impact. The executive team are in a much better position than your group to assemble the full financial context for their decision. The CEO should pre-commit to moving at least one of the recommendations from the workshop on to the next stage of the process.

Find a suitable location

You need to find a space that is big enough to accommodate the group but with the capacity to allow break outs. These do not need to be separate rooms but, as a minimum, there should be space in a room where groups can be separate. There are pros and cons for holding the workshop off site or on site. Your final decision will be based on your individual circumstances. Off site is always more relaxing and interruption free but it can add to cost and complexity. If you have suitable space in the business and want to use it, be firm about managing interruptions. If you prefer to go off site but do not like the cost and hassle perhaps one of your key partners may have space you can use without incurring a fee.

When booking an off site space, think of practicalities. It is really nice to have an off site at the beach or a winery, but will that mean extra travel time for your participants? Near the airport and major travel links is good.

Design a clear agenda

Make sure your agenda is clear and allows enough time to address each topic adequately. Lean on your facilitator here. The time needed to have breakout groups feed back to the larger group and to articulate areas of consensus are often underestimated.

Select scene setters

The group you assemble will be from different parts of the business, and may include board members and some key external stakeholders. They all will have different levels of understanding of the business challenges and the external context in which you are about to make decisions. That means you will need to get them on the same page. The agenda needs a section on business performance and strategy as well as one that covers the business environment including trends, best practice, impact of technology, etc. The latter is where it may be appropriate to lean on partners to present. This section of the agenda is important but don't let it drag on. Sixty to ninety minutes is enough.

Agree the rules of engagement

Agree upfront the rules for the meeting. I'm sure you already know what makes a good meeting and what makes a bad meeting; however, in our experience we have observed that in innovation workshops it's good to ban mobile phones to prevent distractions and encourage open debate to allow every voice to be heard.

We also believe it is important to aim for consensus. You need to agree which pieces of treasure you find are the most valuable. Business is not a democracy. In the end the leader of the business is responsible for its welfare and has the final say, but going for consensus is fun and motivational and has a practical benefit. When it comes time to deploy innovation, the ideas that have the support of all stakeholders will be easy to deploy, whereas those that divide a room of your best and brightest come with a high degree of difficulty.

Some ideas should be exempt from the treasure hunt process completely. We have all heard the phrase 'Turkeys don't vote for Christmas'. If you know that you have initiatives to consider that will directly challenge many of your stakeholders' future livelihoods, it's best to handle that in another way.

Whatever your rules of engagement, the important thing is to get everybody to agree to them at the start so that the meeting can run the way you want it to run.

Do not leave without an action plan

Above all, do not leave without an action plan. If one of your goals is to recommend three initiatives to the executive management team for resourcing, name who will present it and get a date from the CEO for when it will be considered. If another is to get more information on a particular initiative, then make somebody responsible for doing it and get a date when they must report back to the group. While you are on a roll, why not set the date for the next workshop?

Management review of outcomes

It is up to the management team, led by the CEO, to give final approval as to what projects will be pursued. If the golden rule has been applied properly, no proposals will reach the management team that do not offer value for the customer and the business, and align with the purpose of the organization. While frontline team members are able to judge what initiatives will best improve value for the customer, the management team are best equipped to assess financial and strategic impacts for the business. There is plenty of advice around on how to assess an innovation idea for investment[12] and how to build a portfolio of innovation initiatives.[13] We would only add that these decisions will depend on the specific circumstances of the business and whatever methodology is chosen for selection the criteria should be different for innovation than for BAU projects.

EXERCISE
Testing the treasure hunt

If you are still not sure the workshop format will work for you, try this short exercise, which is a snapshot of how it will work:

1   Pick the three most important things your business should do to give customers a better shopping experience. Rank them. Pick the three most important things that could be done to run the business more efficiently. Rank them.

2   Apply the golden rule. Does your ranking match the golden rule ranking? If not, why not?

3   Message a couple of colleagues and ask them to do the same exercise.

4   Have a coffee and discuss the results. Can you agree on the top two initiatives the business should resource?

Conclusion

There needs to be a process to filter innovation ideas, otherwise the wrong initiatives can be pursued, leading to wasted resources and, in extreme cases, wasted careers. Applying the golden rule (solves a customer problem, does something positive for the business and aligns with your purpose) ensures that only the most sustainable ideas are pursued, and innovation impersonators are unmasked before too much damage is done.

Externally, tech companies, design agencies and advisors have a powerful motive to control the innovation agenda and are well connected in most businesses. Internally, managers with rank (especially those who regularly visit trade shows, participate in best practice study tours, or attend conferences) feel entitled to pursue pet projects.

Applying a proper process to filtering innovation ideas using the golden rule protects the business and protects the careers of those who champion initiatives, including external partners. Management are the ultimate custodians of the golden rule and always have the final say because they are in the best position to weigh all the consequences of action. External stakeholders are vital partners in innovation and will be of more value to your business if they clearly understand the agenda for innovation and what the golden rule tells them about expected outcomes.

How you run the filtering process will be dependent on your innovation maturity. Some of the masters of retail innovation like Amazon and Starbucks run devolved processes. For those who are early in their quest we recommend using our idea treasure hunt process. This face-to-face format including a wide range of stakeholders and led by the CEO will motivate the team and help facilitate the cultural change you need to embed into the operating fabric of your business to make your innovation quest successful.

Now it is time for action. If you are a retail CEO, have the team work with you to select an external facilitator and design a series of idea treasure hunts. If you are a member of the management team, make the case for the treasure hunt in a management team meeting by using the exercise in the previous section to illustrate its power. If you are a team member, do the exercise with your colleagues and write to the CEO with the results.

Now that you have an aligned management team and some valuable ideas to pursue, it's time to prepare to execute. In the next chapter we outline the process for getting innovation-ready.

Notes

1   Galloway, S (2017) *The Four: the hidden DNA of Amazon, Apple, Facebook and Google*, Random House, New York, p 28
2   Domino's purpose and values [Online] https://www.dominos.com.au/inside-dominos/corporate/vision-and-mission (archived at https://perma.cc/95RG-AA9J)
3   Vuong, B (2018) *Pizza Restaurants and Takeaway in Australia*, Industry Market Research Report, IBISWorld
4   Roy Morgan Research (2016) The Domino's effect, or why Eagle Boys stopped soaring [Online] http://www.roymorgan.com/findings/6907-dominos-effect-or-why-eagle-boys-stopped-soaring-201607270911 (archived at https://perma.cc/6YBU-79RY)
5   Reynolds, B (2016) You wanna piece of me? Pizza Hut's franchisors pricing win, Legal Vision [Online] https://legalvision.com.au/you-wanna-piece-of-me-pizza-hut-franchisors-pricing-win/ (archived at https://perma.cc/RA2Z-ZRLX)
6   Vuong, B (2018) *Pizza Restaurants and Takeaway in Australia*, Industry Market Research Report, IBISWorld
7   Roy Morgan Research (2016) The Domino's effect, or why Eagle Boys stopped soaring [Online] http://www.roymorgan.com/findings/6907-dominos-effect-or-why-eagle-boys-stopped-soaring-201607270911 (archived at https://perma.cc/S5HP-AQTN)
8   Australian Food News (2016) Allegro acquires Pizza Hut Australia master franchise agreement, 9 July [Online] https://www.ausfoodnews.com.au/2016/09/07/allegro-acquires-pizza-hut-australia-master-franchise-agreement.html (archived at https://perma.cc/BK6M-SSJ5)

9   Burgoon, JK, Guerrero, LK and Floyd, K (2016) *Nonverbal Communication,* Routledge, Abingdon

10   Osterwalder, A, Pigneur, Y and Clark, T (2010) *Business Model Generation: A handbook for visionaries, game changers, and challengers,* John Wiley & Sons, New York

11   Osterwalder, A, Pigneur, Y, Papadakos, T, Bernarda, G, Smith, A and Smith, A (2014) *Value Proposition Design: How to create products and services customers want,* John Wiley & Sons, New YOrk

12   Cohen, D, Quinn, B and Roth, E (2019) The innovation commitment, McKinsey Quarterly, October [Online] https://www.mckinsey.com/business-functions/strategy-and-corporate-finance/our-insights/the-innovation-commitent (archived at https://perma.cc/AT7W-THXV)

13   Brache, AP and Bodley-Scott, S (2009) Which initiatives should you implement? *Harvard Management Update* (September), pp 1–5

06

Stage 3: Get innovation-ready

(ANDREW)

Introduction

When I was a kid, I played cricket, mainly because Australian Rules football scared me (this was the dominant code in my hometown of Melbourne, Australia, and it is a sport noted for being fiercely physical). However, I adored cricket. Every Saturday, I would don my cricket whites and hit the field to compete with a group of humans I mostly liked. Dad would always tell me stories about how team sport is an important lesson in life about how to work together. I think he just liked the cheap beer available at the club and a chance to get out of the house.

When I was 14, the end-of-season awards night came round, and I was buzzing. Halfway through the night, the coach got up to present the Coach's Award. Everyone knew what this was about: it was a participation award. My coach introduced it, saying, 'This player brings a lot of energy to the team and always supports his teammates. He tries hard, even though he doesn't have any natural talent for the game.' 'Ouch,' I thought, 'This is going to suck for the poor kid that wins this award – talk about a back-handed compliment!' I think you see what is coming. When my name was called, I was so disappointed. I tried to hide the fact that I cried, but I'm not sure I did a great job. I did later realize that it had been a great lesson.

It taught me to think about my game more deeply, including my preparation for training, my equipment, my mindset, my team and game day itself. It taught me that there is more to success than just turning up and playing the game. We often see people do that at work, and perhaps are guilty of it ourselves. We grow up with an execution mindset and it means we're not always primed to achieve the best we can. (This is especially true in retail, as we discussed in Chapter 3.) What I learned from cricket was to think beyond 'work' to everything surrounding it – my role, my preparation and the best way for me to execute my job. This has helped me in countless retail transformation projects, both as a leader and a team member. And yes, I did go on to win awards at cricket for more than participation!

In this chapter, we talk about stage three, the first where we start the 'innovation work'. This is about taking the broad idea generated in the first two stages of the *ReFRAME* process through to creation and embedding.

Innovation work needs three core characteristics to work: the right sponsorship, cross-functional teams, and adequate resourcing. We call this getting innovation-ready. In this chapter, we will go through the process of setting up our work for innovation success. In order to do that, we need to re-think a few ideas we may already hold (the traditional behaviour of sponsors in an innovation context can often be stifling), and after we have done that, it's time to roll up our sleeves and get innovation-ready!

Getting innovation-ready

Any quest without the right sponsorship, cross-functional teams and adequate resources is bound to be unsuccessful. When it comes to an innovation quest, this preparation is especially important. Even more so in retail, where the margins are tighter and the pace is quicker. We often see innovation attempted using traditional programme management techniques, which all too often leads to:

- more money spent on wasted time and builds;
- more failed and expensive trials;
- poorer outcomes;
- lower employee satisfaction;
- lower customer satisfaction.

Nike is arguably one of the best at getting innovation-ready. In 2019, Nike deployed its Consumer Direct Offense – a series of innovations that took from the best of direct-to-consumer brands to improve the customer experience. After ranking Nike in its 'most innovative retail companies' list, Fast Company wrote about the culture of creativity and experimentation that enables this innovation pipeline to constantly deliver for the company.[1] It listed the four principles that drive innovation throughout the Nike organization:

- To disrupt, go all in.
- Anticipate a product's evolution.
- Direct your partners.
- Feed company culture.

What results is a company that directs its partners (it doesn't outsource innovation entirely – it takes ownership), goes all in on ideas (promotes creativity and doesn't see failure as a negative), and builds for the longer term by anticipating the evolution of the 'thing' they are building. The results of this innovation culture and the Consumer Direct Offense strategy are compelling, with the second fiscal quarter of 2019 seeing:[2]

- 13 per cent currency-neutral revenue growth;
- gross margin increases of 20 basis points;
- 38 per cent growth in digital sales.

FIGURE 6.1 Get innovation-ready

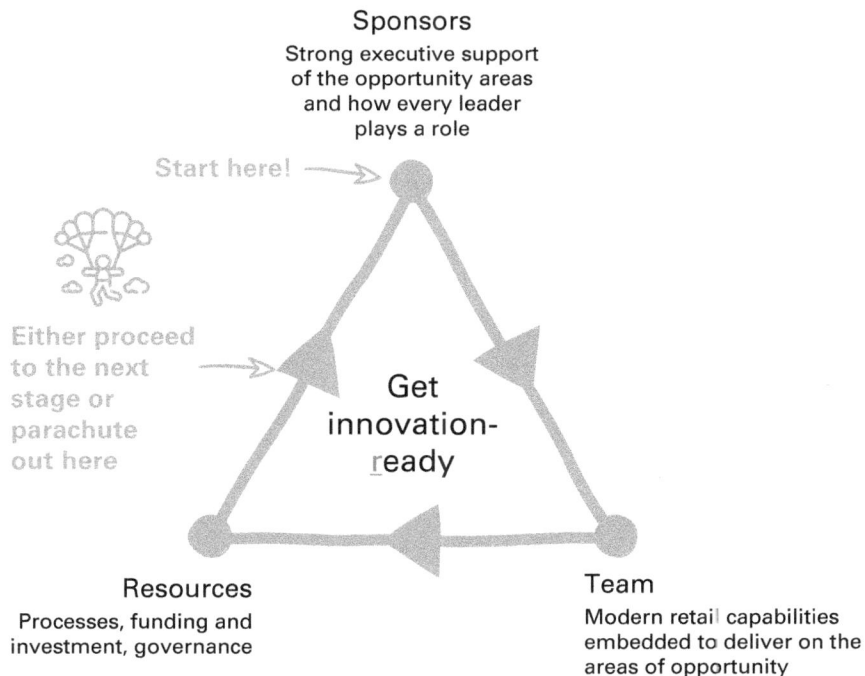

Sponsors
Strong executive support
of the opportunity areas
and how every leader
plays a role

Start here! ⟶

Either proceed
to the next
stage or
parachute
out here ⟶

Get
innovation-
ready

Resources
Processes, funding and
investment, governance

Team
Modern retail capabilities
embedded to deliver on the
areas of opportunity

Big numbers like that are made up of countless smaller innovation stories, with leaders and teams building and delivering their 'things' across all areas of the company. The culture of creativity in Nike should be the goal of your own quest to get innovation-ready. To do so, you must:

1 Put in place the right sponsor (if not you) and sponsorship model. It is more than a figurehead role. There are specific jobs to do and a defined mindset to keep, which we will discuss later in the chapter.

2 Recognize that cross-functional teams need new capabilities. These might include skills like human-centred design, behavioural economics, data science or agile skills that are new to some retailers.

3 Provide adequate resourcing. This is about more than money; it is about providing everything that is needed to create the 'space' to innovate.

Sponsors

Sponsoring a project has historically meant that you are the member of the management team who is accountable for the outcome. The idea that sponsorship is a management role (ie a functional role of managing and being responsible for work outputs), and not a leadership one, is flawed. It is based on the idea that those sponsors who have a higher organizational rank or fancy title are more likely to deliver. This can be true if the sponsor has the authority to remove roadblocks and demand whatever the project needs, eg the CEO. However, it doesn't mean that your 'thing' will necessarily achieve everything it set out to do. Having the CEO remove roadblocks, open doors previously closed, facilitate cooperation (sometimes forced), and more, is incredibly helpful, but CEOs often cannot give the project team the time they need. Moreover, these are temporary advantages that can disappear in a heartbeat if the CEO is distracted by the next 'thing' or leaves the company. Having a great sponsor, backed by an aligned leadership team, who works *for* the project team, who is also able to get those roadblocks removed, means your organization will be able to achieve innovation across the whole business rather than in clumps relying on the CEO's attention.

One challenge for an innovation project sponsor in a results-focused retail environment is that innovation is inherently creative. The sponsor must ensure that the team is creating work that delivers results, whilst also not smothering creativity with cumbersome processes or requests. Such a balanced sponsorship style will encourage a team to be creative and experiment within a structured innovation programme that constantly measures the outcomes.

The three types of sponsor

From our experience there are three types of sponsors of innovation projects.

The 'looking good' sponsor – they are in this because it is going to make them look good. They are subjective and steer the project towards what they think will be the most impressive thing. It can mean they chase a fast delivery, media attention, awards, or other things that ignore the golden rule. These sponsors are tough, and they are destructive. They also love making people build PowerPoint packs. I once had a leader whose intellect was inspiring and who constantly came up with brilliant ideas but who also was desperate to impress both the market and upper management. The pressure on the project teams to show progress was so high that we rushed things to market that ultimately failed. New roles were created solely to build internal documents for senior leaders!

The 'I am very busy and important' sponsor – these absent managers make it hard for teams as they generally devote very little time to the project. This often leads to slow decision-making and slow or no progress due to lack of funds, structure and support. Most people have experienced this style of sponsor. Remember the frustration of having to push a project every step of the way? I certainly do. Tasked with a major programme to increase store productivity, my 'very busy and important' sponsor made it to only one out of fifteen governance meetings, and eventually we declared the programme dead after not receiving funding for two years in a row. They did not provide us with prompt decisions and support, we didn't get the team and support we needed to deliver, nor did we have the resourcing to complete the work. Not being innovation-ready led to a programme of good ideas going nowhere until a new sponsor came in – an 'innovation legend'.

The 'innovation legend' sponsor – this is who you want to be. You see your role as working for the team, giving them everything they need to be successful – which can sometimes mean getting out of their way. When I was leading the retail innovation team at Telstra, we were tasked with opening the flagship store in Sydney. We had very short timeframes and very high ambitions. Our sponsor at the time gave us all that we needed and trusted us with the rest. This allowed the amazing team I was part of to be creative, experiment and try new things (including several first-to-market technologies) and to design and build a store that went on to receive the award of Merit for the Telecommunications category at the Retail Design Institute International Store Design Awards in New York in 2014. The team's incredible abilities were put on show because our leaders gave us all we needed to be successful and then got out of the way so we could get it done.

If you find a leader with an 'innovation legend' sponsorship style, you'll get faster progress, better outcomes and, ironically, they will look better than the 'looking good' sponsor and spend less time working on it than the 'very busy and important' sponsor. It seems straightforward but is strangely uncommon.

There are many examples of 'looking good' and 'very busy and important' sponsors (insert your own favourite example). However, we will focus on the more helpful style of 'innovation legends'. We believe Howard Schultz of Starbucks and Jeff Bezos of Amazon display the characteristics of 'innovation legends'. They both have a proven history of fostering innovation, crafting creative cultures, and delivering results.

The challenges of being an 'innovation legend' sponsor

As an innovation legend, you are responsible for creating the space for the team and sets the structure and can still contribute to the creative process – just remember that you are an equal in the creative work. Objectivity and the team's capabilities must be respected. People often mistake rank or seniority for being smarter or more likely to have the right answers. Shed that view as quickly as possible – it is dangerous and often leads to failed innovation.

In any system where humans are involved, we need to be aware of the individuality each person brings to their contribution. Each leader will have their own style of sponsorship. Think of it more as a job description: these are the things you need to do as a sponsor. Your individual techniques and personality will mean that you do the role in your way. That is okay – in fact, it's great! We just need to be honest with ourselves about our strengths and areas for development as we work towards becoming an 'innovation legend' sponsor. Of course, we also need to be transparent and make sure the team is aware of them so they can fill any gaps.

How to become your own version of the innovation legend sponsor

Let me indulge myself for a minute with a story about a discovery that was crucial to my deployment as a retail innovator. I am an introvert leader. This essentially means I worry a lot about how people are acting and feeling and seek strong one-to-one relationships, but do not have the desire to be the centre of attention in a large room full of people with fancy titles. I hate the idea of meeting with the big bosses or the board, where others thrive on that opportunity. My focus on individual relationships meant that I built a strong and connected network of people from all parts of the business to help me deliver what I needed to. I then gave my team their objectives and told them to tell me when they needed anything, and it was my role to get them just that. To be honest, at the time I considered it was cheating to a degree. It was not until I saw it work that I realized it was a perfectly legitimate way of doing things.

We still had to have the right strategy and bring together the right team, but once that was in place, all I had to do was give them the 'space' to do what they did best. We took world-best practices and ideas, including the Amazon memo system, and we acted. We broke some long-standing corporate rules along the way (a lot without permission and we simply sought forgiveness later).

EXERCISE
Characteristics of an 'innovation legend' sponsorship style

To develop as a sponsor, you must first reflect on your current sponsorship style. A great way to reflect is to go for a coffee and think about your leadership and how you can use that as the basis for your role as a sponsor. This will include areas like how you act and behave when you are part of the process (as an equal), and as the guardian of the structure. It is a hard balance to strike and will take practice.

This exercise is one we use with retail leaders who are looking to adapt their sponsorship style to become 'innovation legends'. Use it as a basis of your reflections with yourself and the team or as the core way you select sponsors for certain projects. Your role here is to find a sponsor who has this leadership style and the knowledge and experience to lead the design, build, deployment and embedding of your 'thing'.

What this is

This is an exercise for those who want to be innovation legends. It is designed to help you assess how you are going on your journey to be the best innovation sponsor you can be. Complete the exercise regularly (to start, try at least every month) and keep plotting out where you rate yourself. You can also provide this to others to rate you (say, your team or your manager) to get broader feedback.

Instructions

For each trait listed in Table 6.1, read the characteristics carefully. Give yourself the 'Me' or 'Not me' score for each question. The answers are weighted, so please answer carefully. Add up the score you get for each section and plot it on the tracking sheet.

TABLE 6.1 Innovation legend sponsorship characteristics survey

Topic	Statement	This is me	Almost or sometimes me	This is not me	Corrective actions
Clarity. How well have you completed the 'Re' – Reset the foundations step of the ReFRAME process?	I have spoken with all members of my innovation project team and they understand and buy into our strategy and purpose.	3 pts	1 pt	0 pts	Sit down with members of the team and ask (without judgement) their different views and why they are divergent. Group them into root causes and discuss (as a group) how you can align them.
	I have ensured that any member of the team could describe in 30 secs the purpose of our work and how it aligns to the strategy.	2 pts	1 pt	0 pts	Run an exercise as a group to agree on your 30 sec elevator pitch that covers what you're doing, what it will deliver, and how it is linked to your purpose. Use clear human language so even people without knowledge of the project will have clarity immediately.
	I have heard all members of my innovation project team describe in their own words how the 'thing' follows the golden rule.	3 pts	1 pt	0 pts	Run a session with the team on how the golden rule works, how it was filtered using it, then get them to rephrase it in their own words on a post-it note (keeping the paper small keeps the description short!).
Decision-making. How well have you achieved a co-creation innovation team?	Decision discussions are led by the expert on the topic or part of the business at the centre of the decision, not me.	1 pts	0 pts	0 pts	Adjust meeting formats to ensure that experts always lead discussions. Run an experiment in project meetings where you only ask questions, not make statements. Use this to take on an investigator mindset rather than an expert mindset.

	2 pts	1 pt	0 pts	
I don't need to get involved in small decisions as they are mostly made within the project team. They come to me when a decision has a bigger impact. Otherwise I am updated in the decision forum or showcase.	2 pts	1 pt	0 pts	Have a coffee with yourself and reflect on why you need to be involved in every decision. It will be one of two answers: 1.You are a micro-manager and need to let go and trust the team you've pulled together (ask them to hold you to account on this). 2.You have selected a team of people without the appropriate skills for the work (adjust the team, if you can).
My opinions (and those of other 'senior' humans) can be overridden by objective evidence easily.	2 pts	1 pts	0 pts	Become more enthralled by evidence. Assess how it is being presented and why senior leaders override it. Include the biases in the next briefing and challenge senior humans to self-reflect.
I, as sponsor, often ask: 'What does everyone think?' before giving my opinion.	1 pts	0pt	0 pts	Run an experiment: in one meeting only ask that question and record your observations. What worked, what didn't, what was different to a normal meeting? Use that as motivation to make asking that question a habit.
I give my time, and that of any other relevant people for regular and consistent forums to get fast decisions (at least once a week).	2 pts	1 pt	0 pts	Slow decisions lead to bad or ineffective project outcomes. Ensure you make the time yourself and for others. Reflect on what stops the team from getting the needed time and how to change that.

(continued)

TABLE 6.1 (Continued)

Topic	Statement	This is me	Almost or sometimes me	This is not me	Corrective actions
Resources. Do the team have all they need to be successful?	I never hear from the team: 'We are constrained because we don't have <something, eg money, time, skills>.'	3 pts	1 pt	0 pts	Analyse the end-to-end process of resource allocation and identify the problem areas and how to adjust the process to avoid it.
	I take action and give clear time frames, acting with urgency, whenever the team needs something.	2 pts	1 pt	0 pts	Have a coffee with yourself and list the reasons why faster and more transparent actions are not happening and identify experiments for you to try that will change that.
	I have strong relationships with the people and teams who provide resourcing (eg finance, project office, chief of staff to CEO).	3 pts	1 pt	0 pts	Draw a stakeholder map and identify where your relationships aren't strong. Use the challenging stakeholders exercise later in the chapter to assist.
Communication. How well are you sharing what you do in the most helpful way?	I ensure we run regular (at least every two weeks) and accessible showcases for all who wish to attend, with specific invites to representatives from across the business (all teams, not just those impacted) and I support and participate always.	2 pts	1 pt	0 pts	Reflect on why these aren't occurring or your role in them is not consistent. Use the showcase materials in this chapter to assist you in understanding their benefit over traditional governance and use the tools to give you confidence in running them.

I ensure we use multiple mediums to communicate to all layers of the organization, both central support and frontline.	2 pts	1 pt	0 pts	Sketch (or use lego if you're feeling creative) the organization represented as personas. How do they like to be communicated with, how often, and what do they care about? Use that as a basis to reflect on your project communication strategy.
I have created a way and encourage people outside the project team to put questions and ideas to us and we respond regularly within a reasonable timeframe (48 hrs is a long time).	2 pts	1 pt	0 pts	Ideas and improvements can (and should) come from everywhere. Diverse views will make your 'thing' better. Set up an inbox or use a platform your organization has to capture these ideas and have a process within the project team to respond.
The senior leadership team (CEO and direct reports, board) are regularly informed of my programmes of work and mention my work in their updates.	2 pts	1 pt	0 pts	Some humans find this challenging or redundant; however, having a supportive senior leadership team means faster and more effective support to your project team. Therefore, as a leader, it is your responsibility. Find your own style that makes you feel comfortable and is reflective of how they like to be updated. Use the challenging stakeholders exercise as a guide.

Now, plot your answers on the scale (see Figure 6.2) and keep track of how you progress over time.

FIGURE 6.2 Innovation legend sponsorship tracking sheet

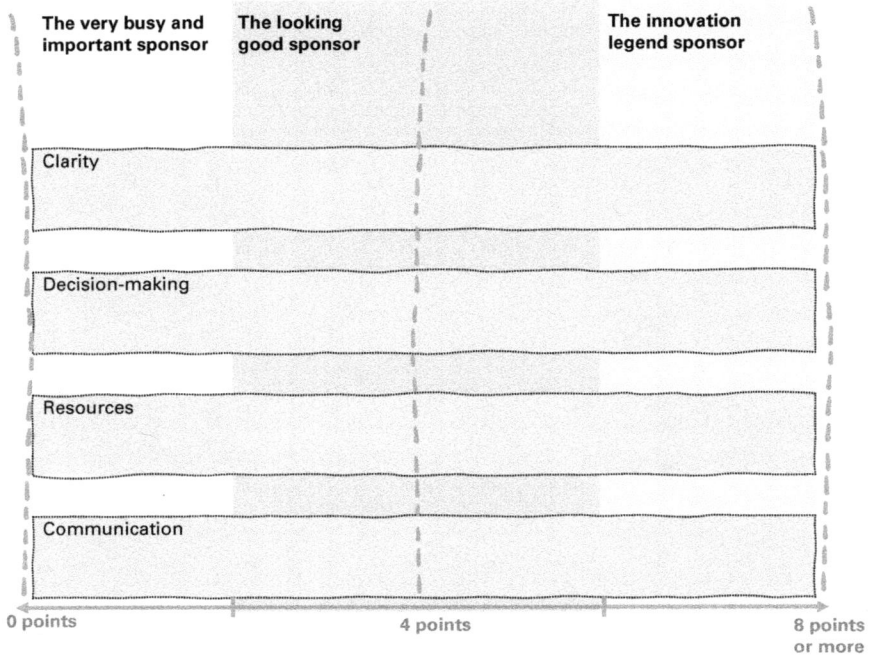

The very busy and important sponsor	The looking good sponsor		The innovation legend sponsor	
Clarity				
Decision-making				
Resources				
Communication				

0 points   4 points   8 points or more

FINDING YOUR INNOVATION LEGEND SPONSORS

In this chapter we talk about how those leaders who will be sponsoring innovation projects can become their own version of the innovation legend sponsor. As a senior leader or portfolio manager, your role might be finding those people. Your job shifts to one where you must become accustomed to the characteristics of this new style of sponsor, and support the transition of each of your project sponsors to this new style of project leadership. Use the previous exercise when selecting your project sponsors to assess how quickly they can achieve this sponsorship style, as well as throughout your coaching and support of them.

Remember, culture change is hard. You may face internal objections to these changes and people will feel like they miss the old control of more direct leadership. Stick with it! Give it a few weeks and have regular retrospectives with the team. Take some of them for a walk or have an open group conversation about what is working and what isn't. Courage here is important. Being transparent about your initial objections and how you overcame them will be powerful to share with the team.

This is a very personal challenge for a lot of leaders. It feels like you are relinquishing control, and that is something humans have evolved to hate to do. You will be fighting regular battles with yourself on this. To overcome them, I suggest keeping up the 'coffee with yourself' routine regularly and reflecting on your progress using the checklist.

The team

Now it is time to think about the team who are doing the work designing and building your 'thing'.

Teams have historically been allocated work based on ownership of an area of the business. For example, the visual merchandising team would lead innovation projects related to their area. Then, for a while in 2015 or so, the trend was to have a dedicated innovation team – a hero group of creative minds who come into different areas of the business and solve specific problems in new and innovative ways.

Both approaches have had limited success across the retail sector. The specialist teams doing their own work are inefficient. They have to balance innovation and business as usual, and often projects end up poorly implemented, if at all, as there is no cross-functional team involvement to support the project with skills or implementation. The dedicated innovation teams often lack specialized working knowledge of the 'things' they are tasked to build and can come in to conflict with those who 'know what they are doing'. This political layer can lead to projects stalling, taking too long, missing the mark in design and build or not being transitioned effectively due to their lack of support from the broader business.

In our experience, the answer is to put innovation projects in the hands of cross-functional teams. These allow us to bring together all the skills needed to deliver brilliant outcomes, including area specialization, technical capability, design capability and execution skills. We call this co-created innovation. If we use the visual merchandising (VM) example, the VM team will still own the customer or business challenge they want to solve but a cross-functional team – perhaps including people from the frontline, customer experience design and IT – come together to design and build the 'thing' as a team.

As we get further into the *ReFRAME* process, particularly Chapter 8 – Stage 5: Make the design and scale it, we will talk more about how these cross-functional teams co-create innovation. To deliver in this co-created innovation space, new skills are often needed – ones that are often commonly misunderstood. We are going to take an overview of these new skills, explain what each is (and isn't) and when to recruit in, engage external support, or train up within your organization.

The skills and why they are important

1 **Behavioural design** has lots of names – service experience design, customer experience design, human centred design, behavioural economics, etc. All are part of a group of skills that bring in the processes and principles of evidence collection, human behavioural characteristics, and good design practices to the way you choose and build innovations in your business. They enable you to become incredibly human-focused and deliver projects that are relevant, useable, and aligned with the golden rule.

    To support innovation projects across your organization, a balance of the following behavioural economics and human-centred design skills is a good idea:

    a) **Behavioural economics:** Behavioural economists use evidence-backed individual human traits to make assumptions smarter when designing an experience for a group of humans (eg customers). Behavioural economics introduces psychology into traditional economics. It looks at the choices that humans make in a situation, why they make them, and how to influence them. This is a highly specialized field and still evolving as a discipline.

    b) **Human-centred design (HCD):** HCD has been around for centuries, giving us fridges that have handles and buttons in spots that are easy to reach, cars that open when we touch the handle to save us getting the key out, even the flow of a house to suit how the inhabitants live. The principles of HCD (how real humans interact in the real world with the actual 'thing') are now being used to design products and experiences everywhere. HCD is increasingly important in retail.

Customers are demanding more from every experience and expect a deeper level of engagement. HCD skills help retail brands to become more human. Examples of it being used well come from digital-first brands like Allbirds or Stitch Fix as well as traditional retail brands like IKEA, Nike and others.[3]

If you need to recruit HCD skills into the business, be wary. Many people have HCD in their CV but have little experience in design itself. It involves much more than post-it notes and brainstorming. Good HCD comes from people with high levels of empathy and insatiable curiosity that is balanced with an action bias and a commercial focus.

2   **Testing** is a specialized skill that is often undervalued. Testers are people who have a working understanding of both behavioural economics and design, and use methodical and scientific methods to analyse and test how your 'thing' is working compared with what you thought it would do. Most companies can have a team of these talented folk and test as many innovations through them as possible. The more 'things' that go through the testing process, the less expensive your innovation pipeline will be (reducing waste and focusing on the important things that are delivering the results) and the more likely it will be to succeed.

3   **Data scientists** are the super-smart humans who can help you better capture, understand and leverage the information in your organization and beyond. Data science works best as a centre of excellence integrated with your broader innovation teams as data scientists can work across multiple programs at once. The only exception to this would be if the project is a data-focused project, such as cleaning your customer data, in which case having these team members working full time on a project would be required.

Changing people's minds about these skills and knowing when to use them

I have been in many meetings with senior executives who either overtly or through subtext let me know that they believe the skills we have described above to be dark arts, 'faff', and just the latest fad. You should respond with examples of the organizations that build better and more profitable relationships with customers using these techniques. You could cite Apple,

Google, Facebook, Amazon, All Birds, Warby Parker, Bonobos, Walmart and others who all apply these skills in one way or another and continue to grow compared to their competitors in a heavily disrupted market. If you win that debate you might be allowed to hire these skills permanently, but realistically that will take time and you may need to seek external support initially. Stick with it. Like any skill that is unfamiliar, or we do not understand, it's only a matter of time before you won't know how you lived without them!

If this is all new to you, then I would recommend getting an external advisor. Most good human-focused talent firms will assist you in both individual projects as well as implementing a people plan to bring the skills into your organization. To help to start identifying the skills you need across your innovation projects, we have created a team skills canvas that will list the skills you need for specific projects.

EXERCISE
The team skills canvas

What this is

This is an exercise that will help you assess the weight of the skills you need for your innovation project.

Instructions

For part 1 – team skills required in each of the three interaction mediums (pre-show, on stage, off stage) – measure the effort impact of the 'thing' that you're building. The definitions of each are shown in Figure 6.3.

Colour in each square that is applicable, eg if your 'thing' has a high effort impact to the pre-show interaction medium, then colour in all three squares and sum the value of each square. In this example, we would have behavioural design at 4 points, data science at 4 points and specialization at 1 point. Do that for all of the mediums and add them together, and you will have your total skill requirements to plot on the scale on the right.

Specialization in this instance is specialized skills from within your business related to the area of the project itself, eg if the 'thing' you are building is a new element of your order management system, IT specialization will be required.

FIGURE 6.3 The team skills canvas

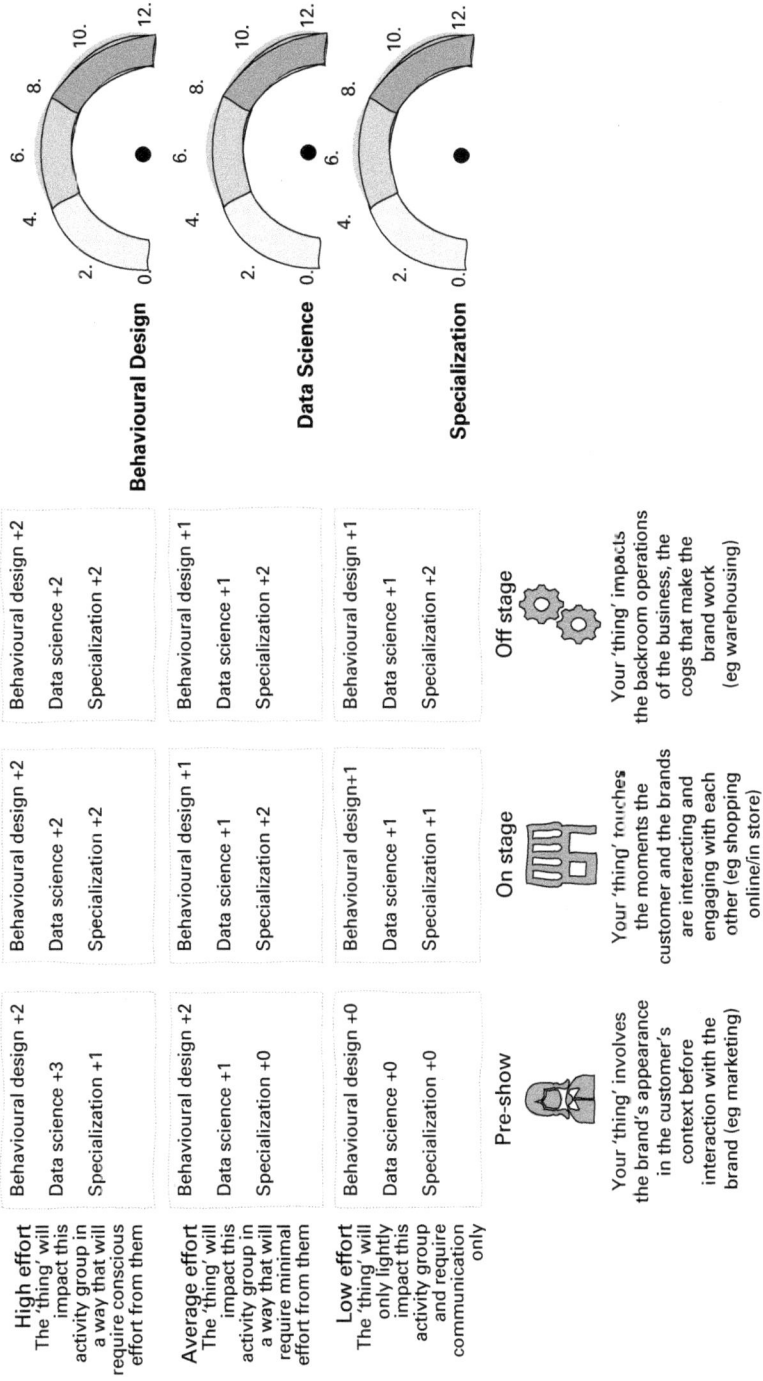

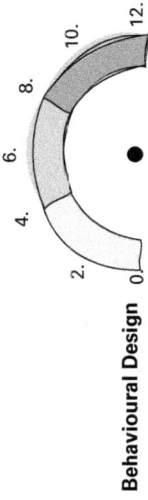

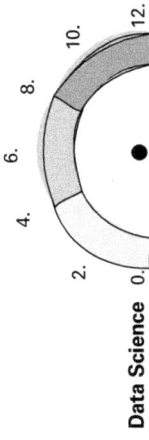

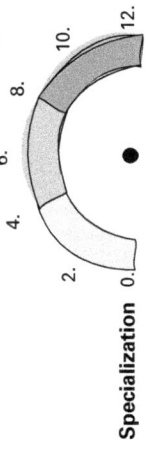

	Pre-show	On stage	Off stage
High effort The 'thing' will impact this activity group in a way that will require conscious effort from them	Behavioural design +2 Data science +3 Specialization +1	Behavioural design +2 Data science +2 Specialization +2	Behavioural design +2 Data science +2 Specialization +2
Average effort The 'thing' will impact this activity group in a way that will require minimal effort from them	Behavioural design +2 Data science +1 Specialization +0	Behavioural design +1 Data science +1 Specialization +2	Behavioural design +1 Data science +1 Specialization +2
Low effort The 'thing' will only lightly impact this activity group and require communication only	Behavioural design +0 Data science +0 Specialization +0	Behavioural design+1 Data science +1 Specialization +1	Behavioural design +1 Data science +1 Specialization +2
	Pre-show Your 'thing' involves the brand's appearance in the customer's context before interaction with the brand (eg marketing)	**On stage** Your 'thing' touches the moments the customer and the brands are interacting and engaging with each other (eg shopping online/in store)	**Off stage** Your 'thing' impacts the backroom operations of the business, the cogs that make the brand work (eg warehousing)

Behavioural Design

Data Science

Specialization

What to do next

For part 2, you will be selecting the team structure and dynamics. You'll need to review the information in each section and answer the guide questions (below) to assist you in forming your innovation team.

Once you have the skills areas plotted on the right-hand scales, you can work out what level of involvement that you need, based on the options below:

- **Pale grey:** A consultative skill of this area should be involved.
- **Mid grey:** A permanent team member should be included.
- **Dark grey:** A permanent team member and support should be included (eg more than one skill from the discipline or a consultant).

Once you have your expertise skills identified, this should form the core makeup of the project team building your 'thing'. Next is to craft the team structure and dynamics. When structuring your innovation team, there is no one answer. There are many options depending on your 'thing'. To help guide you, read each team type below and then answer the guide question to define your team structure and dynamics.

- **Functional:** The project is led by a representative of the area that owns the context your 'thing' will be sitting in, and as close to the humans it impacts as possible. To test that you have the right human, ask yourself: Who is the expert on how the 'thing' will be used day to day, and who is accountable for it in normal operations? If this is ambiguous, then go with the group closest to the customer.
- **Specialized:** The project lead will be from the key area of specialization in the project, eg a technologist. To find this human, ask: Who is the expert in what the 'thing' is and how it is built, but not necessarily involved in its day-to-day use?
- **Blended:** This is the most effective, if it is possible. It is essentially where a functional and a specialized duo work as partners. It requires deep trust and strong relationships between the two areas to be effective. In these blended teams, if there is disagreement the decision of the functional lead should take precedence, as they are closer to the customer.

Guide question

Do you have the people to run this as a blended approach? If not, then is your 'thing' going to have a direct impact on your frontline or your customer? Eg, they will be cognitively aware of your 'thing' or what it impacts, such as a store design, an app experience, etc. If yes, then a functional style is needed. If no, then a specialized lead is appropriate.

The remaining structure and how your team work together can be created using these principles:

- **Breadth:** Are all the teams who are impacted by your 'thing' represented in the core project group? If not, you need to ensure they are regularly represented in the showcase.

- **Depth:** Does each member of the team have alignment and authority from their represented area of the business to make decisions? If not, you need to have a clear and agreed plan to get decisions fast or get a different representative.

- **Location:** Can everyone collocate? If not, then you must have appropriate digital tools set up to ensure the project team spend their full working day as a group.

- **Specialized skills:** Do you have permanent representation of the skills you need from the team skills canvas? If not, can you get them? Can you hire them? If not, you will need to task these to members of the team and be clear that it is their responsibility.

TEAM PRINCIPLES

As a project team, it is important to set the tone of how the team will work together with some team principles. Below are some of our favourites we have collected in our experience. You should get the team in a room and discuss what is appropriate for your project and how it is aligned with your purpose.

- Collective intelligence beats individual intelligence.
- We only win if we all win.
- There are only equals with different specializations and experiences in this room – leave your rank and title at the door.
- Customers and stakeholders are not an interruption – they are the reason we exist as a team.
- Doing good beats looking good, always.

The space

We define 'space' as everything that the team needs for success. Many people think this means 'Give them a room where they can stick up post-it notes.' That is possibly partly true, but there is a lot more to it than that. The four core characteristics of space for an innovation team are time, investment, processes and governance.

We will walk through each of the elements, what they mean, what it looks like (including examples), how to do it, and how to know when you have got it working for you.

Time

Time is a challenging adjustment to make, and will likely lead to the most initial pain. Innovation cannot be an adjunct to the normal day job; it must become the new day job for those who are doing it. It is not about stopping business as usual, but instead redefining work allocation to ensure those who are building are given the time to do it. At the start of the initial planning process everyone should understand and commit to time allocations. Despite our best efforts, there will always be forces pulling you back to the normal rhythm, but if you are to be successful you must avoid that.

Investment

Investment can be a big blocker for innovation in retail. However, it is incredibly important to ensure that your investment strategy delivers on two key principles:

- Capital is invested as efficiently as possible to maximize outcomes.
- Capital matches the phased approach of innovation processes (a funnel where multiple ideas are continuously refined to a working solution).

If innovation funds are not already allocated and quarantined in your budgeting process, we recommend you apply the 70/20/10 system described in Chapter 2.

Processes

A ruthless review of processes and their value will help you end up with a simple set of processes that govern what goes through your pipeline – from initial seed funding of an idea through to a launch to market at scale. The *ReFRAME* model will be a replacement to most of your current innovation processes; however, there will still be other adjacent processes that will need to be considered. Take the time to map out a project through the *ReFRAME* model in your organization and see what other processes impact that work-flow and whether they can stay, need to be adjusted, or need to be stopped.

EXERCISE
The creating space checklist

This checklist will help you create the space for your team to be successful. This is a guide and will require some input from you based on your business structure and process environment, but use this as a starting point.

Time

Time and energy focus are imperative for innovation to remain creative, objective, and built from a diverse set of skills and business representation. The checklist in Table 6.2 will allow you to ensure there is clarity on the team's time and energy. Add on to these any additional team members and ensure you have confirmed the requirements with any of their traditional reporting lines.

TABLE 6.2 Time and energy checklist

Role	Time	Location	Goals
Project lead	Full time on project, no exceptions	Located with the team. If not possible, a constant digital connection in a dedicated space	Fully adjusted to focus on the project (ie for project period this human is solely assessed by project performance)
Key specialist roles	Full time on project, no exceptions	Located with the team. If not possible, a constant digital connection in a dedicated space	Fully adjusted to focus on the project (ie for project period this human is solely assessed by project performance)
Sponsor	Part time on project with an agreed amount of time allocated	Should be able to visit the project location once a week and for hosting showcases	Adjusted to allow for project metrics if not their core business
Part-time or shared specialist skill	Part time on project with an agreed amount of time allocated	As required by the project	Adjusted to allow for project metrics if not their core business
Showcase attendees	No official time allocated	Not required	No adjustment required

Investment

It is important to have a rough estimate of your capital requirements and other financial metrics to measure the project against. Innovation capital must be allocated in smaller but more regular chunks than standard capital. The guide questions in Table 6.3 will allow you to complete a foundation estimate as part of getting innovation-ready. Build on the questions with more specific requirements of your 'thing'. These numbers will then get further revised in the next stage, but you will need to do estimates now to get the seed funding released.

TABLE 6.3 Building a foundation estimate

	Seed funding	Analyse and design	Make the design	Embed
What is it	The funding required to take the idea to its first prototype phase	Additional funding for testing and evidence collection that may be required (some projects may not require it)	The required funds to take the prototype through the levels of build maturity	Any capital or operating expense requirements to embed your 'thing'
How to estimate it	What physical requirements do you need?	Are there any specialist skills needed to test? Eg a full time testing resource, a data scientist, a consultant, etc	What are the estimated costs of building the thing?	What are the costs of any additional operational changes such as support or equipment costs?
	Any specialist skills required to complete this stage?		What are any foreseeable additional costs?	
	What location and travel expenses are needed?		What costs will testing incur?	

Processes

Each part of a business has a role or influence on innovation processes. Use Table 6.4 to assess each of the processes and what may need special attention from the sponsor or a permanent redesign to maximize innovation performance. To do this, review any areas with low scores (high friction), and assess whether you can make permanent change to reduce the friction and increase pace, or whether you can simply temporarily overcome it for this project. Use this as a guide to complete this for your own business processes and organizational functions.

TABLE 6.4 Assessing processes and functions

Function	What they own	Speed	Supportive	Effort
Definition	The processes and approvals they are the functional owner of	How fast is entering and going through the process?	How open are they to innovative projects not from their area?	How much time and energy is required to get ready for and participate in the process?
		0 slow to 5 very fast	0 closed to 5 always supportive	0 none to 5 a lot
Marketing	Approval of any brand representation	☆☆☆☆☆	☆☆☆☆☆	☆☆☆☆☆
	Approval of any marketing materials	☆☆☆☆☆	☆☆☆☆☆	☆☆☆☆☆
	⋮	⋮	⋮	⋮
Finance	Funding releases	☆☆☆☆☆	☆☆☆☆☆	☆☆☆☆☆
	Business case approval	☆☆☆☆☆	☆☆☆☆☆	☆☆☆☆☆
	Benefit reporting	☆☆☆☆☆	☆☆☆☆☆	☆☆☆☆☆
	⋮	⋮	⋮	⋮
IT	Technology selection	☆☆☆☆☆	☆☆☆☆☆	☆☆☆☆☆
	Technology improvements	☆☆☆☆☆	☆☆☆☆☆	☆☆☆☆☆
	⋮	⋮	⋮	⋮
Channels	Channel impacts	☆☆☆☆☆	☆☆☆☆☆	☆☆☆☆☆
	Go to market calendar	☆☆☆☆☆	☆☆☆☆☆	☆☆☆☆☆
	⋮	⋮	⋮	⋮

Governance

Governance is necessary in all organizations. It is especially important in retail, where large amounts of cash and resources are deployed and margins are thin. Formal governance of innovation, however, can be scary and slow down innovation teams. We advocate shifting the oversight of innovation from traditional, formal governance meetings to 'showcasing'. Showcasing is often used in agile methodology; however, the principles are applicable and helpful in all innovation projects to ensure that they can move at a measured and driven pace.

The sponsor, assuming they have an 'innovation legend' sponsor mindset, will be informed and involved in the work and progress and, therefore, the showcase becomes something much less focused on them and more focused on the broader organization. One option is to issue an open invite to all relevant business teams to attend and see the work.

Those who attend can provide their inputs and encouragement, as well as any feedback and helpful commentary. There will still, as per the previous point about processes, be a need for some senior leadership team-specific showcases to highlight the results of testing and gain an ultimate decision on whether to continue, nudge or parachute out of the work. However, this shift in thinking allows a true 'innovation legend' sponsor to continue momentum, gain business-wide support, reduce friction on progress and deliver something the whole organization understands and is proud of.

For those who are new to the term, a showcase is a more modern way to share the progress of a project. In an innovation culture, showcases replace steering committees (in the most part). It is usually made up of a representative from all areas of the business that are impacted (store teams, logistics, finance, people and culture, etc), but should also be opened up and broadcast where possible to all those who want to attend. They are interactive, open and designed to generate a larger volume of more helpful learning, as you are getting input from a larger cross-section of the business at all levels.

This reduces the time it takes to embed your 'thing' as the new normal once it is complete. If run well, showcases generate huge amounts of useful insight for the project teams and can be a great deal of fun. They also give the project team a lot of energy. In a corporate retail environment, showcases should be run in parallel to a more senior and business strategy outcome focused gating process that releases funding and keeps senior stakeholders informed. The showcase material should be used within the gating process to ensure the project team is working on building your 'thing' rather than building documents.

FIGURE 6.4 A showcase model

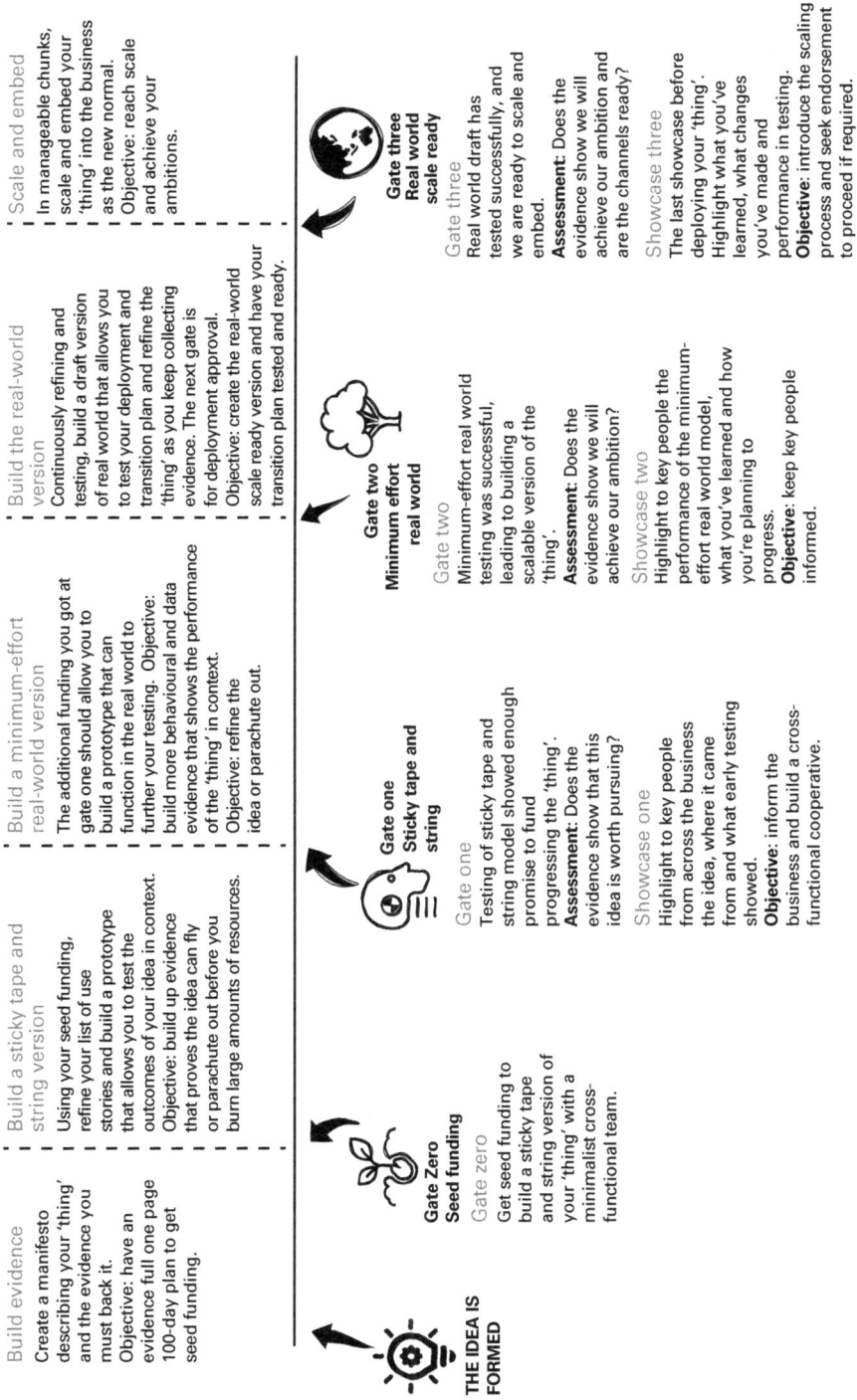

THE IDEA IS FORMED

Build evidence

Create a manifesto describing your 'thing' and the evidence you must back it.
Objective: have an evidence full one page 100-day plan to get seed funding.

Gate Zero Seed funding

Gate zero

Get seed funding to build a sticky tape and string version of your 'thing' with a minimalist cross-functional team.

Build a sticky tape and string version

Using your seed funding, refine your list of use stories and build a prototype that allows you to test the outcomes of your idea in context.
Objective: build up evidence that proves the idea can fly or parachute out before you burn large amounts of resources.

Gate one Sticky tape and string

Gate one

Testing of sticky tape and string model showed enough promise to fund progressing the 'thing'.
Assessment: Does the evidence show that this idea is worth pursuing?

Showcase one

Highlight to key people from across the business the idea, where it came from and what early testing showed.
Objective: inform the business and build a cross-functional cooperative.

Build a minimum-effort real-world version

The additional funding you got at gate one should allow you to build a prototype that can function in the real world to further your testing. Objective: build more behavioural and data evidence that shows the performance of the 'thing' in context.
Objective: refine the idea or parachute out.

Gate two Minimum effort real world

Gate two

Minimum-effort real world testing was successful, leading to building a scalable version of the 'thing'.
Assessment: Does the evidence show we will achieve our ambition?

Showcase two

Highlight to key people the performance of the minimum-effort real world model, what you've learned and how you're planning to progress.
Objective: keep key people informed.

Build the real-world version

Continuously refining and testing, build a draft version of real world that allows you to test your deployment and transition plan and refine the 'thing' as you keep collecting evidence. The next gate is for deployment approval.
Objective: create the real-world scale ready version and have your transition plan tested and ready.

Gate three Real world scale ready

Gate three

Real world draft has tested successfully, and we are ready to scale and embed.
Assessment: Does the evidence show we will achieve our ambition and are the channels ready?

Showcase three

The last showcase before deploying your 'thing'.
Highlight what you've learned, what changes you've made and performance in testing.
Objective: introduce the scaling process and seek endorsement to proceed if required.

Scale and embed

In manageable chunks, scale and embed your 'thing' into the business as the new normal.
Objective: reach scale and achieve your ambitions.

A showcase rhythm should be set based on the project milestones rather than a time, but a rule of thumb should be that they occur at least every month or more often if required. Remember, a showcase is exactly that. It should be used to show actual work, not PowerPoint slides. Although a guide with a presentation is helpful to show project status, spend as much time showing the actual work as possible. Preparation should be limited (as you want your team focused on your 'thing', not on preparing for meetings). **Hint:** Keep in mind that the work is the bit that is impressive. We have been trained to think a slick presentation with few bumps and all the answers equates to good work. That only equates to looking good, not doing good. Show off the rough edges of the work – it helps you achieve your objective, which is to gather insights and reflections on the work you have completed in this iteration.

EXERCISE
The showcase preparation template

Use this template to help guide your preparation for showcasing the work you've completed in this iteration of making your 'thing'.

1. Overview

5 minutes – led by the sponsor. An overview of the progress you have made since the last showcase in the context of the overall project.

Questions to help you frame this section:

- Remind the group what the objective is: What are you doing? How are you doing it? Why are you doing it?
- On the timeline of the whole project and all its milestones, what are we talking about today? Are we on track? Has any past reviews or showcases changed the timeline or project objectives?

2. This iteration

40 or 80 minutes (split evenly between demonstration and discussion) – led by whoever is best placed to talk through it. It is wonderfully powerful if it is a frontline team member or the project lead rather than the sponsor. The place where we show the work we have done as close to real life as possible. Avoid PowerPoint in this section if you can and show the real 'thing'.

Questions to help you frame this section:

- What have you achieved since the last showcase?
- What use stories did you make progress on?
- How did it go? Any challenges needed to be overcome?
- What did the testing show?
- What new evidence did we collect during this iteration?
- Can I see it in real life? (You really should answer yes here, even if it's sticky tape and string!)

3. What's next?

15 minutes (you may not need all of this). This is where we return to our project timeline view and talk about what's coming next.

Questions to help you frame this section:

- What are the next set of milestones and use stories you are focusing on?
- What testing and results should we expect?
- Who is involved from across the business?
- What should we be looking for at the next showcase?
- How long is this iteration going to be?

Hint: With a measured and driven mindset you should be ambitious with timing but not to the point where the team feels they are not building something of quality. Test that with them regularly with a simple question of confidence. 'On a scale of 1–5, how confident are you that you will deliver on the ambition and measures?' Anything less than a 4 requires you to rethink scope and timing. If you get a score below 4, ask the team what they need to change to become a 4 or a 5. It's then your job to deliver on it.

Challenging stakeholders

Tough stakeholders are in every business. Whether it be a CIO, CFO, COO, CMO or any other acronym, it can stifle innovation if you do not have the politics working for you. If the business has **ReFRAME**d, then the leadership alignment exercise from Chapter 4 will have helped create a more innovation-friendly political environment. However, if you haven't

FIGURE 6.5 Winning over challenging stakeholders

The political challenger

Plan A

The things they care about are: (add to this list based on the person)	The priority of this to them out of 5 is: (5 is their highest priority. You can have multiple 5s if that is accurate, but try to provide separation between topics)	Your strength in this area is: (5 is very strong and comfortable talking to this person and responding to the reasons they care about this topic).	The people who can influence them (can be a manager, a peer, or a long-term colleague)	Your relationship with that stakeholder: 5 – Strong and able to influence 3 – They know of me (mild relationship) 1 – They don't know of me (no relationship)
Their KPIs		☆☆☆☆☆		☆☆☆☆☆
Supporting others' work		☆☆☆☆☆		☆☆☆☆☆
Being correct		☆☆☆☆☆		☆☆☆☆☆
Being objective		☆☆☆☆☆		
...		☆☆☆☆☆		

The things they look for are:	The priority of this to them out of 5 is:	Your strength in this area is:		
Detailed risk management		☆☆☆☆☆		
Strong project milestones		☆☆☆☆☆		
...		☆☆☆☆☆		

Plan B

The things they respond to are:	The priority of this to them out of 5 is:	Your strength in this area is:	The people who they influence (can be a direct report, other senior stakeholders etc)	Your relationship with that stakeholder: 5 – Strong and able to influence 3 – They know of me (mild relationship) 1 – They don't know of me (no relationship)
High level of input		☆☆☆☆☆		☆☆☆☆☆
Work outside their area of expertise		☆☆☆☆☆		☆☆☆☆☆
...		☆☆☆☆☆		☆☆☆☆☆

*ReFRAME*d, or one of the stakeholders didn't get as much from the alignment session as the others, this tool (created from our experiences with too many negative stakeholders to reference) will have you moving at a measured and driven pace again in no time.

1 **What to do:** Start with plan A (Figure 6.5). Fill out the template and identify the areas where their high priorities (high stars) and your strengths (high stars) align. Use these alignments to change the way you are interacting with the stakeholder.

2 If plan A shows little or no alignment, then you need to use other influences to gain support from this stakeholder. Plot the map in Plan B to work out the best way to gain the support of this stakeholder via mutual relationships.

Conclusion

In this chapter we learned that we need three things to get innovation-ready:

1 Put in place the right sponsor (if not you) and sponsorship model. It is more than a figurehead role. There are defined jobs to do and a defined measured and driven mindset to keep.

2 Create cross-functional teams with the right capabilities. These might include skills like human-centred design, behavioural economics, data science or agile skills that are new to some retailers.

3 Provide adequate resourcing. This is about more than money – it is about everything that is needed that gives your people the 'space' to innovate.

Getting innovation-ready is the most labour-intensive part of our *ReFRAME* model. There are lots of internal and external challenges to getting it embedded and correct; however, the results are well worth it. Once we are innovation-ready, we are able to start taking our filtered ideas and get them specific enough to test, designed and built. You have done the hard work, now it is time for the fun work! (Just to manage your expectations – it is still hard, to be fair, but much more fun.)

Notes

1 Fast Company (2019) Most innovative companies: Nike [Online] https://www.
fastcompany.com/company/nike (archived at https://perma.cc/5YLZ-99AT)

2 Bowman, J (2019) Nike's Consumer Direct Offense is paying off, Motley Fool
[Online] https://www.fool.com/investing/2019/12/22/nikes-consumer-direct-
offense-is-paying-off.aspx (archived at https://perma.cc/2T8S-LW3G)

3 Sharma, A (2018) From Muji to Ikea: Why the best retailers think like UX
designers, Fast Company [Online] https://www.fastcompany.com/90177301/
from-muji-to-ikea-why-the-best-retailers-think-like-ux-designers (archived at
https://perma.cc/479X-LJS2)

07

Stage 4: Analyse and design the solution

(ANDREW)

Introduction

In 1957 when Ford released the Edsel, they did so with the belief that they had created something they thought the world needed – a medium-priced car that had inclusions that the team at Ford thought would redefine how people drove. On launch day (which they called E-Day) three million people ventured to the showroom. However, only 69,000 sold in its first year and the whole range was removed in 1959 after Ford lost $2 billion on the project.[1] Ford didn't need to lose all this money, but they took an idea that had passionate executive support (it was even named the Edsel after Henry Ford's deceased son), and went into design, production, marketing and launch with a product that the consumer eventually decided they didn't need or want. Continuing to spend money on a project that is untested is dangerous and often wastes resources and careers. This is common in retail where a good idea with strong executive support often skips ahead without the idea being properly defined or tested with the people who will ultimately determine its success.

To avoid blowing all your capital, the following three-step process will ensure that your projects are properly defined and backed by evidence before scaling:

1 Narrow down the specifics of an idea to truly understand what you want to deliver and how it achieves the outcomes you want.

2 Collect evidence, both data and behavioural, about the environment surrounding the idea that you want to innovate.

3 Analyse the evidence to assess whether the initiative will work in the intended environment, deliver the outcomes you want, and work in the way that you expected.

Analyse and design the solution

Too many business leaders think that once a project is formed and agreed then the next step is to build it. However, even with a brilliant idea filtering process, progressing without testing a more defined version of your innovation idea is fraught with danger.

FIGURE 7.1 The analyse and design the solution process

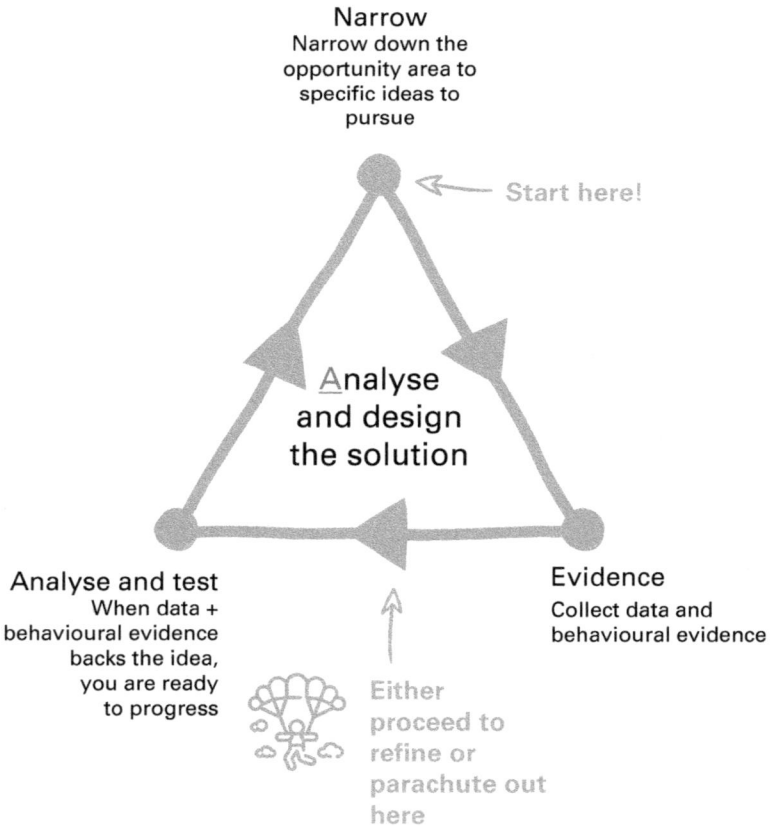

Narrow
Narrow down the
opportunity area to
specific ideas to
pursue

Start here!

**Analyse
and design
the solution**

Analyse and test
When data +
behavioural evidence
backs the idea,
you are ready
to progress

Either
proceed to
refine or
parachute out
here

Evidence
Collect data and
behavioural evidence

Putting your innovation project (let us call it the 'thing') through this testing process has two primary benefits:

- Evidence collected from the environment the 'thing' is going to exist in (for example; a store with a certain type of customers) means that you can objectively assess how it is going to influence that environment and deliver on the desired outcomes. In other words, you can confidently say how it will work, how humans will use it and what it will deliver.

- Testing the conceptual form of the 'thing' you want to innovate not only allows you to collect specifics for the design phase, but also assists you in future stages of the process like scaling it. Our process specifically records learning that will help reduce time to scale.

If you skip this stage, you risk wasting time and money on designing and building something that may not influence its environment in the way you intended. Our process is design-led to ensure all projects are backed by evidence and will influence the environment in the way they were intended to do.

Using a design and evidence-based process like this has been proven to improve outcomes. The Design Value Index assessed organizations over a ten-year period and found that design-conscious companies like Apple, Coca-Cola, IBM, Disney, Herman Miller and Nike saw a 219 per cent greater return on capital investment than non-design-conscious companies between 2004 and 2014.[2] The Premier's Design Council of Canada found that 48 per cent of projects with additional design investment recovered total costs within a year or less after the market launch, and 90 per cent of projects achieved payback within three years.[3]

This stage of the **ReFRAME** process reduces innovation costs and increases returns by reducing project time and the investment required in change management whilst delivering better outcomes. Another benefit is that it enables more ideas to be tested, which means your innovation pipeline will be larger but cost less overall as only ideas with a high chance of success get deeper investment.

Narrowing down the specifics

The first step is to narrow down to a level of specifics so you can truly understand the 'thing' you want to deliver and how it will achieve the outcomes you want. In this step you will:

- understand what elements make up the idea;
- take them to a level of specificity that is useful;
- articulate the environment around the 'thing' and quantify how the project will come to life in that environment, influence change (eg reduce digital transaction times) and deliver the outcomes you were targeting (eg reduce cost to serve).

An idea without specifics is a guess. This step isn't about PowerPoint packs or huge documents, it can be as simple as one diagram hand-drawn on a whiteboard, as long as it explains the idea in full, where it sits, the unique humans it impacts, the processes or business operations it involves, and anything else that is pertinent. We do not care about the colour of the 'thing' or its name yet, but we do care about finding all the characteristics of the 'thing'. Without this step, the danger is that you may jump ahead to the design-and-build phases with the team still guessing some of the elements and choosing to add specifics that are untested. In other words, you will be wasting money, time and people's focus.

Two of my favourite sayings that I have collected from smart leaders in my time are: 'Feedback is a gift' and 'Never underestimate the power of a story about your own failings'. So here I go with both in one go: When I was leading an innovation team at Telstra the business had a problem: stores didn't know what we wanted them to know and weren't completing the changes or tasks we were asking them to do. At least, not en masse. As a team, we set ourselves the challenge of getting stores the information they needed in a timely manner and in a way that they could absorb it.

We had a brilliant idea: the back of house menu board! Well, we thought it was brilliant, and so did everyone we told about it. A digital screen in the back room of every store with a menu on it that we could adjust and change as needed. The screen would be centrally controlled, easily updated, and in a location that every store team member could see it every day. Sadly, several months later, it was rare that I didn't walk into a store and see the screen switched off, 'out of order' signs taped to it and team members laughing at the initiative.

The problem we had not identified was that the screen interface was not intuitive and the choice and placement of the technology not aligned with how the store teams behaved when checking for new information. For example, we thought store leaders would run meetings around the board with our content available for this; however, most back rooms did not have the space, nor is this actually how or where store leaders did this activity. This meant our great idea was a screen that was more difficult to use and made the task longer than simply printing the content and putting it on a notice board or reading it out to the team in the usual way. My failure as sponsor was that I let my subjectivity and those of other leaders who thought the idea was amazing be enough to skip a testing phase and instead moved forward to selecting a vendor and constructing it. We failed to get specific enough on the core characteristics of the idea and the environment it was going into, nor did we test any of that before we started building it. The team did exactly what was asked of them and the vendor is one of the best I've worked with. This was my error as sponsor for not following a proper and thoughtful process.

People often ask why these issues aren't taken care of in the filtering stage (stage 2). The filtering stage is only intended to select the best ideas to pursue and is designed to be quick. The detail of the elements that make up the idea, getting to a fine level of specificity and considering how it will come to life and influence its environment, is not necessary before the idea gets a sponsor and team to build it (stage 3). It would be a waste of time and money to do otherwise.

To execute this step, you will need the right people assigned to do it. If you have followed the process correctly from stage 3, you will have them already. If you don't, then you may need to return to the previous stage in the *ReFRAME* process and get innovation-ready. Without the right cross-functional team with a breadth of skills, the steps in this stage will be harder to execute and may include errors that will ultimately impact how well your 'thing' achieves its set outcomes.

Sometimes we get enthralled by an idea, thinking that it is obviously great, and we don't need to get specific. We are trained to think that skipping a step makes things faster. It doesn't. In fact, slowing down and applying this step of the process will speed you up in the long run and produce better outcomes for the business.

The only prerequisite to complete this step is the space to do it, which should have been created in stage 3. Do not try and fast forward to stage 5 because, no matter how tempting it might be and how confident you are in the 'thing' that you're building, your outcomes won't be as strong without this stage.

EXERCISE
The narrowing canvas

What this is

The narrowing canvas is a guide to take your idea down into a useful level of specificity that we use to test our 'thing' effectively. The canvas includes some example groups of a typical retail business and the types of questions that will help guide you on their level of involvement.

Instructions

1 Complete the narrowing canvas (Table 7.1) for each of the primary groups by answering each question as either true or not.

2 A score is given to each statement that reflects the complexity or impact of that statement. If the statement is true, then you add the associated score to that group's total.

3 Calculate the score for each group and then use the involvement scale (below) to understand how involved they need to be in the design, like the example in the narrowing canvas.

4 For each of these core groups, write them a one-page memo that explains (in their context and language) what the 'thing' is, why you are building it, how it will change the way they do or think about things, and the value it gives them. Use both measurable and estimated value types (eg time saving is measurable, enjoyment is estimated).

5 The answers to the narrowing canvas and the memos you write will be used to create your use stories in the next part of this chapter.

6 Depending on the complexity of your project and the scale of its impact, it may be worth conducting a narrowing canvas exercise for internal functions of the business, like finance or IT. This is particularly pertinent if your 'thing' impacts their area either directly or indirectly. The canvas includes some example areas of a typical retail business and the types of questions that will help guide you on their level of involvement.

Hint: Do not use jargon, just very clearly articulate what the 'thing' is, how it works, how they use/access/etc it and what it means for them. You may need to add more groups depending on your business, which is ok, just do not leave anyone out! You don't need to actually send them the memo, but the exercise of producing one that is clear and easily understood helps you get to a level of clarity that jargon and PowerPoint alone can't get you to.

TABLE 7.1   The narrowing canvas

Group	Questions	Score
The customer	This changes how I perceive your brand and its values	2 pts
	This changes how I use your products or services	2 pts
	This changes how much I pay you	1 pt
	This stops me from doing or getting something I currently do	5 pts
	This changes the way I do or get something (but I can still do it or get it)	5 pts
	This creates a new way for me to do or get something	5 pts
	This changes the products and services you offer me	5 pts
The channels	This changes the tools I use to work	5 pts
	This changes the products and services I sell	5 pts
	This changes how much I earn or how I earn it	5 pts
	This changes the way the channels are connected or integrated	5 pts
	This introduces new functionality to my work	5 pts
	This changes the channel aesthetics	2 pts
	This changes the customers I work with	2 pts
The product	This adds new products and services	5 pts
	This removes products and services we offer	5 pts
	This changes our go to market pathway	5 pts
	This changes the customers we offer products and services to	5 pts
	This changes the customer breakdown	2 pts
Finance	This changes our profit	1 pt
	This changes our expenses	2 pts
	This changes our prices	2 pts
Marketing	This changes our brand image	5 pts
	This changes our go to market pathway	2 pts
	This changes our customer breakdown	5 pts
HR/people	This changes the way our people work	5 pts
	This changes the skills we need	5 pts
	This changes the way our people earn or are rewarded	5 pts
Operations	This changes the way we deliver products or services	5 pts
	This changes the way we support our channels	2 pts

(continued)

TABLE 7.1 (Continued)

Group	Questions	Score
IT/technology	This changes our technology map	5 pts
	This requires IT work	5 pts
	The way a system is being used is changing (not the system itself)	2 pts

Assess the scale of involvement

Assess the scale of involvement by answering and scoring the questions. If the statement is correct, then it scores the points listed next to the statement. If the statement is incorrect, then the score is 0.

- *0 is 'Invite me'*: The group who scored this (eg the customers or finance) are welcome to participate and add value, but are not required on the project team directly.

- *1–4 is 'Inform me'*: You should keep this group informed appropriately and they should participate in your showcases.

- *5 and above is 'Involve me'*: With a score of 5 or above, the group who got that result should actively be involved in the design, building and testing of your 'thing'. For example, if it is a technology project and IT got a score about 5 (I assume, well above) then they need to be part of the core project team.

Depending on the complexity of your project and the scale of its impact, it may be worth conducting a narrowing exercise for internal functions of the business, like finance or IT. This is particularly pertinent if your 'thing' impacts their area either directly or indirectly.

Create a list of use stories

To create a full list of use stories for all the statements that were correct in the narrowing canvas, ie those that scored points, we need to start with big themes and narrow from there. There are three levels in use stories that are used for different elements of the build process:

- **Big theme** – These are the top-most level of describing areas of the 'thing' in the form of a general task or ambition. An example might be that our 'thing' is about improving how a family coordinates their night as a family. A big theme might be 'reduce order input time by two minutes'. It is not specific enough yet to let us move on to the design phase, but it does allow us to group things into useful collections for design.

- **General ambitions** – These are the next layer down, getting more useful, but not specific enough for us to use within a design. If we keep our example going it might be 'reduce duplicative effort', or 'reduce the number of screens'.

- **The use story** – Before we get into creating specific use stories for how we do those things, it is often necessary to run a prioritization at the 'general ambition' level. This ensures that we do not waste effort creating use stories for ambitions that will not make the final list for your 'thing'. To do this, use the ambition prioritization exercise below.

EXERCISE
Ambition prioritization

What this is

To prioritize your general ambitions, we use a modified version of the golden rule. To help you remain objective in your assessment, use members of your frontline teams or members of any team who is impacted to support rating the human impact of each part of your 'thing'.

The big themes

The big themes will be the first level breakdown of the ambition you have selected from your idea filtering session in stage two of the **ReFRAME** process. For this example, let's assume our ambition is to improve in store productivity; a big theme from within that could be 'Reduce order input time by two minutes':

1 In a room (or a virtual equivalent), discuss and create the big themes and place sticky notes on a wall or write them on a white board. No idea is bad, as there will be a prioritization exercise coming later. A great way to do this is to have each member silently and individually write their ideas down and then group like-minded themes and eliminate duplicates.

2 As a team, you should discuss the language to ensure it is clear, without jargon, and unambiguous in its intent.

The general ambitions

1 For each of these big themes, as a team, break it down into general ambition statements. As an example, if the big theme is 'Reduce order input time by two minutes' some general ambitions may be: 'Reduce duplicative effort in the form customers fill out' or 'Reduce the number of screens in the order form', etc. Place each of these ambitions under the big themes, creating a pyramid with the big theme at the top.

2 At this point, if possible, bring new people with fresh eyes into the room to assess what you have done and provide any additional ambitions or adjust existing ones.

The gravity issues (immovable requirements)

Next, we need to assess whether the ambition is a genuine requirement for our 'thing' or not. A requirement is defined as something that, if not included, means the 'thing' will not function.

This is a matter of engineering and facts, not opinions. For example, if the technology team say 'You must use the current system' then that is a requirement (or a gravity issue as we call it) as it is out of your control. 'Reduce the number of screens in the order form' is a good way to achieve your big theme but is not a requirement for it to function:

1 Check if your ambition can be altered to ensure it is objective and jargon free.

2 If the group agrees it is a requirement, it will not need to go through the impact assessment (the next step) so you can confirm it as an ambition of your 'thing' (circle it, put a green sticker on it, whatever works for you).

3 If it is not a requirement, you need to assess its impact for prioritization.

Assessing impacts

Any ambitions that are not gravity issues now need to be assessed for their impact so you can prioritize which are included in your scope:

1 Human impact: What is the scale of impact on the humans your 'thing' is intended for? The scale is 0–5 and is based on the size of impact it has on your 'thing' achieving the outcomes you are targeting. For example, 'Reduce duplicative effort in the form customers fill out' will score medium (3) if inputting the same information multiple times is repetitive and time wasting, or it will score very high (5) if it causes a common error that makes the customer start the process over again and redo everything.

2 Business impact: As per human impact, this is an assessment of the scale of impact the general ambition has on your desired business outcomes. For example, if you are wanting to reduce labour investment in stores, then 'Reduce duplicative effort in the form customers fill out' will score very low (0) as it is the customers who fill out the form, not the frontline teams. However, if the form is also used by frontline teams, then it will score highly (4 or 5).

3 Place a sticker, a dot, a tick or whatever tickles your fancy for each point scored on both business and human impact (use two different colours to differentiate the two types of impact).

The prioritized list

Your fully prioritized list should be formed as follows:

1 Requirements that you need to include to ensure your 'thing' will function get a straight pass and will be prioritized ambitions.

2 As a group, identify the ambitions with the biggest impact. Depending on the priority of your business and your 'thing', you can choose to weight human or business impact differently. Eg human impact could be worth 2x the value of business impact if you are currently on a 'customer obsession' strategy.

3 You should now have a list of ambitions that include all requirements, as well as a prioritized view of other ambitions.

4 Now it is time to allocate your estimated resources. Start with a score of 100 units of effort. Effort is an estimated value to help with prioritization. Don't overthink it; if things change, you can include or exclude ambitions later. As an example, if you have $5 million estimated funding, then you can equally divide it up into a number of units.

5 Allocate estimated effort to each ambition until you run out of effort units.

Once completed, you should have something that clearly articulates which ambitions are included in the design of your 'thing'.

Now for the use story

To create the list of use stories that will allow us to design and build our 'thing', you should use the helpful template of the 4 Hs, overleaf. A use story needs to be very specific and allow the project team to have no doubt about what capability they are building. If there is ambiguity in the use story, there will be ambiguity in the finished product. Depending on the depth and breadth of your project, your use story list could be two stories or 200, so you will need to spend time ensuring you have got this right. Don't let you or the team get caught up in worry about losing or missing use stories, though; as you build your 'thing' it is not uncommon for you to collect more, change or remove them. Any new ones will need to either be incorporated into your design (eg if they are important to you achieving the outcomes you set out to achieve), or put into a backlog for later improvements (eg they won't stop you from achieving your targets, but will add value if added via another phase of this project or a new project entirely).

EXERCISE
Create a use story using the 4 Hs

What this is

The 4 Hs are human, habit, hope, hypothesis. Depending on the project, you will create tens or hundreds of use stories. The simple flow of creating a use story is shown below.

Instructions

Work in order. The questions here are general and will act as a guide. As a project team, add more specific ones that are applicable to the 'thing' you are designing.

1   Outcomes
    As a group, define the metrics you are seeking to impact with your 'thing':
    a. *Data metrics:* What metrics that you have a baseline for are you wanting to move with these outcomes and by what margin? You don't need exact numbers, but a directional ambition is important (eg move 10 per cent of sales to digital channels).
    b. *Behavioural metrics:* Essentially choices, what are the behaviours you are looking to influence in a group of humans (eg customers or store teams)?

2   Boundaries
    Facilitate an activity with your core project team to discover the boundaries in which your 'thing' will be operating:
    a. *Gravity boundaries:* What elements of the environment cannot be changed as part of implementing your 'thing' (ie like gravity – eg a system constraint, or a law)?
    b. *Elastic boundaries:* What are the things that will require additional resources (time, effort, energy, people, money, etc) to overcome that you don't currently

have access to but is likely you can get (eg a process change, a minor system adjustment, or additional people or skills)?

3   Environment

With a group that must include any specialists needed for the project, define the environment that your 'thing' is being designed for:

a. *Physical boundaries:* This includes places or objects that the 'thing' will be connected to or placed into. For example, a new point of sale will have a technological and physical store environment.

b. *Organizational boundaries:* What processes or organizational elements are part of the environment that your 'thing' will be operating in? This must include internal and external elements (eg a law or shopping centre requirement).

4   Forming and testing the use story

Create your use stories using the formula below:

As a *(who the* **human** *is, eg the customer)* I want to be able to *(the* **habit** *that is changing, eg use the app to search for stock in a store)* so I can *(the* **hoped** *benefit, eg save time and a store visit)* because *(the evidence that forms the* **hypothesis***, eg 87 per cent of interviewees said time was important).*

Hint: The principles to guide the creation of your use story: is it testable (the human will comprehend it and confirm that it is real), specific (it provides clear direction for designing and building the 'thing'), objective (evidence backed), and does it clarify (it explains your answers in the canvas clearly)?

5   Check each user story with the checkpoint questions below, one for each of the earlier groups:

a. *Outcomes:* Does your use story support the shifting of these data and behavioural metrics?

b. *Boundaries:* Does your use story operate within these boundaries?

c. *Environment:* Can your use story operate within these environments?

Collecting evidence

Collecting evidence enables you to objectively assess your idea and work out how the 'thing' will impact its surroundings. This evidence is then used to assess if the 'thing' should be made but will also help save time in forming a testing plan when you get into the next stage of the process.

This step is simple to comprehend, but very difficult to execute. We will help you understand the different types of evidence and how to collect them. After that we talk about how to use the evidence to assess whether your idea will create the change it is intended to achieve.

> Facts are stubborn things; and whatever may be our wishes, our inclinations, or the dictates of our passions, they cannot alter the state of facts and evidence.
>
> John Adams[4]

After collecting evidence, you are going to have:

- a better design of your idea;
- a more accurate understanding of the outcomes you can expect;
- the ability to save time by eliminating ideas that will not work.

If we look back to my back of house menu board debacle, this step would have saved me. We would have found out that the routine and layout of every store was very different to what we thought, which meant our technical design was poor and not user-friendly, therefore the screen was unhelpful as anything but a bulletin board for paper printouts. If we have had a greater understanding of the environment and tested the idea, we would have had evidence that would have allowed us to refine the idea to suit the environment it was going into and delivered a project that met the expectations our egos had of the project.

There are two types of evidence to collect to assess your innovation: quantitative data and qualitative behavioural evidence.

Data and behavioural evidence

QUANTITATIVE DATA

Quantitative data is numbers and facts. It is the type of data you use to diagnose most business problems. In projects, it sometimes feels like there is never enough access to the right data to make decisions. Sometimes. the data exists in your organization but not in a format that makes it easy to use. If this is the case, then you may consider using an external agency with data science skills to help. Alternatively, if you find that you do not have enough data internally you can use third parties to help you collect it.

You do not need a lot to get started, but the more data you have, the more helpful evidence it will be.

There are several types of quantitative data that are helpful pieces of evidence. Often people think of data as only that which is in the reports they generate in their business already; however, there are many forms of data to collect. When innovating, the most helpful forms of data have the following characteristics:

- A baseline: You have some historical measurement of how this data has changed over recent history. The longer the history, the better quality of insight you can derive of what impacts the measure and by what margin.

- Constantly measurable: Innovation moves at pace, and therefore so must the flow of information and evidence. If the data isn't currently measured constantly, can it be? If not, what alternatives are there that can get you the same level of insight?

- Broad and deep sample size: It needs to be a decent enough sample of outcomes that you can draw conclusions that are robust. For example, if you are assessing the impact a new rostering tool has on productivity, you will need to have all the store types represented (breadth) and a number of each of those types (depth) to collect reliable outcomes. If you can't control depth and breadth, then you will need to increase the overall sample size to reduce your margin of error.

- Numerical outcomes: This might seem obvious to some, but quantitative data must be numerically represented. It can be defined with words but needs to be a numerical measure. In our rostering example, productivity will be a number (x products per hour per full-time equivalent).

QUALITATIVE BEHAVIOURAL EVIDENCE

If you have ever had the 'But I don't understand why people aren't using it?!' conversation, then you did not collect enough appropriate behavioural evidence. Behavioural evidence is qualitative data that helps you understand context. Retail is a human business, and you need to put your ideas in *their* context, not your own. Behavioural evidence is a collected set of information that helps you see how your customer connects with your 'thing', ie how it fit into their broader life and the choices and actions they make.

You will need to collect behavioural evidence from interviews and observations. Interviews should be conducted with customers and your team after observing their behaviour. If you have never collected behavioural evidence before, you may want to consider getting external help. If you do want to keep it in house, a good start would be to design out a rough plan for how you want to observe and conduct interviews and to practise it within the team. Using your in-store cameras or live web tracking are good ways to start, as they are resources you already have. When it comes to the real thing, in depth observation of behaviour (in a customer's home for example) and interviewing them in-store, at a central location or in their home will require permission to ensure customers and team members are comfortable before the process begins. If it is your team's first time doing this, stick with in-store interactions, as they are a good way to get your confidence up in observing and asking objective open-ended questions. Talk to your legal team about any waivers or permission forms you may want to get the participants to sign. This is not only the right thing to do but also protects you from any privacy issues raised by respondents after the event.

To demonstrate the type of evidence that needs to be collected, let's use the example of a toy retailer operating in a mall whose customers spend a lot of time in the mall after school drop-off to get their errands done. In this case, you need to observe how they get to the mall, where they park, where they go first and for what reasons, and so on. Then when they get to your store, you want to know where they go in store, what they look at and what they miss. You then need to ask them to describe the experience from their point of view using open-ended questions that are not judgemental or overly targeted or leading. You want to understand what they were thinking and feeling whilst they were doing what you observed. Only towards the end of the conversation can you ask more specific questions like 'What if it was like this?' Collecting behavioural evidence helps you to understand the customer better and how their behaviours will be influenced through the design of your 'thing'.

It is at this point some may ask why the quantitative data alone is not enough. Quantitative data is used to diagnose problems, to calculate risk and analyse all sorts of business problems. In this stage of the *ReFRAME* process, both quantitative data and qualitative behavioural evidence are important for different reasons. Quantitative data helps you objectively understand current performance and changes in performance after the 'thing' you are building is deployed, but it does not tell you why performance changes (or does not change). Qualitative behavioural evidence does this. It helps you understand how the 'thing' impacts the choices humans make and their perceptions, ie the reasons the performance changed.

There are loads of ways to collect behavioural evidence, and if you are doing this already with slightly different techniques, then, great! I would still recommend being curious and open to different ways of doing it and see whether our recommendations can help you evolve the way you do it.

Hint: You do not have to reinvent the wheel each time you collect evidence. Sometimes, several innovation projects may be happening at once in the same environment and impacting the same people. In this case, the evidence collected can be used across multiple 'things'. Make sure all the teams involved in innovation are communicating and sharing so you minimize effort and cost.

People capability can be a challenge in both collecting and analysing behavioural evidence. If you do not have these skills in your organization now (behavioural economists, human-centred designers, data scientists, etc) you will need to either recruit them or train your current team. The team skills canvas exercise from stage 3 will tell you what skills you need. These new skills are becoming more and more important to modern retailing and add value not only across innovation projects but also in business decisions generally. Alternatively, there are plenty of great consulting firms that could help you on a contract basis whilst you build up the capability. If you do not have the capacity to hire, train or contract then simply use the behavioural evidence collection card (below) as a guide with the project team you have assembled. You should select the best members of the team to do this. To help you find the best members of the current team, use these questions as a guide:

1 Do they have good observation skills (someone who can observe, take notes and generate insights from what they see)?

2 Do they have high levels of empathy (someone who can easily put themselves into other people's shoes and is curious but not judgemental as to why other people do things in certain ways)?

3 Do they feel comfortable conducting an interview (someone who is comfortable talking to strangers, can follow up on good insights and is able to communicate and take notes at the same time)?

The evidence you need to collect will change with each project; however, our behavioural evidence collection card process will help guide you.

The behavioural evidence collection cards

We have created templates of evidence collection cards (and other tools) that provide a process to flow and some example questions. You can find them online at www.koganpage.com/RIR

Behavioural evidence collection comes in three forms: observation, one-on-one interview and group interview.

OBSERVATION
Observation should involve as little interference as possible. Essentially, you want to watch how a human behaves within your digital or physical environment. It is the 'what' and 'how' of a human's choices and actions.

Write short factual notes on what you see. After the observation, write out your deductions and reflections. Do this straight away before your brain takes over and starts inserting what it wants to hear!

INTERVIEWS

The interviews, whether one-on-one or group, are used to gather information about 'why' they made those choices and took those actions. The process is simple enough, but doing it well is difficult and is something that should be practised if your team have not done it before. They should use the evidence collection card as a guide. During the interviews, your objective should be to gather what the human was thinking and feeling, and what led to those thoughts, feelings, and actions.

Analysing the evidence

So, you have more specifics on the 'thing' you are wanting to create, a heap of evidence from the data sources you have, and behavioural context of the humans involved. Awesome! Now you need to test how your 'thing' impacts and aligns with that evidence. The decisions you can make are:

- move forward (proceed);
- change the specifics of the idea (pivot); or
- parachute out and go back to the filtering of ideas.

This is the final step to take before moving on to the fun bit – stage 5: making the design and scaling it! When evidence backs up an idea it is what we call a 'BOOM!' moment. This means that everything is going smoothly, and the parachute can stay safely under your seat. If the evidence does not back up the idea, then it's better to parachute out now at 10 feet rather than continuing to progress and needing to leap from the aircraft at 10,000 feet. Improving cultural objectivity and awareness of biases, not to mention a healthy love for evidence, will mean that you will consistently become stronger and faster at this part of the process.

Completing the evidence assessment

The goal of this step is to have a good level of confidence that the 'thing' at this level of specificity will both deliver the outcomes required and fit in the environment. 'Fit', in this context, means that it makes sense to the humans who will use it and has a logical and objective connection to the problem you are solving.

Let me again use my back of house menu board failure as our example. If we had collected evidence about how our 'thing' would fit into the daily work rhythms of our frontline teams, on the different environments the screens were going into (the different sizes and shapes of back of house), and the content going on them, we would have very quickly realized that it would not work. In other words, we would have discovered that our assumptions of its use were wrong because we had misinterpreted the environmental, behavioural and technical context it was going into. In hindsight we should have pivoted the solution to be portable and improved the user interface to make it more aligned with the store operating rhythm.

EXERCISE
The evidence assessment tool

What this is

The evidence assessment tool is used to assess whether the evidence collected indicates that your 'thing' will deliver on its intended outcomes. It forces objective assessment of the evidence and the context to reduce influence from our somewhat pesky levels of subjectivity.

Instructions

List the pertinent evidence that you have collected under the headings quantitative or qualitative.

For quantitative evidence, you are looking to check that your data is helpful.
Hint: When listing your quantitative information below, include any helpful context, such as other variables that may have impacted the changes.

- Does it have a useful baseline?
- Is it constantly measurable?
- Did you have an appropriate sample size?
- Is it a numerical outcome?

For qualitative evidence, list the observational variables you found using plain human language. Avoid superlatives or hypotheses that can imply whether an observation is good or bad for your project. **Hint:** When listing your qualitative data, group it by the primary actor, such as the store team member, or the customer.

FIGURE 7.2 The evidence assessment tool

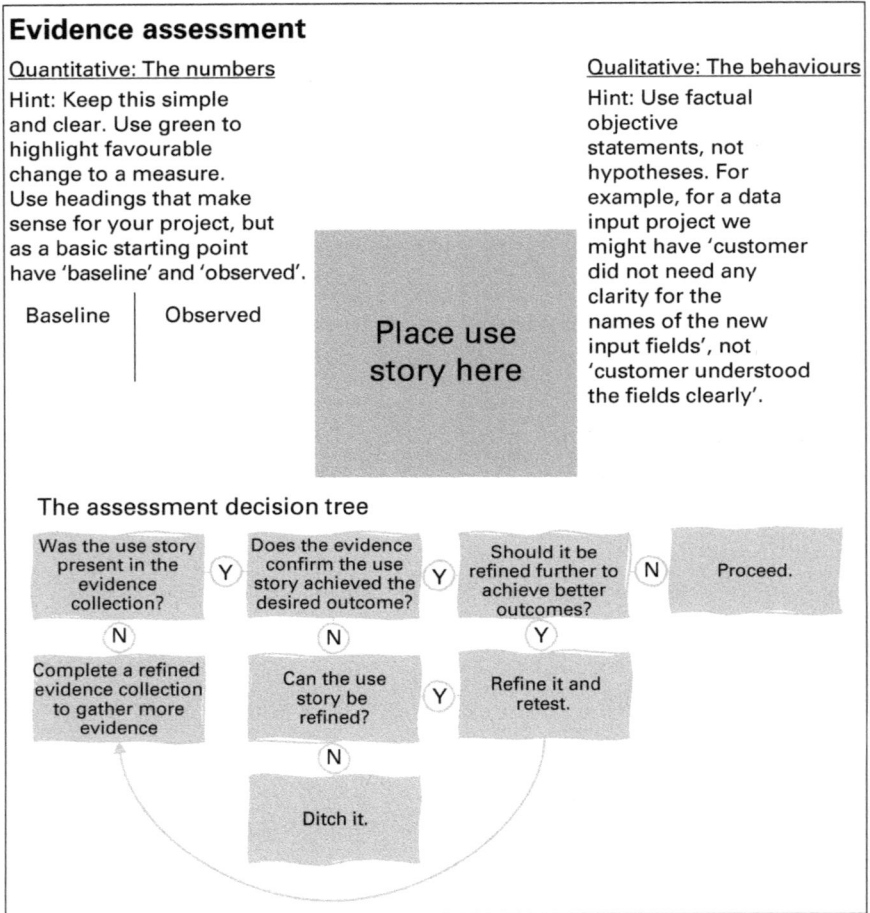

Evidence assessment

Quantitative: The numbers
Hint: Keep this simple and clear. Use green to highlight favourable change to a measure. Use headings that make sense for your project, but as a basic starting point have 'baseline' and 'observed'.

Baseline | Observed

Place use story here

Qualitative: The behaviours
Hint: Use factual objective statements, not hypotheses. For example, for a data input project we might have 'customer did not need any clarity for the names of the new input fields', not 'customer understood the fields clearly'.

The assessment decision tree

Was the use story present in the evidence collection? — Y — Does the evidence confirm the use story achieved the desired outcome? — Y — Should it be refined further to achieve better outcomes? — N — Proceed.

N | N | Y

Complete a refined evidence collection to gather more evidence

Can the use story be refined? — Y — Refine it and retest.

N

Ditch it.

Place each use story one at a time in the centre of the tool (Figure 7.2) and look for quantitative and qualitative data that confirms that use story was met and what impact it had on the measures. Follow the decision tree to complete the assessment.

When we created our back-of-house menu boards, the evidence we collected was during deployment. If we had collected evidence earlier, then we would have known to either pivot or parachute out. This simple exercise can save you and your business a lot of time and effort.

Innovation biases

A likely enemy to progress will be subjectivity. Our brains have evolved over centuries to find the path of least resistance. If it is our own idea, it's natural to go through this process with an ambition to prove that we are right. This biases the process and leads to invalid conclusions. It is important to remember when assessing evidence, you are not proving anyone right or wrong, you are assessing the impact an idea has on an environment and humans. Try to remove your prejudices. A fabulous leader I used to work with called this keeping your strong opinions but holding on to them loosely. To do that you will need to keep an eye on your biases. To help you with that, we have produced a set of innovation biases to help you stay objective (Figure 7.3). Set a coffee date with yourself and think about how you, your team or your peers and leaders show these biases. Not to mention, how you can create a culture where people are constantly assessing whether these biases are impacting your work every day or not.

Conclusion

In this chapter we have explained the three steps of stage 4 of the *ReFRAME* process. They are:

1 Narrowing down the specifics of an idea to truly understand what you want to deliver and how it achieves the outcomes you want.

2 Collecting evidence, both quantitative and qualitative, about the environment surrounding the idea that you want to innovate.

3 Analysing the evidence to assess whether the initiative will work in the intended environment and deliver the expected outcomes in the way that was expected.

There are some key risks to completing this stage:

• People capability: The cross-functional team should ideally include behavioural economists, human-centred designers, data scientists, etc. These are not common skills in the retail industry. Make sure you have a plan to overcome any skills gaps in the team that may influence the outcomes of this process. If none of the specialist skills you need are available to you then the behavioural evidence collection card and evidence assessment tool can be used by the existing team as a guide.

FIGURE 7.3 Innovation biases

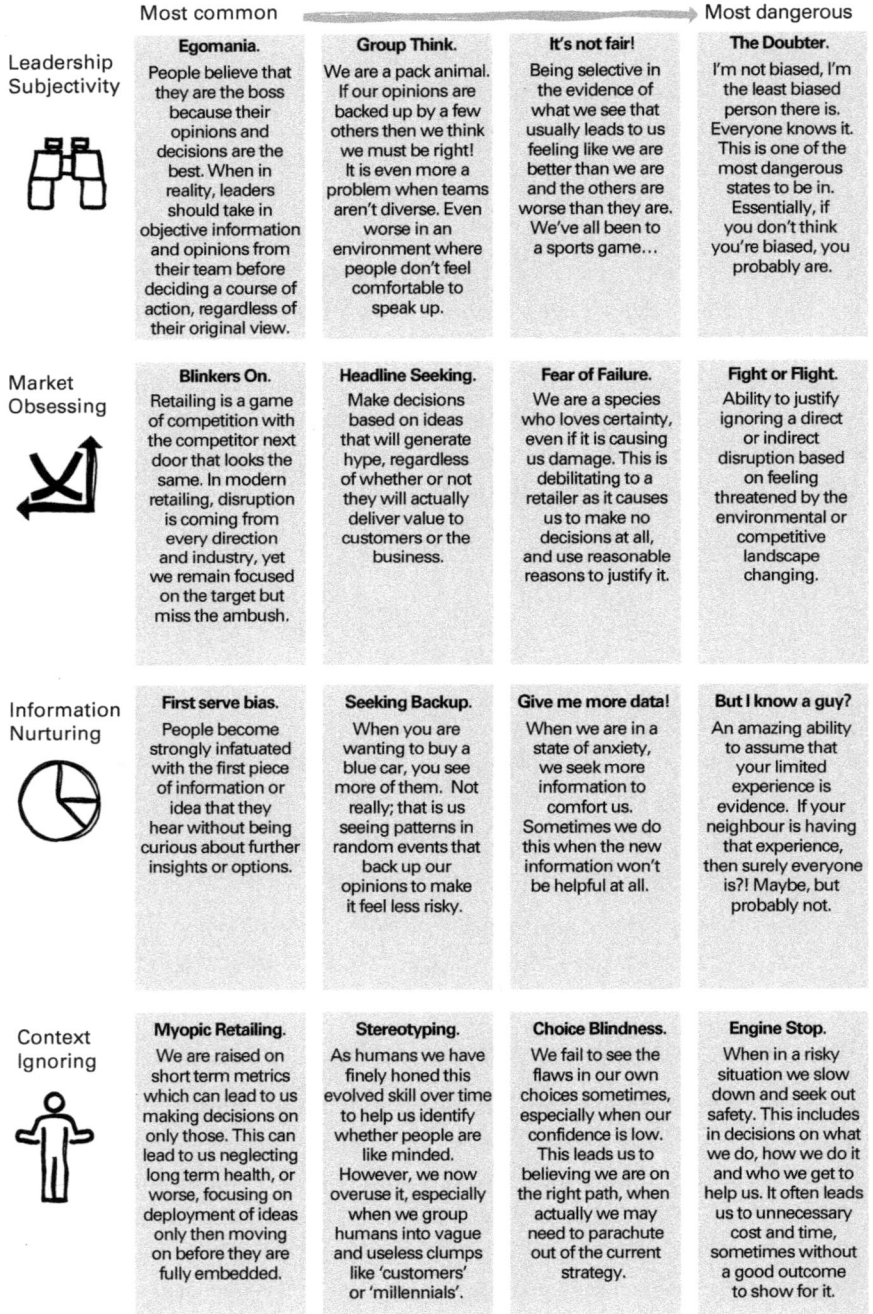

Most common ➤ Most dangerous

Leadership Subjectivity	**Egomania.** People believe that they are the boss because their opinions and decisions are the best. When in reality, leaders should take in objective information and opinions from their team before deciding a course of action, regardless of their original view.	**Group Think.** We are a pack animal. If our opinions are backed up by a few others then we think we must be right! It is even more a problem when teams aren't diverse. Even worse in an environment where people don't feel comfortable to speak up.	**It's not fair!** Being selective in the evidence of what we see that usually leads to us feeling like we are better than we are and the others are worse than they are. We've all been to a sports game…	**The Doubter.** I'm not biased, I'm the least biased person there is. Everyone knows it. This is one of the most dangerous states to be in. Essentially, if you don't think you're biased, you probably are.
Market Obsessing	**Blinkers On.** Retailing is a game of competition with the competitor next door that looks the same. In modern retailing, disruption is coming from every direction and industry, yet we remain focused on the target but miss the ambush.	**Headline Seeking.** Make decisions based on ideas that will generate hype, regardless of whether or not they will actually deliver value to customers or the business.	**Fear of Failure.** We are a species who loves certainty, even if it is causing us damage. This is debilitating to a retailer as it causes us to make no decisions at all, and use reasonable reasons to justify it.	**Fight or Flight.** Ability to justify ignoring a direct or indirect disruption based on feeling threatened by the environmental or competitive landscape changing.
Information Nurturing	**First serve bias.** People become strongly infatuated with the first piece of information or idea that they hear without being curious about further insights or options.	**Seeking Backup.** When you are wanting to buy a blue car, you see more of them. Not really; that is us seeing patterns in random events that back up our opinions to make it feel less risky.	**Give me more data!** When we are in a state of anxiety, we seek more information to comfort us. Sometimes we do this when the new information won't be helpful at all.	**But I know a guy?** An amazing ability to assume that your limited experience is evidence. If your neighbour is having that experience, then surely everyone is?! Maybe, but probably not.
Context Ignoring	**Myopic Retailing.** We are raised on short term metrics which can lead to us making decisions on only those. This can lead to us neglecting long term health, or worse, focusing on deployment of ideas only then moving on before they are fully embedded.	**Stereotyping.** As humans we have finely honed this evolved skill over time to help us identify whether people are like minded. However, we now overuse it, especially when we group humans into vague and useless clumps like 'customers' or 'millennials'.	**Choice Blindness.** We fail to see the flaws in our own choices sometimes, especially when our confidence is low. This leads us to believing we are on the right path, when actually we may need to parachute out of the current strategy.	**Engine Stop.** When in a risky situation we slow down and seek out safety. This includes in decisions on what we do, how we do it and who we get to help us. It often leads us to unnecessary cost and time, sometimes without a good outcome to show for it.

- Subjectivity: Humans are good at it, so use the innovation biases taxonomy to help you and your broader team overcome it.

- Complacency: Organizations can get complacent and start accepting mediocre outcomes in exchange for faster delivery times or reduced human capital consumption. Do not come up with reasonable reasons to simply 'get through' this part of the process. Stay vigilant!

My days of back of house menu boards are well and truly behind me. If you want to avoid my mistakes, get enthralled with evidence (both quantitative and qualitative) and believe in the process.

In the next chapter we move on to the most fun part of the process, which is making the design and scaling it! We cover the steps needed to end up with a version of your 'thing' that can become embedded as the new normal.

Notes

1 Walgrove, A (undated) 4 failed products that will teach you a lot about business, Growth Lab [Online] https://growthlab.com/famous-product-ideas-that-failed/ (archived at https://perma.cc/9YKB-LLFV)

2 Design Management Institute (2015) The Design Value Index [Online] https://www.dmi.org/page/DesignDrivesValue (archived at https://perma.cc/N7DE-YB4P)

3 Design Forward Alliance (undated) Good design is good for business (and more) [Online] https://www.designforwardsd.com/the-value-of-design (archived at https://perma.cc/6MZU-FNSH)

4 Gordon, W (1788) *The History of the Rise, Progress, and Establishment, of the Independence of the United States of America*, p 296

08

Stage 5: Make the design
and scale it

(ANDREW)

Introduction

There is much written about how perfect the world looks from an aircraft flying at altitude. Fields look squarer and more consistent in colour. Roads become outlines of images as they smoothly bend and turn across the earth. Streetlights form stunning patterns and brake lights on cars weave their way through towns almost blurring into a single red spark. It is true, there is no greater a feeling than the freedom of flying an aircraft. Sitting in a cockpit, in control of this well-engineered (hopefully) piece of machinery gliding through the sky looking down at the earth below. When I was learning to fly, this view was a constant, but lovely, distraction from the job at hand.

One of my least favourite lessons on my pathway to becoming a commercial pilot was learning how to navigate once lost. As every student pilot can attest, there is something incredibly uncomfortable about having a hood on you that means you can't see out of the aircraft, blocking that usually engrossing viewpoint. All you can see is the basic instruments as your flight instructor takes you to an unknown location before removing the hood and saying, 'Ok, get us home.' What follows is utter panic. Your brain usually stops working as it is overloaded with the things you need to do. Find yourself, plan your trip home, notify air traffic control, and, preferably, don't run into any other planes whilst doing it all.

Having managed to find my way home, albeit after a good five minutes of wasted time as I tried to make the shape of the lake below me to fit the one on the map where I thought I was (it wasn't), upon landing I learned that this lesson wasn't just about how to navigate when lost. It was about appropriate pace and prioritization. No matter how urgent the imperative feels, the same rule always applies. Aviate. Navigate. Communicate. This mantra is drilled into pilots' heads from day one of training. At times of high stress, you will have people talking in your ear, instruments throwing information at you, a co-pilot usually in the same situation and an aircraft at altitude ploughing forward through the sky. It is designed to make you feel calm in times where your instinct is to panic. It helps you be thoughtful, but action focused. The summary is:

1 **Aviate:** Get control of the aircraft, understand its situation and ensure it is safely in your control.

2 **Navigate:** Find where you are and plot your flight plan to your destination (and make sure you have fuel!).

3 **Communicate:** At that point, communicate your plan and ensure everyone is kept informed on your progress.

What I learned from my pilot's training I have taken into every part of my career, and nowhere has it been more valuable than during times of high innovation. The mantra is designed to help you get into the mindset that we call 'measured and driven'. Be smart, take in information and analyse it, be decisive and always communicate clearly. There is always going to be distractions, noise, people talking to you or demanding things from you, expectations on you from yourself and others. Sound familiar? Retail is a noisy place that is constantly ploughing through the sky with bad weather. As we navigate our way to a resilient and innovation-focused retail business, we need to be measured and driven to ensure we make it to our destination despite the noise.

The pressure and noise of progress is one that constantly surrounds retail innovators. As you make your 'thing' it is incredibly common to hear people say 'But we can fix that later', or 'I don't think it'll work like that in the real world', or the worst, 'That just works that way because it is in trial mode, it'll be better when it's real'. We have all been there, desperate to get something finished or succumb to the pressure to deliver progress, so we keep our engine roaring and don't check the map. Not a great strategy.

To be clear, we are not advocating for slow and steady; that will never work in retail with its rapidly changing environment. Instead, we now know that pace through processes instigated with a 'measured and driven' mindset is the way to achieve innovation that delivers the highest outcomes for retailers. It is the fastest way to delivering peak outcomes and it avoids veering off course and wasting time and money, whilst ensuring we are not unduly risking customer experience.

To bring the mindset to life in this chapter, you will learn that to reach scale with an innovation (we define scaling as taking your 'thing' from a thought to a real world product that is ready to reach scale), using the measured and driven mindset is much faster than simply running at ideas and building them without structure.

We will describe each step within this stage and show you how to know when you are ready to move on, and when to parachute out. The three steps are:

1 **Ideate and build.**

2 **Test.**

3 **Refine.**

This stage of *ReFRAME* is a little unique as it is the only one in the process that is repeated through several levels of maturity. Essentially, as your 'thing' goes from an idea to real-world scale ready it will need to grow up and keep being refined.

The levels of maturity are:

- **Sticky tape and string:** If it holds together long enough to gain insight on how it will work and what it will do, then that is perfect! Low cost, low-fi production (think a polystyrene model of a new shelf system with sharpie-drawn products on it).

- **Minimum-effort real world:** Often called a minimum viable product or similar, this is the maturity level that you can put it into a real-world environment and get humans who aren't biased to test it (think a web page or animation that mimics what a new piece of software would do so you can get insight on how it is being interacted with).

- **Real-world draft:** The most skipped level of maturity. It is easy after the first real-world test to progress to scale, but without a more robust draft being tested in the real world, your 'thing' will likely not achieve the outcomes it needs to or could do.

- **Real-world scale-ready** (nothing is ever final): This is the most mature stage before your 'thing' is ready to scale (think testing it in a store with the same level of support that the team and customers would get in deployment – no hand-holding!).

The steps of this stage of *ReFRAME* done right and with the measured and driven mindset will:

- deliver in the fastest possible timeframe without sacrificing quality;
- deliver the best possible outcomes that drive the highest results;
- achieve a product that most smoothly transitions to the new normal in your organization.

The pace of this stage is specifically designed for retail and its disrupted environment. It comes from research that looked at data, helpful examples from other retailers and non-retailers, as well as our own personal experience and that of our clients. It allows you to reduce waste and improve outcomes by having a robust testing methodology at every step.

Innovation mindsets

We humans are a strange species. It is incredibly easy at this point to be enthralled by the 'thing', telling everybody about it (maybe even externally to your organization) and building up pressure on the team building it to skip steps. This is dangerous, and often leads to good ideas failing to deliver as expected.

Before we get into the steps to take your 'thing' to scale, we need to understand the measured and driven mindset more. It is your greatest defence against moving on too quickly.

There are a lot of innovation mindsets out there, each with their distinct advantages and challenges. The measured and driven option is one that provides the right level of balance to achieve maximum outcomes in retail and is also the most easily replicable across already existing organizational retail cultures. Let us look at how a few of the mindsets work to give ourselves some context.

The illusionist mindset

Amazon are often heralded (including by us) as one of the masters of innovation. Amazon's process of innovation is covered in Chapter 3. Its approach, style and ideas are often mirrored by other retailers, including Starbucks, which has a 100-day 'idea to action' principle reminiscent of Amazon's rapid deployment approach. Amazon's strategy is one of constant growth, and its innovation at pace style helps it expand incredibly quickly.

However, Amazon often produces innovation that does not always follow the golden rule of always adding value to your customers, your business and be aligned to your purpose in an obvious way. For example, Amazon Go was the first store in the USA to allow customers to walk in then walk out with their cold brew and salad, and have no interaction with a register or checkout. To achieve this stunning experience, the store is packed with cameras and sensors and is supported by a remote team that is watching video footage of interactions to help the 'machine' learn when it is correct or not. The sheer amount of technology, data and labour required to make an Amazon Go transaction happen means that it is very unlikely to be scalable in the near term, but the learning that Amazon is getting about human behaviour, technological capability and product performance is valuable to them on their larger ambition. Not to mention it impresses the market, investors and customers. This kind of innovation belongs to the illusionist mindset. The illusionist gets innovation in market to wow its stakeholders, provide information and learning, but is not primarily concerned with producing something that is scalable or provides a net benefit to the operating model, at least not immediately.

The perfectionist mindset

The perfectionist mindset is one of design at scale. Never losing focus on the human at the end of the innovation and not moving on to the next stage until it is achieving close to 100 per cent on progress milestones. Although the perfectionist mindset delivers beautiful experiences, it also has drawbacks.

Apple is rarely first to market. Instead, Apple takes the time to ensure it delivers to the perfectionist design principles of the organization. When it does release something, it is usually a well-designed, human-focused product that delivers strong financial results and has created a user following that is fiercely loyal. Take the iPod, for example. It was not the first MP3 player to market but its design meant Apple dominated its competitors for many years. Fixing major pain points such as naming conventions, searching and finding media as well as partnering with the music industry to help users find more music they love (even though it did take some time for Apple to be fully embraced by artists and labels), allowed the iPod and iTunes to reshape the music industry. This style requires high effort and high levels of investment, and is ideal in a market where time is less relevant than market perception.

The measured and driven mindset

Sitting between the illusionist and the perfectionist mindsets is what I call the measured and driven mindset. This mindset embraces evidence collection and testing, never loses sight of the humans involved and has the right amount of pressure on milestone achievement to maintain progress. It might feel slow to deliver at the start, but once the pipeline is full of projects at different stages, the market will see the company constantly delivering new ideas and iterative improvements alongside major overhauls.

This measured and driven mindset is ideal in markets where you can afford a little bit of time (how much time is usually a reflection of the health of your balance sheet), but few mistakes, and when customer experience is everything – ie retail.

Focusing on internal capability, building experiences and innovation around your organizational purpose, cutting costs smartly balanced with new investments, whilst balancing risk, are all characteristics of the measured and driven mindset. Implementing this mindset helps overcome the objections often found in retailers looking to try to become innovative.

EXERCISE
The measured and driven characteristics survey

What this is

Now that we have narrowed down the traits that represent the measured and driven mindset, conduct this assessment of you and your organization, and ask others to complete it as well. Remember, feedback is a gift, so having more information from multiple sources will support you in creating a measured and driven mindset. Use this as a basis to regularly test yourself and adapt your style to suit each of the traits you see in the survey.

Instructions

Table 8.1 assesses your own mindset; Table 8.2 assesses your organization's 'mindset' (or environment). For each topic in Tables 8.1 or 8.2, read the statements from each of the three columns and circle the one that is most like you or your organization, whichever you are assessing.

For any of the topics where you or the organization are more aligned with the *hinder* or *neutral* statements, then take the time to reflect on how to progress them towards the characteristics of the *help* column. What are the characteristics in you or your organization that would need to change? What processes need to shift? What leadership adjustments are needed? To be most effective, only take on one personal topic and one organizational topic at a time. Once you move it to the *help* column, then move on to the next topic of change.

TABLE 8.1 Your measured and driven mindset

Topic	Hinder	Neutral	Help
Evidence-led	I have strong opinions and it can be difficult to sway me from them	I have strong opinions but listen to good evidence	I actively question my opinions and seek evidence myself
Purpose-led	I choose work based on how it helps my personal mission	I lean on the commercial side more, but always ensure there is at least a loose link to our purpose	I am driven by our purpose and most of my work is to deliver on that
Optimism	I am a pessimist by nature and always plan for the worst	I am an optimist that always starts with yes	My evidence-led nature means I'm realistic
Human-focused	Humans are predictable and will do what I tell them	Outcomes are most important, but we do make sure it makes sense to people	Human drivers are how I do my work, how do we adjust behaviour and choices, not force them into our way
Outcome-led	My job is important, and I focus most of my time ensuring people see me working hard	Outcomes are everything, and we manage the project to ensure we get them	Outcomes are easy if we remain focused on testing all the way through the project
Balanced risk	I am risk averse	I don't think too much about risks	I ensure risk is controlled, but don't fear it

(continued)

TABLE 8.1 (Continued)

Topic	Hinder	Neutral	Help
Creativity	I usually don't get along well with creative types	Creativity has its place in some projects	I actively promote creative thinking in all our work
Failure	Failure is not acceptable	Failure is why we have risk controls	Failure is something that is part of innovation, and we ensure it is always learned from

TABLE 8.2 Your organization's measured and driven environment

Topic	Hinder	Neutral	Help
Outcome style	Direct commercial results are all that is reported	We have some secondary non-commercial measures	We have commercial, human and organizational measures in place
Purpose-led	We don't have a clear purpose	We have a purpose but it rarely influences our work	We have a strong, clear purpose used to guide decisions
Skills and capabilities	We have traditional retail structure and skills	We have some data, design and creative skills in house	We have transformed to included data, design and creative skill teams across the business
Leadership	Our leadership team aren't working together on innovation	Our leadership team support each other's work	Our leadership team is co-dependent and work together on all work
Processes (challenger)	Our processes are strict and cumbersome	Our processes mostly don't hold us back on innovation work	Our processes actively support and promote innovation and its measures
Failure	Failure is not acceptable	Failure is mostly hidden or unspoken in our business	Failure is recorded and learned from with no negative consequence

How the measured and driven mindset changes your innovation outcomes

When discussing how the measured and driven mindset changes things, a common question is whether being measured and driven takes the creativity out of the process. The answer is it does not if it is done right. 'Measured and driven' simply means a disciplined approach, just like a musician making an album with a finite amount of studio time or a writer working to a deadline. Retailers need to produce outcomes in a timeframe, and that requires innovation to be disciplined.

Another common question is about what we mean by measured. Does being measured mean it is all about numbers? In this instance, we mean measured as balanced, considerate and thoughtful – using evidence to make decisions, but still being decisive.

MEASURING INNOVATION

Innovation can be measured, but not necessarily by the accounting methods you have always used. MIT's Sloan School of Management defines the goal of innovation measurement as

> not identifying metrics – there is no shortage of measures to choose from. Nor should the goal be to find the perfect metric since that quest is often futile. Rather, the crux of effective innovation measurement is to understand the problem that measurement should solve for the organization and, based on that insight, to design and implement a useful and usable innovation measurement framework appropriate to the organization's needs.[1]

Translation: at each step in this process, depending on the type of 'thing' you are building, you should have different measurable outcomes. A rule of thumb is that you start with an ambition sentence, such as 'Grow digital sales', and as you keep progressing the idea it should become more and more specific. In this stage of the process that will start to become actual numbers as we test the idea at different levels of maturity until we have a confirmed idea of how large an impact it can make. Innovation is a process, like any other, and if it is focusing on outcomes then it can and should be capable of being measured and targeted.

The importance of resources

Resources are important in determining the scale and ambition of your innovation pipeline, but innovation can be achieved by companies of all sizes. Amazon and Apple were not always the trillion-dollar companies that they are today, and there are plenty of examples of new retail brands with innovation ingrained in the way they create products and experiences. Sometimes, a lack of deep pockets can drive its own form of innovation creativity. There are some adjustments to the process for small businesses, which we get into in Chapter 11.

So, with our mindset adjustment done, we are ready to start the process.

CASE STUDY
Warby Parker

Warby Parker is a vertically integrated direct-to-consumer eyewear brand that was born online but now also operates 120 physical stores.[2] In 2020 Warby Parker generated $245 million in funding and had an estimated market valuation of $3 billion.[3] However, Warby Parker is dwarfed by the market leader, Essilor Luxottica, which operates, owns or licenses 80 per cent of the eyewear brands in the United States,[4] operates 4,348 stores,[5] generated an estimated $10.5 billon in gross sales in North America in 2019,[6] and has a market capitalization of $54 billion.[7] In 2015 Fast Company named Warby Parker the most innovative company of the year. It was no small feat for a five-year-old company to beat the likes of Google, Amazon or Apple to the coveted top spot. In its announcement, Forbes described Warby Parker as the 'first great made-on-the-internet brand'.[8]

In this case study we will discuss what makes investors and customers so passionate about Warby Parker, how their process of innovation works and how it has embedded innovation into the operating fabric of the business. We will show how Warby Parker's focus on innovation as a growth strategy has allowed it to evolve beyond their original great idea and seen it to continue to take share in a market dominated by the biggest optical company in the world.

Warby Parker was founded in 2010 by four students at Wharton School of Business, who decided that the eyewear industry was ripe for disruption. One of the founders, Neil Blumenthal, had previously worked in the industry with the not-for-profit VisonSpring,[9] but that was not the sole inspiration for the business. Instead, like Netflix, the inspiration for Warby Parker came from a frustrating customer experience. Warby Parker was created over the course of many conversations, long email chains and beers after another one of the founders, Dave Gilboa, lost his glasses and, due to the high cost of replacement and his low student income, had to spend an entire semester of grad school with broken glasses.[10] 'I'd just bought the iPhone for $200 and it did all these magical things that people wouldn't have believed even a few years earlier... meanwhile, a pair of glasses: The technology has been around for 800 years. It didn't make sense that I was going to have to pay that much for a new pair of glasses,' he recalls in an interview with Fast Company.[11]

The business idea was simple. Sell glasses online at value and provide a home try-on programme to offer that in-person experience since the glasses were not sold in stores. Five frames were shipped to customers for free. After trying them out for five days to see which ones they liked, the frames could easily be shipped back with the pre-paid return label. Warby Parker targeted a low operating cost model, including buying materials direct from the source to construct its own frames and lenses. This enabled it to achieve a $95 price point, including prescription lenses,[12] which represented great value in the market at the time. The idea was popular with customers. Warby Parker soon had a waiting list of 20,000 orders and met its first-year sales targets within three weeks.[13]

After launching online, the Warby Parker team noticed that customers started asking if they could visit the Warby Parker office to try on the frames. The team happened to be working out of co-founder and co-CEO Neil Blumenthal's apartment at the time, so he took a risk and invited customers over. Since Warby Parker didn't have a showroom or an office yet, Neil's dining table was the first display and co-founder and co-CEO Dave Gilboa's laptop was the first cash register. Despite the rudimentary nature of the retail environment, the response from customers was clear – they wanted the opportunity to touch and feel the frames. It also became clear to Warby Parker that they could use those moments to build in-person connections. After including a showroom in their first office in New York City, which was very successful, the founders decided to test physical retail.

The innovation journey from there came through heavy experimentation and a willingness to be creative and think differently. Warby Parker is brand first, with its experiences being agnostic of the medium. In other words, it is focused on the customer experience and less concerned with the medium itself. This means it aims to give consumers choice and be where the customers are – whether that's online, in-store, or via social platforms. There was also an economic imperative. As many digital-only businesses realize, achieving growth in online and social marketing channels eventually becomes too expensive. To enable sustainable growth, the founding team realized they needed a physical presence to enhance brand consideration in ways that a digital-only strategy could not.

In 2011, they converted a vacant garage in SoHo, NYC to create the Warby Parker Holiday Spectacle Bazaar. The space was transformed into a holiday shopping destination with offerings from brands they admired and their glasses.

The learning and testing continued in 2012, when they launched the Warby Parker Class Trip, a mobile showroom that travelled across the country. They retrofitted a yellow school bus with leather couches, wood shelving to display the glasses, and vintage books. The Class Trip visited 16 cities, parking in three different locations within each city, allowing the team to gather an enormous amount of data (not only which cities performed well, but which neighbourhoods and, sometimes, which street corners – detail mattered). This patient collection of data through a thoughtful and creative testing strategy ultimately informed their retail strategy helping them determine where to open stores and what experiences to offer. Also, they describe how the mobile nature of the showroom taught them about the importance of flexible technology. That meant building tech such as point of sale in-house (which they call 'point of everything' as they want their retail experiences to be about experiences, not just sales) so that they weren't tied to a giant cash register like so many other inflexible retail environments.

Ultimately, it was a combination of these experiences and learnings, coupled with excitement from customers, that gave them the confidence to open their first flagship store in 2013 in New York City's SoHo.[14]

One of the Warby Parker values is 'Learn. Grow. Repeat.' It is apparent to all of us who are observing from the outside that this value is key to implementing their new ideas, as managers encourage their teams to experiment and test their ideas, tracking and sharing the results to ensure company-wide learning.

By 2020, Warby Parker had opened 120 stores and had been reported by Fast Company (2015)[15] and the *Wall Street Journal* (2014)[16] as hitting industry-leading productivity numbers like $3,000 per square foot from its physical locations. Warby Parker prides itself on an operational culture that is all about creating incredible experiences for customers. This has allowed it to continue to create new value through innovation beyond the original core idea. Table 8.3 shows some key initiatives that Warby Parker has introduced over the years as it has evolved into the al -channel retailer it is today.

TABLE 8.3   Warby Parker's innovation initiatives

Initiative	Description	Launch date
Home Try-On	5 frames are shipped to customers for free. After trying them out for 5 days to see which ones they like, the frames can easily be shipped back with the pre-paid return label	2010
Buy A Pair, Give A Pair	A core part of the original model, for every pair of glasses bought, Warby Parker distributes a pair to someone in need	2010

(continued)

TABLE 8.3 (Continued)

Initiative	Description	Launch date
Personalization	An ongoing innovation in Warby Parker is its focus on personalization, including the Frames Quiz, which recommends style choices based on preferences, and the introduction of frames in a greater range of sizes, from extra-narrow to extra-wide (and many widths in between)	2010–20
Prescription Check	A telehealth service designed by Warby Parker that, if you are eligible, allows an eye doctor to assess how you're seeing through your glasses and provide an updated prescription	2017
Virtual Try-On (augmented reality)	A feature available on Warby Parker's iOS app for the iPhone X and above that virtually places frames on the user's face to help them find the best frames from wherever they're shopping	2019
Scout by Warby Parker	Warby Parker's first-ever daily contact lens that comes in an innovative, space-saving flat pack that uses 80% less packaging	2020

Introducing the three steps of making your design and scaling it

This stage of the **ReFRAME** process moves your 'thing' from a formed idea to a scalable version through four levels of maturity. Through each stage of maturity, the three steps are going to be repeated. For the first level of maturity (before we have built anything), the three steps will be:

1 Ideate.

2 Prototype and test.

3 Refine.

After this we will have a working prototype, what we call the **sticky tape and string** model. This is the first stage of maturity. Having a model adjusts the steps slightly for the remaining three levels of maturity:

1 Build.

2 Test.

3 Refine.

Within this process you will be using the showcase model we discussed in Chapter 6. This replaces the traditional steering committee to provide a more transparent and learning-rich engagement and steering process.

FIGURE 8.1   Make the design and scale it

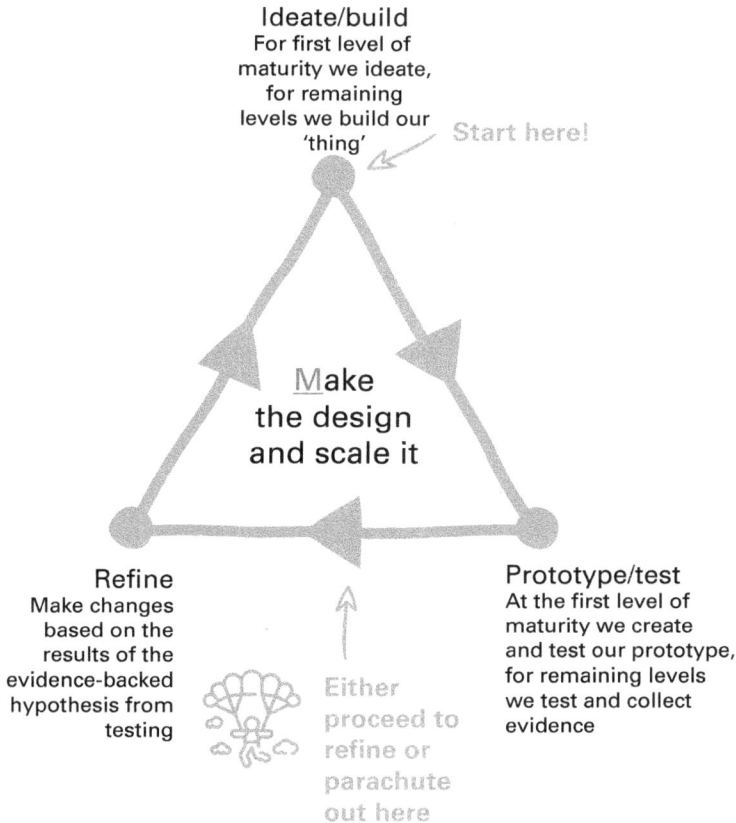

Ideate/build
For first level of
maturity we ideate,
for remaining
levels we build our
'thing'

Start here!

Make
the design
and scale it

Refine
Make changes
based on the
results of the
evidence-backed
hypothesis from
testing

Either
proceed to
refine or
parachute
out here

Prototype/test
At the first level of
maturity we create
and test our prototype,
for remaining levels
we test and collect
evidence

The levels of maturity and how to know when to proceed

At each level of maturity there are tests that tell you whether to proceed to the next level of maturity, pivot or parachute out. The maturity blueprint (Table 8.4) is a worksheet that will guide you as you complete each iteration of this phase. It includes the identifying characteristics of each level of maturity, specific requirements of that level and how to know when you are ready to elevate your 'thing' to the next stage of life.

TABLE 8.4 The maturity blueprint

Sticky tape and string	Ideate	Test	Refine
At this level we are testing whether what you're creating does what it's meant to do, and does it appear to be able to deliver on its ambition after some basic objective testing?	Basic build, eg polystyrene (physical) or a powerpoint (software)	Complete testing card with the project team and a small sample of the end-humans	Refine the idea and use stories based on evidence and decide on the next build phase activity
Ready to proceed when (the basic proceed criteria): 1. It has shown objectively measured capability to deliver on its ambition 2. The end-human behaviour has been tested 3. The mock-up has confirmed your user stories (some minor adjustments are ok)			

Minimum effort real-world	Ideate	Test	Refine
Often called minimum viable product, here we recreate how the 'thing' will act and impact its environment and the people who use it and whether it is likely to achieve its ambition	Get your 'thing' to a point where it can be tested in the real world, still low-fi, but refined	Use the same testing card but using the refined low-fi model in the real-world environment	Final adjustments to the high-level use stories, decision point for a parachute out or pivot
Ready to proceed when: 1. Your 'thing' met the basic proceed criteria above 2. Have run a showcase 3. No major pivots or errors			

Real-world draft	Ideate	Test	Refine
During this level of maturity we want to progress our 'thing' to a point where it is 80% complete and ready to go to a few test locations in the real world	Much longer build phase (up to 6 weeks per iteration) Run showcases regularly	Testing transition and embedding as well as the 'thing' itself Minimize hand-holding	Begin the backlog of use stories that don't impact the outcome Refine the transition components
Ready to proceed when: 1. It met the basic proceed criteria above and had regular showcases 2. The transition and embedding of the 'thing' has been tested 3. No major pivots or errors			

Real-world scale ready	Ideate	Test	Refine
Progress the 'thing' to a deployable state, any training or information materials are produced as is anything else that is needed to move into the embedding phase	Build now is focused on smoothing rough edges and improving transition ease	Test must be same as your scale environment, ie same training and support levels	Build your refined transition plan Refine your backlog
	Ready to proceed when: 1. Your 'thing' met the basic proceed criteria above and had regular showcases 2. The outcomes remained the same (or improved) in the scale environment 3. No major pivots or errors		

DEFINING OBJECTIVE MEASURES

Objective measurement allows us to proceed, pivot or parachute out of our 'thing' with confidence because we are informed and removing unhelpful emotional and subjective opinions from our decisions. In an innovation context, we are not just measuring the outcome we are wanting, or trying to prove the idea will work. We want to understand how and why we got there, whether there is a chance to improve that result and how to do that. If we use an example of an Olympic runner wanting to improve, we don't just care about the time it took to finish the 100 metre sprint, but why it was at that speed and what opportunities are there to improve.

When creating your measures, ensure that:

1 *Data collection is not dependent on the person doing the measuring.* In other words, the actions or opinions of the person doing the measuring don't influence the outcomes. For our runner, the measurement of the data example, we have a stopwatch measuring point A to point B.

2 *Behavioural observations have depth and breadth.* One-off behavioural observations can be helpful but are not objective until you have sufficient depth (the reasons behind our runner's behaviour and choices), breadth (different examples of the behaviour and choices of different runners) and integrity (they do not contain ambiguously worded questions, leading questions or the opinions of others).

3 *You are collecting evidence from the entire context around the 'thing' you are measuring and consider any other influences on that object.* If we continue our runner example, we also observe the differences in track, wind direction, hecklers or supporters, clothing choices, mindset, breakfast, how they got to the track, etc. Remember rule one: we don't choose what to observe – we observe everything so we can maintain objectivity and get a true understanding of the situation.

Once you have selected your measures, check that you are achieving all the metrics above. A good rule of thumb for objectivity is that, if you have people arguing about the results, objectivity is probably the problem!

Ideate and build

If this is your first session after progressing from analyse and test, then you are here to turn your idea into a sticky tape and string model. To do that, you need to create a blueprint. Depending on the nature of your 'thing', you will need to take the use stories you have created in analyse and test and start making tangible examples of a solution that solves them.

For an example, let us assume your 'thing' is a piece of software that is meant to reduce the time it takes to submit an order. Let us say it currently takes 20 minutes and you want it to be less than 5 minutes. Your use stories will be things like 'I only have to input each bit of information once' and 'I can submit the order in one system in less than 5 minutes'. There will be more but let's keep it simple for the example. The sticky tape and string model could be creating a PowerPoint that has clickable links and forms a demonstration of what the software should do. The PowerPoint will allow the team to see whether the model delivers on the ambition.

It is important to make sure you are working within the boundaries you have. In this instance that could be system constraints that stop you changing the aesthetic of the software, but in the end you need to have a perfect replication of what the experience will be (albeit it won't do anything yet). You will be ready for the test phase when you have a replica of your 'thing' that can be assessed against the ambitions of the project. Using the software example, if your sticky tape and string model replicates how it could work in the real system (ie it captures everything the real system would need), within the boundaries of that system (ie it is actually possible to do in the system), then you are ready to test whether your two use stories are achieved!

Hint: The build phase is a good place to constantly assess the work against the golden rule. You do not need to wait for the testing phase for that. The whole team should always be asking 'Is every decision or choice we are making going to add value to the customer and our business, and is it aligned with our purpose?'

EXERCISE
The ideation process

What this is

To create your sticky tape and string model to test out your idea in its most lo-fi version, our simple process allows you to work quickly, cheaply and get great results. It can, and should, also be fun and creative.

Instructions

1 You will need the use stories you produced in the previous analyse and design stage of the process to start this step.

2 Work through each part in succession.

3 The questions here are general and will act as a guide. Add more specific ones that are applicable to the 'thing' you are building.

Prerequisite

Use stories should be collated into groups with similar characteristics. If you have not done that, go back to Chapter 7 and do that now, as it is important in the next parts of this step.

1. Boundaries

Facilitate an activity with your core project team to discover the boundaries in which your 'thing' will be operating.

- *Gravity boundaries:* What elements of the environment cannot be changed as part of implementing your 'thing' ie like gravity (eg a system constraint, or a law)?

- *Elastic boundaries:* What are the things that will require additional resources (time, effort, energy, people, money, etc) to overcome that you don't currently have access to but it is likely you can get (eg a process change, a minor system adjustment, or additional people or skills)?

- *Anything else?* Are there any other boundaries or constraints on your work?

2. Format

To choose the best format to build your sticky tape and string version of your 'thing', you need to base it on what you are creating. Here are some examples:

- *Screens:* When creating content, software or any other user interface 'things' then you need to use something similar. A PowerPoint with clickable links is good for software. A simple image, movies, or animation on an in-store display will work to test the changes you are proposing. Think about how to get as close to the end outcome with the least effort.

- *Physical environments:* Depending on what part you are changing; the physical environment simply needs to interact with the humans in it as it would in the real world. If there is a pole in the way, put a coat rack there, if it is a shelf, raise a table or cut out polystyrene.

- *More:* You can also (or perhaps should) have a combination of elements together. Use your imagination and leverage the team's skills.

3. Context

To work out where to build your prototype, you need to think about how to get the best outcomes. Remember, we want to get an objective and accurate test, so best outcomes equals the most realistic.

- *The humans:* Where possible, you should test with the humans that will be using it. Do you need to build your prototype somewhere outside the office? Backroom of a store? Make sure it is easy to access and as close to the real environment as possible without spending money or time on building something new.
- *The future:* Consider future reiterations of your 'thing'. If you are creating a new store environment, is a lab location better so it can evolve? What is the best location for future iterations of your 'thing'?
- *The materials:* To keep costs down, where is the easiest place to get all the materials to build your sticky tape and string version?

Now it's time to build your sticky tape and string prototype.

Hints and tips

- Never lose sight of the fact that you are building this just to make sure your 'thing' is plausible. It will not always look pretty, but it will ensure you are spending your resources wisely and can move faster in the next build phases.
- As you are building the first 'physical' version of your 'thing', you may learn new things that will change your use stories based on what is possible – that is great! You can do this if you record the changes and assess how they go in the test phase.
- Stay objective and do not make changes or adjustments based on personal views or team opinions. Note them down and look to test those hypotheses in the testing phase.

EXERCISE
The build process

What this is

Although the process steps are the same, the build phase will get more detailed and focused as you progress through the levels of maturity.

Instructions

1 Work from left to right.

2 The questions here are general and will act as a guide. Add more specific ones that are applicable to the 'thing' you are building.

To prepare to reprioritize your use stories, group the outcomes of your testing phase into:

- Positive test – the testing proved your hypothesis about that use story.
- Negative test results – they did not prove your hypothesis correct.

1. Reprioritize

To reprioritize your efforts, you will need to do one of four things with each use story:

- *Remove:* If a use story was shown to be not possible, not effective or to have no value, then remove it.
- *Refine:* Adjust the use story based on the evidence to improve its performance.
- *Proceed:* It worked delightfully, so we should keep it.
- *Park:* In technology projects they call it a backlog. Putting it here means it is useful, helpful and performed but was not the best use of the project's resources. Keep an index and don't forget they exist as they can be useful in future improvements to your 'thing' as well as other projects.

2. Design

The design phase should be conducted by designers or the experts in the field of the 'thing' you are building. Below are some areas to guide you, but you should expand it based on the specifics of your 'thing'.

- *Human elements:*
  o What will reduce the training or support required to use your 'thing'?
  o What elements of your 'thing' were mentioned most in interviews and observations?
  o What other observations will influence the use stories as they are now?
- *Physical elements:*
  o What physical elements of the 'thing' did not perform as expected?
  o How can we make it more efficient or human friendly?
  o Were there any structural barriers that negatively impacted or could positively impact it?

Questions may need to be expanded based on context. Any story adjustments you do make should be driven by the evidence you collected. Be wary of biases creeping in!

Hints and tips

- Depending on the level of maturity you are working on, be reminded of what to expect based on the maturity blueprint. Not until the real-world levels of maturity should you have something that resembles the quality you pictured when designing your 'thing'.

- During the build phase, the experts in the area should be leading the build, whilst the humans impacted should be the decision-makers. For example, for a technology programme, the technologists do the 'work', but the humans or designers lead the 'what should be built'.

- Stay objective and don't make changes or adjustments based on personal views or team opinions. Note them down and look to test those hypotheses in the next testing phase.

Test

Time to test! This testing is slightly different to the evidence collection we did in stage 4. In this stage, testing is more refined and specific and includes recruiting a set of humans that is representative of those who will use your 'thing' when it is completed. If you do not have the luxury of a user experience testing team, then a simple technique can be used here to help:

1 **Always use humans who are not involved in the project.** This allows you to test the idea to find out if it works, and how likely it is that the 'thing' is going to deliver on the outcomes you need it to. Ideally, these humans will be invited from the end-human group, ie customers or frontline team members, depending on your 'thing'.

2 **Test in a real environment** wherever possible, like a store after close or a lab store area if you have it. You will be amazed how often the environmental context influences the test in ways you were not expecting.

3 **Test performance in three areas:**

  a. **The human element:** This is behavioural assessment. How did the person who is helping you with the test respond? Did they see the value straight away, did they understand the intent, can they articulate how it would fit into the context of the real world? Our frontline teams and customers are the best people to tell us if we are focusing on something stupid – here is where we find that out!

b. **The use stories:** How well did we achieve against each of the use stories and ambitions? Have a list of all the use stories and ambitions and record how well the model achieved against them. Include any context that would be helpful, eg 'User submitted in 7 minutes, but there was one section that took 2 minutes. Team member said that this section is information that is already in the system.'

c. **The new elements:** If you didn't learn anything new, you may not have been paying attention. There is always a new element that you were not thinking about. A new user story, perhaps, or something about the environment that changes, or even the language that customers or frontline team members use that doesn't align with how central support talk about it. These little things can make a big difference, so make sure you are looking for them and record them.

4 **Be clear, but don't lead.** Explain your project clearly, but not in a way that influences their point of view. Don't use statements like 'We are fixing this problem' or 'We are building this amazing thing'. Continuing our order improvement example, this is the moment to test our clickable PowerPoint model in a store after close with the store team. The project's intent should be explained in broad terms, an insight should be given into how the PowerPoint itself works the way it does and then the test can proceed. Here are a few ideas to help:

a. **Don't correct or advise the human taking the test.** Let them explain what they are doing and thinking without you reacting in a way that can influence their behaviour. For example, if they say something like 'I don't like the wording on this input field, it doesn't make sense', your response should be, 'Tell me what you mean by that?' to get more useful and helpful information. Saying 'Oh it means the customers preferred delivery date' doesn't give you good information about the test and could become a reasonable reason that leads to you not taking action to improve the clarity of the field.

b. **Write down everything you see.** Not just the actions, but also the context around them. For example, do not write 'Team member successfully submitted'; write down their reactions, where they paused, any references they had to make to other systems or documents, any comments they said out aloud, etc. The more you write down now, the better your insights will be. They don't need to make sense to you in the moment.

c. **Have specific roles for people in the team who are observing.** But don't overcrowd the human in the test. Perhaps someone is timing each step and recording the process steps whilst another is recording the reaction and behaviours of the team member helping you test.

d. **Leave your pride at the door.** The person you are building this for is the team member or the customer; don't defend your decisions or the limitations of the system, they shouldn't care about that. Just keep asking neutral open-ended questions that don't take a position. It will mean you get more helpful information.

The testing card and other resources to help you test your 'thing' are available online at www.koganpage.com/RIR

Now it is time to decide whether we refine or parachute out. If your 'thing' doesn't reach its ambitions and doesn't deliver on the golden rule after testing, you need to objectively decide whether to proceed and refine it, or whether to cease work on the idea and return to other ideas in your pipeline. If it does not work, do not worry, you just failed fast and cheap! That is the best way to do it. Remember, parachuting out of a crashing plane is better than strapping in and staying on board. If you are choosing to refine the idea, that can take one of two forms – pivot or continue.

Refine

Proceed

If most of your hypotheses and use stories were confirmed (ie progress was seen, there is a clear path to refine and the ambitions can be met), then you should proceed with your process in building the 'thing'.

Using all that incredible information we have discovered, we are ready to refine. This means that we adjust use stories or the way the 'thing' responds to them to ensure that we maximize the outcomes. For example, for the section that added two minutes to the process, assess the impact of removing it and using the information already in the system. Once changes have been made, the impact on resources, ambitions and timing needs to be reassessed. In many projects, now is the time that larger amounts of money and resources are going to be used, so a showcase and refined business case with more accurate financial and customer experience metrics should be completed.

EXERCISE
The refine process

What this is

An exercise that will enable you to assess evidence from testing and make the decision as to whether to proceed, pivot or parachute out. Depending on the specifics of the 'thing' you are building, some of the metrics will need to change. However, the principles should remain consistent.

Instructions

1   Be objective and start from left then go right.

2   Let evidence not your opinions lead the way as you complete the refine process.

3   Use the questions as guides to help you create a refine template that suits the 'thing' you are building.

1. Analyse: No opinions, just results

Data evidence

- What percentage of use story was represented?

- What success rate did each use story have?

- What metrics changed (time, conversion, upsell, whatever measures your 'thing' is targeting)?

Behavioural evidence

- Human comfort:
    o   What percentage of people tested felt comfortable about your 'thing'?
    o   How many times on average did things need to be explained?
    o   How many attempts did it take to feel comfortable using it without support?

- User ratings (we recommend a five-star rating system).

- What was the anecdotal feedback from humans in the test?

- Did the 'thing' change behaviour as anticipated?

2. Assess: Review and reflect

Progress

- How have the metrics changed since the last test?

- Have the new or adjusted use stories performed as expected (ie improved the 'thing')?
- Have we had to adjust our expectations downward?

Milestones

- How many of the milestones we had planned to achieve have we completed successfully?
- If we had to adjust milestones as a result of the evidence, what would that adjustment look like?

The 'thing'

- After these results, how many of the use stories would need to change?
- Does the evidence rate the performance of the 'thing' to be high (>80 per cent of use cases successful), medium (50–79 per cent) or low (<50 per cent)?

3. Decide: Be decisive

Evidence

- Are our results improving?
- Does the evidence show that a change in use stories will lead to the set ambition?
- Is the sentiment of the humans we are building the 'thing' for positive or optimistic?

Environment

- Is continuing the best use of these resources?
- Do we have time to deploy this and still achieve our ambitions?
- Is the project strongly supported by the business?
- Are there are other options that existed that could perform better?

The options

- Proceed: If the majority (>60 per cent) of your answers are in the affirmative, then you should proceed with the next level of building the 'thing'. Group all the refinements you need to make by use story. If it is a new use story, or a deletion of an old one, then keep them separate. This will help you in the next build phase.
- Pivot: If there is progress, but not enough evidence to suggest the 'thing' as it is now is going to deliver the outcomes you want or has proven that other options are better suited to deliver the outcomes, then pivot proudly!

- Parachute out: If there is high risk or evidence showing that you will not achieve the outcomes you set out to, then it's time to parachute out. This is a smart and courageous decision to invest resources in better ways.

CAN I REALLY PIVOT?

We adore a pivot. A pivot is a medium to change to the solution while maintaining your ambitions. In other words, you are still focused on the same imperatives, but the solution is changing quite a bit. At this point you need to repeat the sticky tape and string phase as most of the information you have gained will no longer be relevant. A pivot is a save! It does not mean continue. It is very important that if you pivot all the changes you make go back to the test phase. If a pivot is the best option for you, take it! Be proud of the pivot!

Staying objective

This stage of the process may feel a little repetitive; however, it is a move slow to go faster approach. In the end, by using this method, your 'thing' will be more likely to be easy to use, helpful and useful, and achieve the outcomes you want. This means that if we drew it as a curve, jumping straight to building the final version might feel faster, but it ultimately stalls or slows down and delivers lesser outcomes.

Most people (including me when I first started) assumed that this much 'work' means a more expensive project (especially if it is a technology project). It does intuitively feel that way. Our process tests ideas strongly through a thorough approach to ensure that a project will either a) deliver on its ambitions, or b) tell you to parachute out before it becomes a plane wreck.

Discipline is hard! Putting innovation ideas through this process can sometimes feel painful. It is true that a small and relatively easy idea might be able to be delivered without following each step of the process. However, I would recommend against doing it (at least early on in your *ReFRAME* quest). Once you have deployed the *ReFRAME* process a few times you and your team's intuition will be able to guide you to occasionally break the rules. Just make sure you never become complacent. This is a robust model that we know works, and every time you bypass it you are increasing your risk.

Plenty of people innovate, deliver work and feel confident about their strategic direction based on intuition or experience in their field. Intuition and experience are both helpful within the **ReFRAME** model; however, designing for scale needs to consider details. Very few people can truly understand how to make every detail of a 'thing' perfect for its end use purely from intuition and experience. So, use your marvellous intuition and experience but have faith in the objectiveness of the process to make you look even smarter!

To help with that, promote constant conversation within your organization to help people understand the definitions of subjective and objective, how to identify bias and have the courage and openness to speak up about it. Regardless of seniority! (Leaders fall into this trap the most, as they think they are hired as leaders to be the smart one with all the ideas.)

Objective (adjective): Not influenced by personal feelings, tastes or opinions.

Subjective (adjective): Influenced by personal feelings, tastes or opinions.

We have provided a list of biases in Chapter 7 to watch out for throughout this process as well as some heuristics (rules of thumb) in this chapter to keep you on track.

If you have not already, have a coffee with yourself and do an honest and self-critical self-assessment, and identify any of the biases that relate to you. If you feel you can't do that well, then ask someone in your team to do an assessment of you. Use the innovation biases and heuristics (Figures 7.3 and 8.2) as a guide, and talk about this with your team regularly. Help each other be aware of these at each step in this stage. Ultimately, it will give your 'thing' the best chance of success.

Conclusion

The pressure to deliver in most retail environments is high! There will be those who want to slow you down to ensure you have the evidence, or demand that the 'thing' is refined more. At the same time, others will be pulling you forward telling you to hurry up as we need this 'thing' to meet cost cutting quotas or sales experience targets. Being measured and driven is the perfect balance for retail and you should feel comfortable explaining why it is important:

- The pace itself is specifically designed for retail and its disrupted environment.
- It comes from research that looked at data, helpful examples from other retailers and non-retailers, as well as our own personal experience and that of our clients.

FIGURE 8.2   Innovation heuristics

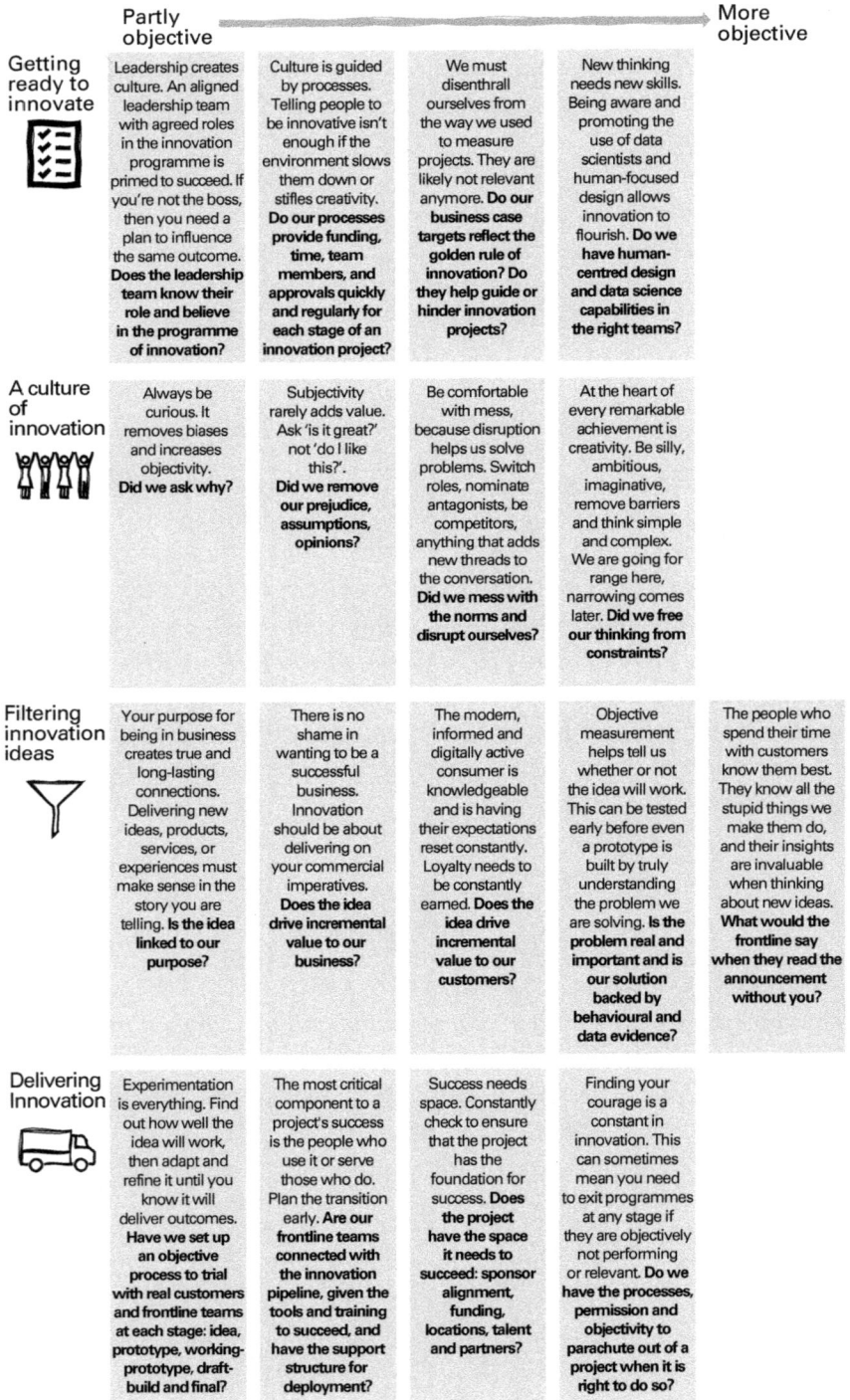

Partly objective ———————————————————————————→ More objective				
Getting ready to innovate	Leadership creates culture. An aligned leadership team with agreed roles in the innovation programme is primed to succeed. If you're not the boss, then you need a plan to influence the same outcome. **Does the leadership team know their role and believe in the programme of innovation?**	Culture is guided by processes. Telling people to be innovative isn't enough if the environment slows them down or stifles creativity. **Do our processes provide funding, time, team members, and approvals quickly and regularly for each stage of an innovation project?**	We must disenthrall ourselves from the way we used to measure projects. They are likely not relevant anymore. **Do our business case targets reflect the golden rule of innovation? Do they help guide or hinder innovation projects?**	New thinking needs new skills. Being aware and promoting the use of data scientists and human-focused design allows innovation to flourish. **Do we have human-centred design and data science capabilities in the right teams?**	
A culture of innovation	Always be curious. It removes biases and increases objectivity. **Did we ask why?**	Subjectivity rarely adds value. Ask 'is it great?' not 'do I like this?'. **Did we remove our prejudice, assumptions, opinions?**	Be comfortable with mess, because disruption helps us solve problems. Switch roles, nominate antagonists, be competitors, anything that adds new threads to the conversation. **Did we mess with the norms and disrupt ourselves?**	At the heart of every remarkable achievement is creativity. Be silly, ambitious, imaginative, remove barriers and think simple and complex. We are going for range here, narrowing comes later. **Did we free our thinking from constraints?**	
Filtering innovation ideas	Your purpose for being in business creates true and long-lasting connections. Delivering new ideas, products, services, or experiences must make sense in the story you are telling. **Is the idea linked to our purpose?**	There is no shame in wanting to be a successful business. Innovation should be about delivering on your commercial imperatives. **Does the idea drive incremental value to our business?**	The modern, informed and digitally active consumer is knowledgeable and is having their expectations reset constantly. Loyalty needs to be constantly earned. **Does the idea drive incremental value to our customers?**	Objective measurement helps tell us whether or not the idea will work. This can be tested early before even a prototype is built by truly understanding the problem we are solving. **Is the problem real and important and is our solution backed by behavioural and data evidence?**	The people who spend their time with customers know them best. They know all the stupid things we make them do, and their insights are invaluable when thinking about new ideas. **What would the frontline say when they read the announcement without you?**
Delivering Innovation	Experimentation is everything. Find out how well the idea will work, then adapt and refine it until you know it will deliver outcomes. **Have we set up an objective process to trial with real customers and frontline teams at each stage: idea, prototype, working-prototype, draft-build and final?**	The most critical component to a project's success is the people who use it or serve those who do. Plan the transition early. **Are our frontline teams connected with the innovation pipeline, given the tools and training to succeed, and have the support structure for deployment?**	Success needs space. Constantly check to ensure that the project has the foundation for success. **Does the project have the space it needs to succeed: sponsor alignment, funding, locations, talent and partners?**	Finding your courage is a constant in innovation. This can sometimes mean you need to exit programmes at any stage if they are objectively not performing or relevant. **Do we have the processes, permission and objectivity to parachute out of a project when it is right to do so?**	

- It allows you to reduce waste and improve outcomes by having a robust testing methodology at every step of the way.

Just like a lost pilot trying to find their way home, there is a lot of character testing in this stage of the process. Having a process enables you to be robust, thoughtful and objective in solving the problem and building the best 'thing' you can which ultimately delivers the highest possible outcomes.

Measured and driven as a mindset will take some practice, but remember, do not expect perfection. Being measured and driven makes you feel confidently uncomfortable. You know there is progress; trust in the results and move at pace. **Hint:** Use the innovation biases and heuristics guides (Figures 7.3 and 8.2) to maintain objectivity throughout and you will feel more confident.

So, now that we have designed and built a 'thing' that is tested and ready for the real world at scale, it is time to plan to make your 'thing' the new way we do things around here.

Notes

1 Sloan Review (2017) Creating better innovation measurement practices, MIT Sloan [Online] https://sloanreview.mit.edu/article/creating-better-innovation-measurement-practices/ (archived at https://perma.cc/L3PG-YZT3)

2 Warby Parker (2020) About us [Online] https://www.warbyparker.com/history (archived at https://perma.cc/XDH3-AAGR)

3 Crook, J (2020) Warby Parker valued at $3b, raises $245m in funding, Tech Crunch [Online] https://techcrunch.com/2020/08/27/warby-parker-valued-at-3-billion-raises-245-million-in-funding/ (archived at https://perma.cc/C8A6-9BR6)

4 Swanson, A (2014) Meet the four eyed eight tentacled monopoly making your glasses so expensive, Forbes [Online] https://www.forbes.com/sites/anaswanson/2014/09/10/meet-the-four-eyed-eight-tentacled-monopoly-that-is-making-your-glasses-so-expensive/#7ae4111a6b66 (archived at https://perma.cc/P7LS-5U6T)

5 Statista (2018) Market value of eyewear in the United States from 2014 to 2025, by product type [Online] https://www.statista.com/statistics/1054371/us-eyewear-market-size-by-type/ (archived at https://perma.cc/3AHH-YTNN)

6 Globe News Wire (2019) EssilorLuxottica EssilorLuxottica: Full year 2019 results / Uplift in Sales and Net Profit growth / Strong foundation to accelerate synergy delivery, Globe News Wire [Online] https://www.globenewswire.com/news-release/2020/03/06/1996288/0/en/EssilorLuxottica-Full-year-2019-results-Uplift-in-Sales-and-Net-Profit-growth-Strong-foundation-to-accelerate-synergy-delivery.html (archived at https://perma.cc/V4XS-NSUL)

7 Forbes (2019) EssilorLuxottica Company Bio [Online] https://www.forbes.
com/companies/essilorluxottica/#4fffb6d46b51 (archived at https://perma.cc/
AG8Z-M9CR)

8 Fox, M (2015) Warby Parker Steals Innovation Thunder from Tech Giants,
CNBC [Online] https://www.cnbc.com/2015/02/13/warby-parker-steals-
innovation-thunder-from-tech-giants.html (archived at https://perma.
cc/75YJ-CRUG)

9 Inc (2015) The mistake that turned Warby Parker into an overnight legend
[Online] https://www.inc.com/magazine/201505/graham-winfrey/neil-
blumenthal-icons-of-entrepreneurship.html (archived at https://perma.
cc/6SS5-DGT3)

10 Warby Parker (2020) About us [Online] https://www.warbyparker.com/history
(archived at https://perma.cc/Z7JA-G4P4)

11 Chafkin, M (2015) Warby Parker sees the future of retail, Fast Company
[Online] https://www.fastcompany.com/3041334/warby-parker-sees-the-
future-of-retail (archived at https://perma.cc/JE5H-KM5X)

12 Howland, D (2018) Warby Parker raises 75m reaches profitability, Retail
Drive [Online] https://www.retaildive.com/news/warby-parker-raises-75m-
reaches-profitability/519209/ (archived at https://perma.cc/SG37-8E7W)

13 Inc (2015) The mistake that turned Warby Parker into an overnight legend
[Online] https://www.inc.com/magazine/201505/graham-winfrey/neil-
blumenthal-icons-of-entrepreneurship.html (archived at https://perma.cc/
A2Z6-BYRD)

14 Warby Parker, 2020, discussing the Warby Parker story and culture on
background with the author.

15 Chafkin, M (2015) Warby Parker sees the future of retail, Fast Company
[Online] https://www.fastcompany.com/3041334/warby-parker-sees-the-
future-of-retail (archived at https://perma.cc/JE5H-KM5X)

16 MacMillan, D (2014) Warby Parker adds storefronts to its sales strategy, *Wall
Street Journal* [Online] https://www.wsj.com/articles/warby-parker-adds-
storefronts-to-its-sales-strategy-1416251866 (archived at https://perma.cc/
L5MA-S7CF)

09

Stage 6: Embedding and making it the new normal

(ANDREW)

Introduction

It was a beautiful sunny morning at 6am (a time of day I don't often see when I'm on vacation) and I was sitting on a cushion with my legs crossed trying to work out how to get my mind to be open and free instead of focused on the torment coming from my hips. I was learning how to meditate from an instructor in Indonesia. I have always found the idea of meditation tantalizing but was suddenly questioning my judgement. Clearly sensing my discomfort, the instructor came and placed his hand on my shoulder in a comforting way. I was ready to receive some reassurance, some guidance, or hopefully permission to extend my legs. He leaned into my ear and said, 'We are judged by what we finish, not what we start.' Silence. That was meant to be helpful? Shaming me into sticking with it did not feel like good value for money. However, he was right, and I eventually appreciated the advice.

When I returned home, I reflected that in my corporate world, finishing wasn't as important as looking good. We often half-deployed things to look good and if they don't work blame the stores or regional managers for not using them properly. We then get energized by the next exciting project or idea that will make us look good. I decided things needed to change. I would take the advice I received that painful morning in Indonesia and shame everyone else into finishing what they started, too. It worked! People realized that, although physical deployment is one thing, there is so much more to embedding your 'thing' in the business. The job is not done until it becomes the new normal. In this chapter we learn about how to embed new initiatives into the fabric of the business so you too can feel good about finishing the job in its entirety.

So many innovations get to a trial or start to scale but ultimately fail. They either don't end up scaling or they scale but do not reach the outcomes they set out to achieve. Most often, it is the process of transitioning the 'thing' to become the new normal that was missing. Usually this part of the process was not thought out, or even planned at all. Too often we see people simply sending out a communication and flicking a switch and expecting their 'thing' to work immediately. Even the most well designed, thoroughly tested 'thing' does not achieve its peak success if the transition was handled poorly.

Remember all those project meetings where you discuss the idea, what it's going to achieve, who it's for, and how much it will cost to build? You sit in meeting rooms, design sessions, steering committees and make decisions for the 'end user' (I hate that term, but I won't subject you to that rant right now) and who gets to use your 'thing'. Sometimes you might even plan a rollout timetable and hold briefing sessions with the communications team to discuss how you announce to the stores and the market.

This is admin, at best, and is not transition planning. If you do things this way and your 'thing' miraculously becomes embedded in your business then you either got lucky, or you have missed opportunities everywhere and could be achieving much better outcomes. Most likely, though, your 'thing' resists being embedded. It results in conversations after deployment like 'How many stores are using it, and who are the bottom 20 per cent? Can we get their regional manager on a call to get them to tell us how they are going to get usage up?'

That is a weird human condition. It is part of what I call 'the force field'. A field that covers the entrance to our central office building that when we walk through it, we forget that we are human, in a human industry, selling to humans via humans or machines built by humans. Change is an important thing to consider because humans hate it. One of the reasons we hate it is due to a biological instinct, often unconscious, that something that has stood the test of time must be valuable. Dr Heidi Grant Halvorson describes the reason this is important when you are innovating:

> It's not impossible to overcome an unconscious bias, but if you want to succeed you need to start by realizing that it's there. Change and innovation requires

that we not only convince others that new can be good, but that we address their (often unconscious) assumption that what's been around longer looks, works, and tastes better.[1]

Change is hard and slow when humans are involved, and therefore we need to be planned and prepared for it. Without a good transition plan, you are throwing your idea off a cliff and hoping the wind picks it up. Transition and embedding are execution steps of the process. It is equally about the project team and sponsor as any other phase. We cannot check out early or assume that the hard or important work is done.

When it comes to the difficulty of organizational change, one of the most cited statistics is that 70 per cent of all attempts end in failure. We know innovation is hard, but there is no evidence of an absolute failure rate of 70 per cent. The original source for this claim, a 1996 book by John Kotter,[2] does not suggest there is any science behind the statistic and subsequent empirical studies have shown that success and failure is based very much on context and measurement.[3]

McKinsey, once a strong proponent of the 70 per cent myth, now has a more nuanced view: 'around 60 per cent of change initiatives are somewhere between a base-hit and a home run, and only 1 in 10 are strikeouts'.[4] McKinsey now says that one in ten projects fail completely or mostly, and six in ten are more successful than unsuccessful. The remainder are not failures but are not successes either. In summary, fully embedded change that delivers great results is elusive. All your previous efforts are wasted if in the end your 'thing' does not embed and become the new normal.

In this chapter we will demonstrate how to embed your 'thing'. There are three steps to the process:

1 Building your transition plan and testing it.

2 The process of deploying your 'thing'.

3 Embedding your 'thing' as the new normal.

After that, you must pull the cord! Unplugging early life support is the best measure of a successful embedding process, well, that is assuming that it is no longer required! When early life support is ready to be unplugged, you can celebrate that your 'thing' is the new normal once you pull that cord. In this chapter you will learn about when to know it is time to do that and how to do it properly.

FIGURE 9.1   Embed as the new normal

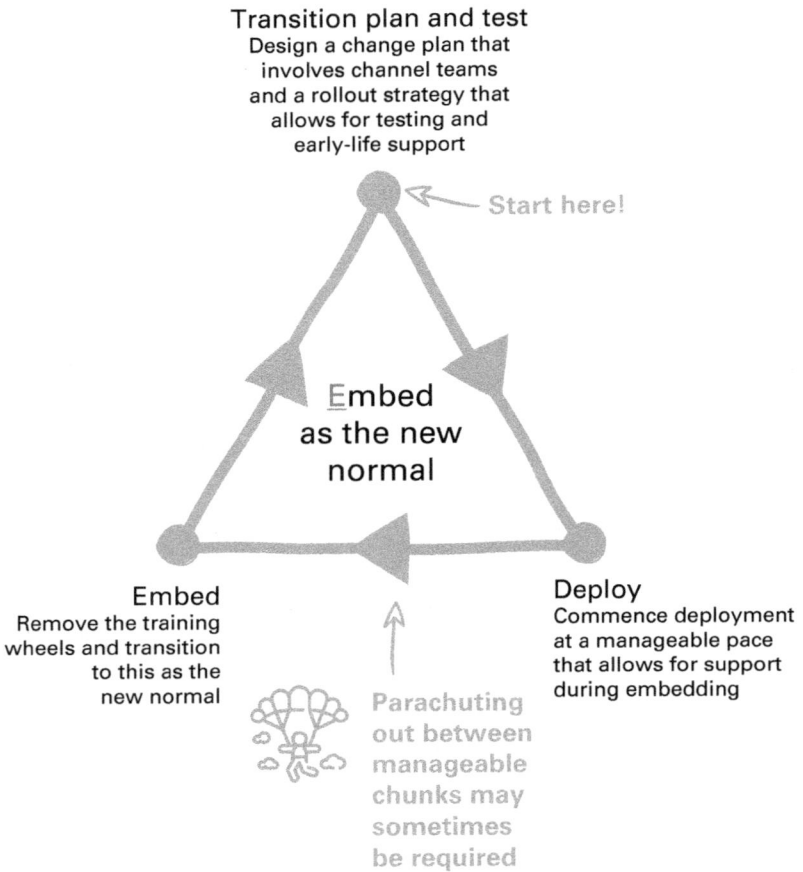

Transition plan and test
Design a change plan that
involves channel teams
and a rollout strategy that
allows for testing and
early-life support

← Start here!

Embed
as the new
normal

Embed
Remove the training
wheels and transition
to this as the
new normal

Parachuting
out between
manageable
chunks may
sometimes
be required

Deploy
Commence deployment
at a manageable pace
that allows for support
during embedding

Transition planning and testing

You now have a 'thing' that, because of your testing in stage 5, works well and can be used with little or no training, that adds incremental value to your customers, and is already operational in some part of your business. Great news! Now you are ready to embed it. A successful transition has these characteristics:

- It is done in manageable chunks (no whole network overnight deployments here).

- It has a thoughtful and considered communication plan to let everyone know about it, when it's coming, why it's coming and how it impacts them (there is a nifty exercise for this included in this part of the chapter to help you).

- It has a thoughtful and personalized engagement plan for the humans impacted by the change (yes, this is different to communication – each touchpoint should be planned like a customer journey).
- It has a temporary early life support plan that is constantly learning from each deployment and has two-way dialogue.
- It includes ongoing testing and learning to support refining the 'thing' even further.
- It has measures to assess the performance of the transition plan, not the humans involved (do not target usage – that is lazy, and if you feel you need to do that then something has gone wrong).

This seems like a lot, but most can be worked through as you are designing and building. Remember the hint in Stage 5 to keep asking ourselves 'What does this look like at scale?' If you have done that well, it will make this stage of the process significantly easier.

Whenever I feel slowed down by transition planning, I find it helpful to recall some disaster stories from when I was on the receiving end of badly managed change. We have all been there. About a year into my retail career I was working in stores during the most challenging embedding process of all… a new customer resource management system. It went from something old, but fast and simple once you had the hang of it, to something new, complicated and slow. There was minimal training, communication was not clear, and the customer migration from the old system to the new was bumpy and painful for all involved. It was the worst time in my retail life. Customers were so entrenched in the pain of the change they even knew the new system's nomenclature. What made the deployment worse for the store teams is that we were performance managed for our use of the system. If we followed the path of least resistance and used the old system, we were reprimanded. It was no doubt incredibly complicated and challenging for the central support team, but it was nevertheless the most poorly executed change I have ever witnessed. Now, having managed several major changes myself, I can see how it happened. The bulk of the effort in any new initiative is building the 'thing' that is going to deliver the benefits. Once the 'thing' is built, it feels finished. If the deployment is difficult it's easy to blame stores for not liking change. Hot tip: if you have to performance manage humans to use your new 'thing', you did a bad job of designing and making it.

Focusing on the embedding phase will deliver the outcomes of your well-designed 'thing' much faster than a 'deploy and hope' strategy where you simply put your 'thing' out there and send an email telling people to use it and then managing their performance, like my customer management system experience.

There are powerful and unstated things that must be considered with any transition plan, and you cannot just deploy it and hope for the best (or worse, performance manage). You are not just transitioning from old to new, you are transitioning the way something works with your 'thing' and doing it in the context of the human at the end of it. These all need to be part of your transition plan. Our transition plan model (Figure 9.2) will act as a guide as we discuss each step in detail.

Build the support ecosystem

Building the support ecosystem means assessing all the impacts of the change and how to prepare for them. At the end of this section is a transition plan template (Figure 9.2), which acts as a checklist on everything we are about to cover. Complete the transition plan checklist and this will be your blueprint for deployment preparation.

Humans going through organizational change will have different levels of motivation toward self-directed learning about your new 'thing'. Some will seek it out willingly, others will need additional coaxing. Having a plan that enables either preference of learning will improve the awareness and understanding of your 'thing' and positively impact the change.

This support ecosystem is broken up into four parts:

1 **Learning:** Investment in learning is essential to the successful embedding of your 'thing'. It is often hard to ask store management for time off the shop floor or to arrange training before open or after close, however, time invested here can mean a significant difference in customer and team member experience if it is done right.

2 **Failure support:** When things go wrong, how are your teams accessing support for the first 90 days and where does this support live after that (it must have a home)?

3 **Training and knowledge impacts:** What are the impacts on existing training and knowledge management practices? Imagine one year from now as new people enter your business; how do they learn about your 'thing', what it does and how to use it?

FIGURE 9.2 The transition plan

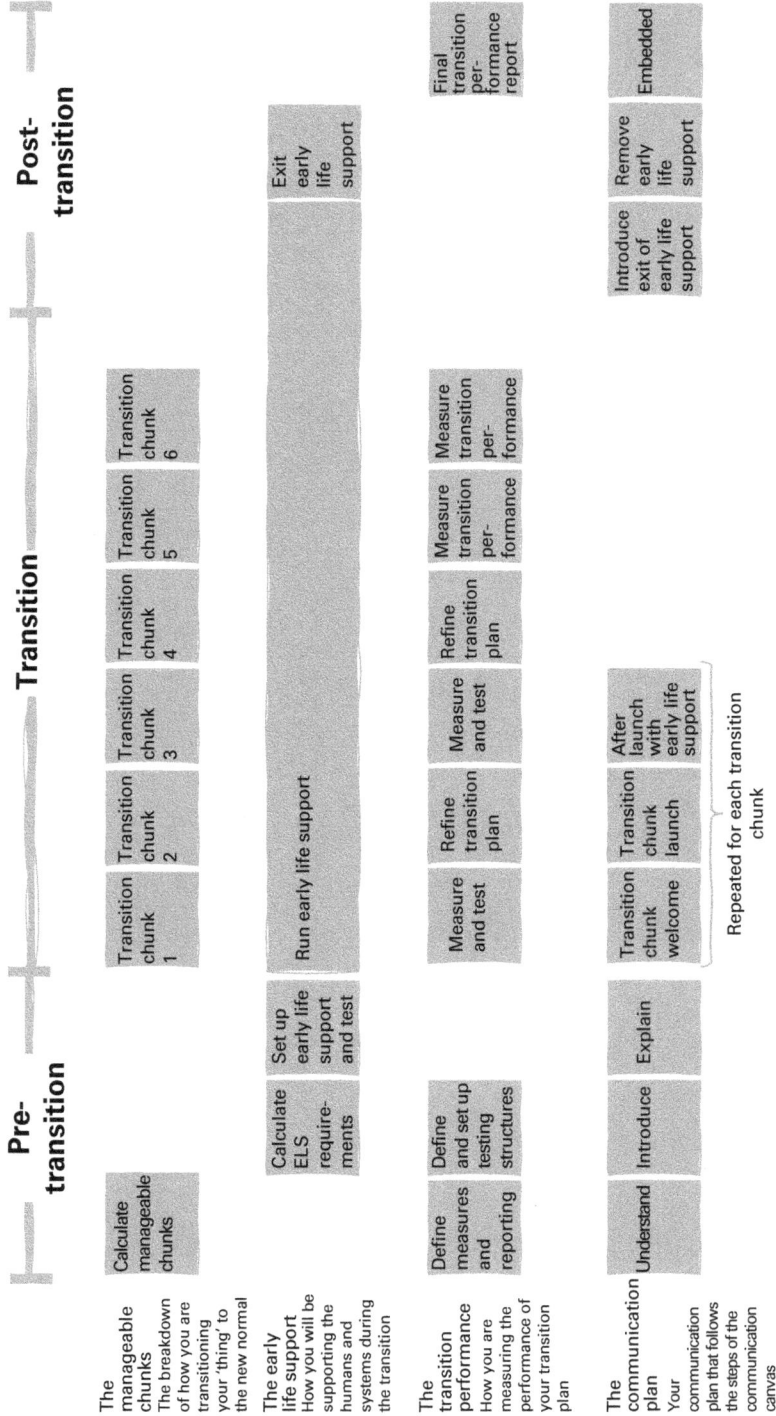

4 **Environmental changes:** If your 'thing' is changing something in the environment, then you need to support the humans you are impacting to gain the new skills they need. This includes practising before they are facing customers with it. Test the practice time required with real humans, not theoretical benchmarks, and make sure you plan for the average time needed, not the highest performer.

EXERCISE
How to prepare your support ecosystem

What this is

This is a guide to help you ensure you have the appropriate support ecosystem for your 'thing' as it is getting embedded.

Instructions

Complete the questions in each of the four sections. The specifics of your 'thing' may need information beyond what is included in this guide sheet, so get the project team together to discuss any additional requirements. Once you have your support ecosystem designed, you should include it in the tests you conduct as you build your 'thing', especially in the final level of maturity, 'real-world scale-ready'. Don't forget to assess and refine with each deployment.

Learning

First, you need to identify what needs to be learned:

1 Why did you build the 'thing'?

2 How did you build the 'thing'?

3 What new information do the humans it is impacting need to know about the 'thing'?

4 How does it change the way they work?

5 Does this replace or augment other ways they work?

6 How do they use the 'thing'?

7 Where do they get help learning about it or if something goes wrong?

8 What else do they need to know about the early life support they will receive, including when it will end?

9 Can they suggest improvements?

10 Does this impact them in any other way (eg remuneration)?

11 What is coming next?

Then you need to design how the knowledge will be delivered:

12 Do they need time off their normal working schedule to do this?

13 Do they need live instruction?

14 How do they best learn?

15 How do you ensure that everyone who needs it has access to this? (There will always be someone who can't make the training, so design for it!)

Failure support

Failure support must be designed and cannot be simply absorbed in normal operations without first assessing if that would lead to reduced performance or productivity. During your testing phases, identify the common questions and stumbling points to design your support ecosystem:

1 What are the common points of failure?

2 What are the common questions asked by humans during testing?

Then design the intuitive process for getting support:

3 Who is providing the early life support?

4 What role does the project team play initially?

5 Who will take over normal support operations once early life support is ended?

6 How do you transition from project support to early life support and finally to normal support operations?

7 What are the measurements and service level performance measures you are committing to?

Finally, use these questions to test your support plan:

8 If failure happens, is the step to resolution obvious and the path of least resistance? If not, how can you make it so it is the intuitive and obvious first step?

9 Are the people or systems providing the support knowledgeable comfortable and able to give support?

10 Are there measures in place to support deciding when to transition from project team to early life to normal support operations?

Once the support ecosystem is in place and understood, it is time to think about how to communicate the change.

Training and knowledge impacts

Identify and adjust current knowledge management platforms and content. To help you identify the areas:

- What processes does your 'thing' impact?
- What content exists that refers to your 'thing' or anything it has replaced or augmented?
- What guides or support documentation refers to your 'thing' or anything it has replaced or augmented?

Now identify any training materials that need to be adjusted:

- Is your 'thing' referred to in any induction or onboarding training?
- Are there any elements of your business that your 'thing' impacts that requires training? For example, does a system that your 'thing' is augmenting, or a business rule, now need to be changed?
- Imagine a year from deployment – how will people first learn about your 'thing'?

Environmental changes

If the humans impacted by the deployment of your 'thing' need to learn new skills or adjust the way they interact with the environment around them, then you need to prepare them for that. Think of this like a change of set, props or stage location for an actor. They need to rehearse before they go on stage.

- Does it involve a change to their physical environment, eg a new technology or store design? If yes, they will need time to rehearse the changes. Ensure that is involved in your transition support plan.
- Does it involve a change to a process or technique that guides the way they conduct their daily activities? If yes, you will need to help them understand the change. Give them tools to help them adapt the way they do things (and each person will have their own way), and give them time to rehearse.

Plan your communication

If team members do not normally read communications sent to them, it is your responsibility to find the reason and improve. Do you send too much information? Is the medium conducive to them being able to access it when it suits them easily? Is your writing style clear? Whatever the reason, you need to either fix it for all your company communications or come up with a way to do it differently for the specific deployment of your 'thing'.

Your objectives in planning your communication must be:

1 **Communicate deeply and with a desire to connect with the humans of your organization.** The result should be a meticulously planned timeline of engagement starting early and going longer than what you might think is 'reasonable'. There is minimal risk in communicating longer than needed; however, there is a risk in over-communicating (too much information at one time). You need to find that balance for your organization.

2 **Map an engagement and change journey for the humans you are deploying to in the context of their lives and work, not your project and its characteristics.** This means that you cannot plan for the 'average person'. There are full time, part time, casual, working parents, young, old, technically savvy, technically uncomfortable. Some take a train to work, others drive. Some have years of experience, others are brand new. Each will be absorbing your information in different ways.

Some rules of thumb to help you:

- Use simple human language – imagine it was your first day and you needed to understand what it meant.
- Make it accessible in multiple forms (in and out of the office).
- Make it engaging. Humans like to be engaged with exciting and interesting content.
- Be genuine and truthful. If things aren't perfect, tell them so and advise them of your plan to improve over time.
- Address their doubts. They will have them; address them directly and honestly.
- Share the way your 'thing' has been created, including the testing plan that involved their colleagues. If possible, include any frontline or customer voices in the communication.
- Give them a chance to respond and be ready to listen deeply and reply promptly.

FIGURE 9.3 The communication canvas

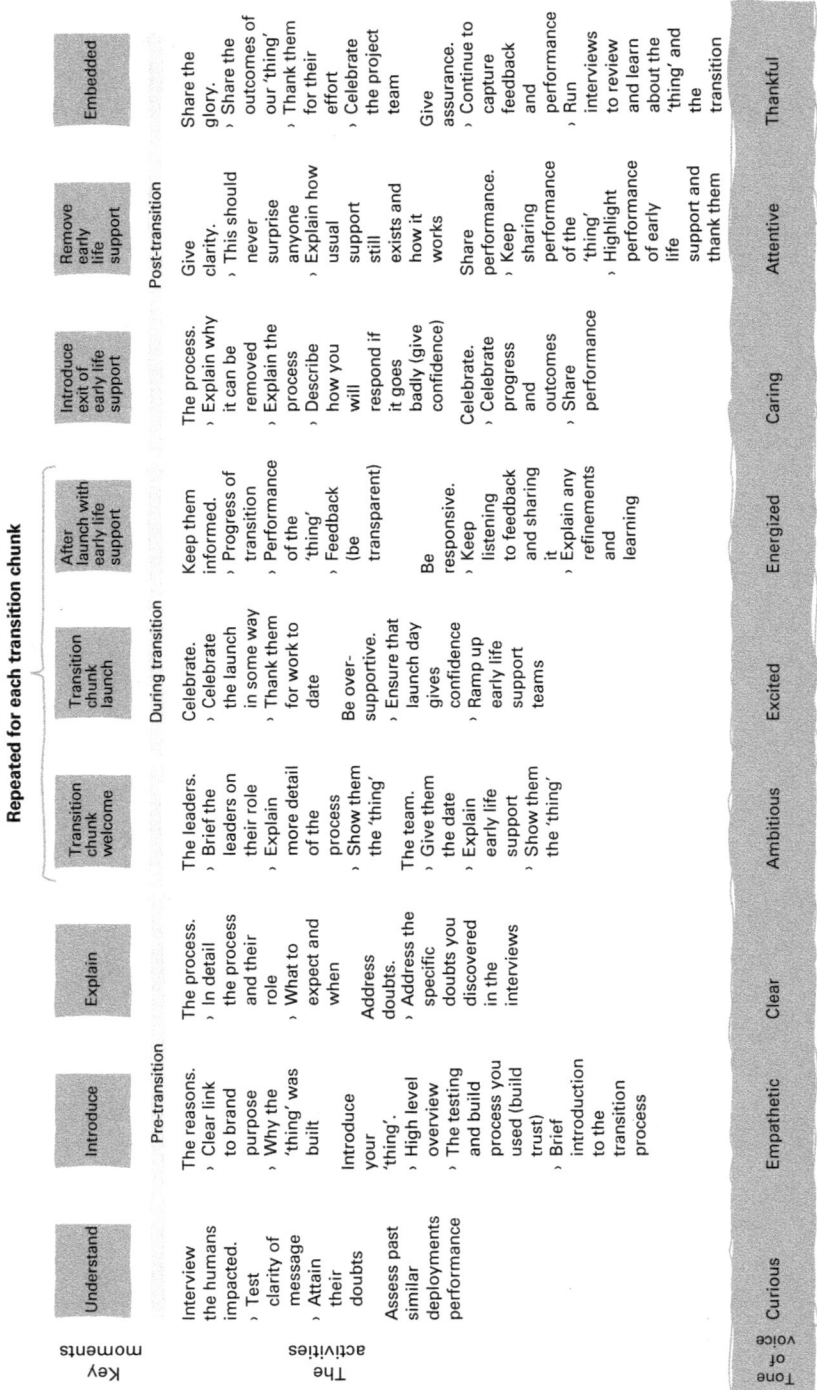

Repeated for each transition chunk

Key moments	Pre-transition			During transition			Post-transition		
	Understand	Introduce	Explain	Transition chunk welcome	Transition chunk launch	After launch with early life support	Introduce exit of early life support	Remove early life support	Embedded
The activities	Interview the humans impacted. › Test clarity of message › Attain their doubts Assess past deployments performance	The reasons. › Clear link to brand purpose › Why the 'thing' was built Introduce your 'thing'. › High level overview › The testing and build process you used (build trust) › Brief introduction to the transition process	The process. › In detail the process and their role › What to expect and when Address doubts. › Address the specific doubts you discovered in the interviews	The leaders. › Brief the leaders on their role › Explain more detail of the process › Show them the 'thing' The team. › Give them the date › Explain early life support › Show them the 'thing'	Celebrate. › Celebrate the launch in some way › Thank them for work to date Be over-supportive. › Ensure that launch day gives confidence › Ramp up early life support teams	Keep them informed. › Progress of transition › Performance of the 'thing' › Feedback (be transparent) Be responsive. › Keep listening to feedback and sharing it › Explain any refinements and learning	The process. › Explain why it can be removed › Explain the process › Describe how you will respond if it goes badly (give confidence) Celebrate. › Celebrate progress and outcomes › Share performance	Give clarity. › This should never surprise anyone › Explain how usual support still exists and how it works Share performance. › Keep sharing performance of the 'thing' › Highlight performance of early life support and thank them	Share the glory. › Share the outcomes of our 'thing' › Thank them for their effort › Celebrate the project team Give assurance. › Continue to capture feedback and performance › Run interviews to review and learn about the 'thing' and the transition
Tone of voice	Curious	Empathetic	Clear	Ambitious	Excited	Energized	Caring	Attentive	Thankful

Now we know our objectives and some rules of thumb, it's time to use the communication canvas (Figure 9.3) to develop your communication plan.

This is an area that some people find challenging, and you may too. That's ok – you are certainly not alone. If you don't have a communications team to support you, there are some key skills that good communications people have that might be worth hiring, even temporarily to support deployment of major change. If that doesn't make sense then just prepare them yourself. Hearing personally from sponsors of work is incredibly powerful, especially when you ditch the professional corporate lingo and replace it with human, real and emotive language. You will be surprised at the change that can have in the support your 'thing' gets.

The process of deploying

Now we move to executing on your transition plan. Your plan must achieve the following:

1 **It must scale up in manageable chunks:** This is an objective calculation and is based on fastest route to outcomes, not fastest route to full deployment (see below what we mean by manageable chunks).

2 **It must have a temporary early life support plan that is constantly being improved:** This was designed in your support ecosystem and should run for 90 days after full deployment and have an agreed plan to transition to normal support (if required) after that.

3 **It must test how people respond:** This will allow you to assess the early life support functions so you can adjust up or down based on the support required.

4 **It must include ongoing testing and learning to support refining the 'thing' even further:** This might just be to add more use stories to the backlog, but every opportunity to learn should be taken.

5 **It must have measures to assess the performance of the transition plan,** not the humans involved (remember, do not performance manage their usage, that is just passing the responsibility onto them for your 'thing's' ineffective design and usability).

Managing change can be challenging, especially if it is a big project. Change professionals are much more common than they used to be, and they may be something you want to consider if you do not have that skill internally. It is also possible to do this on your own. Just follow our guides and make someone accountable for the planning and execution of each of the transition plan elements. We have found that when it is no one's job, it never gets done. If you do not manage your stores directly (such as a franchise or licensed model) then that makes things harder, but this step cannot be skipped. You will have regional teams or store owners in your network that should be just as passionate about the 'thing' as you are. Help them drive the process. Give them the templates with as much filled in as you can. Make it as easy as possible for them to use the tools you provide and manage the transition themselves.

Manageable chunks

Retailers often deploy based on organization or by geography. These are not necessarily manageable chunks. The primary goal of each deployment is to maximize the outcomes achieved by deploying your 'thing'. Therefore, the size of each stage of the deployment should be calculated with the following in mind:

1 **Stability of your 'thing' as it expands:** This is especially pertinent for technology deployments. Stability in this context is the ability of your 'thing' to endure pressure from new use and probable errors in build, without impacting business; for example, if something goes wrong, will the 'thing' still endure and allow business to continue? Do not trust the provider's bold assertions about stability. Stuff goes wrong, so keep it to a manageable and controllable release so you can respond to any instances of instability. You should have a good understanding of stability of your 'thing' from testing phases.

2 **The capability of your early life support to perform:** You need to be immediately responsive, more than normal service level agreements, when deploying something new. So, you need to ensure there are specific, short-term levels of extra support for all those impacted by the deployment of your 'thing'. You only get one launch, and you need to make the most of it. It is the least your 'thing' and the team who built it deserves after all this effort!

3 **Impact assessment on customer experience:** The bigger the impact if things do not go to plan, the smaller the deployment chunks should be. A new font on the web page is different in scale of impact to a new point of sale system.

4 **Impact on your organizational experience:** The bigger the impact on your people if things do not go to plan, the smaller the deployment chunks should be. A change of planogram (a guide for store teams on where and how to place products in store) is significantly less of an impact than a whole new product range being added.

5 **Your ability to revert:** If things do not go smoothly, is it easily and immediately reversible? If a flick of a switch can return things to a state of stability that people know, then the lower the risk, and the larger the chunks can be. If it is not reversible at all, then keep those chunks small to minimize risk to your brand and experience.

6 **The size of the deployment support team available:** This considers things like how much time your transition team can spend with stores, how involved they can be in supporting the transition, etc. This must be for the full 90 days of early life support.

The 'deployment chunk assessment' will help you decide on the size of the chunks you should proceed with. In Table 9.1 I have used an example of a retailer broken up into four main trading areas with approximately 150 stores in each area. I have assumed that each area has a field leader (eg regional manager) and area managers responsible for between 10–20 stores. If your numbers look significantly different to this then adjust as necessary – ie less regional support means you should decrease the size of the chunks and therefore risk.

Even if your 'thing' is not going to impact stores, the manageable chunks assessment will allow you to assess complexity and use that to plan for how large the deployment chunks to customers are and the support you require if things go wrong. For example, if you are updating new app functionality, your deployment chunk assessment will likely be complex, and that should mean that your technology and digital customer experience team should deploy the new functionality in manageable chunks to users and ensure you have a support framework set up for those chunks.

EXERCISE
Assessing manageable chunks

What this is

Follow the instructions below to determine a suggested size profile (the size of your chunks). A profile can be stores or market size and will need objective adaption to suit your 'thing' and your business. For example, if you have tens of thousands of stores, even if the profile suggests 20 per cent of your market can transition in one chunk, that will almost certainly need to be dialled down.

TABLE 9.1 Assessing transition complexity

Variable	High	Medium	Low	N/A
Stability	Lots of moving parts, lots of skills needed or a technology deployment	A somewhat complex system but not a technology deployment	Few moving parts, people and is not a technology deployment	
Early life support	We don't have any capability to increase support	We have some capability to improve normal support	We can have a dedicated and responsive support team	
Customer experience	Customer experience will be directly impacted if things go wrong	Customer experience is somewhat impacted	There will be minimal impact to customer experience	
People experience	There is a large impact or new work is required by our people	The impact is minimal, and any work is not new to our people	There is no direct impact and workload doesn't change	
Reversion capability	We cannot revert or it is complicated to do so	We can revert and impact would be minimal	We can revert without delay	
Deployment support team	We have no experts available to support transition	We have some experts available to support all transitions	We have experts to support each transition chunk	
Scores	x3 =	x2 =	x1 =	=0pts

FIGURE 9.4   Transition profile meter

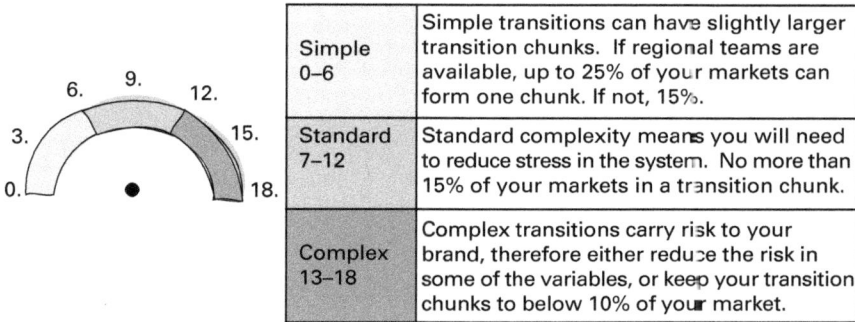

		Simple transitions can have slightly larger transition chunks. If regional teams are available, up to 25% of your markets can form one chunk. If not, 15%.
	Simple 0–6	Simple transitions can have slightly larger transition chunks. If regional teams are available, up to 25% of your markets can form one chunk. If not, 15%.
	Standard 7–12	Standard complexity means you will need to reduce stress in the system. No more than 15% of your markets in a transition chunk.
	Complex 13–18	Complex transitions carry risk to your brand, therefore either reduce the risk in some of the variables, or keep your transition chunks to below 10% of your market.

Instructions

1   In Table 9.1, for each variable, select a statement that most represents your project environment.

2   To calculate your totals, sum how many times your 'thing' fits into each column (high, medium, low) and multiply it by that column's complexity multiplier. For example, high has a x 3 complexity multiplier, so if you have selected high for two of the six topics, you get a score of 2 x 3 = 6.

3   Plot your answer on the meter in Figure 9.4 to ascertain your transition profile.

4   Figure 9.4 will help you translate your transition profile into suggested manageable chunks.

Now that you know how many manageable chunks you are working with, it is time to transition. Complete each chunk with vigour and thoughtfulness; do not get complacent. Think of each step as a mini design project. An opportunity to assess, learn from and refine your idea.

When working in Telstra's retail innovation team, I got some great advice from my boss: 'Hope for the best, plan for the worst.' Your transition plan will cover you for most eventualities but when things don't perform as expected there is no need to panic and rush for the parachute. Remember in our last chapter we discussed how to prioritize at each step? Aviate, navigate, communicate translates in retail into serve, understand, respond. *Serve* your customers and people, *understand* by listening and learning about what is going on in and out of your business, and adjust your business to *respond* and continue to perform. Take what you learn, test it, refine the 'thing' and/or the transition plan if necessary, and then continue.

When it comes to hoping for the best, getting leadership pressure to go faster because your 'thing' is amazing and doing brilliantly is about as good as it gets. 'This is great, can we get it rolled out faster?' 'Can we bring forward the deployment date?' Great compliments, but this speed may introduce risk, and you need to be ready with an answer. The best one is to be direct, say no, and explain clearly that you are on the fastest route to outcomes, which is what ultimately matters. Any deviation and outcomes may be reduced, or the project could be put at risk.

SIDE NOTE

Sometimes, timing is not right for a change and it is outside of your control. Market crash, huge world news, global pandemic, holiday period, etc. Make sure you are taking that into account in your planning time where possible (market crashes or global pandemics are a bit harder) and have a contingency in mind for when they do. If the need really is urgent and the opportunity compelling, then read through our urgent innovation processes in Chapter 10.

Measures

Measuring the performance of your transition plan is different to measuring the outcomes being achieved by your 'thing', but the two are inextricably linked. Some suggested measures for the transition plan are:

- speed to competence (measures effectiveness of training and preparation);
- volume of support enquiries (measures how well your 'thing' is designed);
- efficacy (eg outages, sales or volume changes for same period, etc);
- qualitative feedback (feedback from support and field teams from the humans that are using your 'thing');
- performance (outcomes vs objectives, eg if reduced transaction time was your objective how much has it reduced?).

There may be some changes to these measures based on your 'thing' and its context, but use them as a guide. You can access an example report template online at www.koganpage.com/RIR that will assist you in creating your own. Your transition performance report should clearly articulate a balanced view of every aspect of the transition of your 'thing', including the measures above. It should be designed to be simple and easy to update as your team are busy transitioning your 'thing', so they do not have time, nor reason, to fill out a heap of paperwork just to make you or some other leader more comfortable! Do not overcomplicate it. Just report the things that matter.

Now it is time to transition and embed your 'thing' as the new normal! Use the transition plan we created earlier to help guide you each step of the way.

EXERCISE
The deploying process

What deployments should look like

All the things you have created will form your deployment actions. For each deployment (one manageable chunk at a time) create a timeline of milestones using the guide below as a base and, as usual, make any adjustments you need to based on the specifics of your 'thing'.

What it is

This guide will assist you with your deployment steps and understanding the process flow of a deployment, and what you should be doing at each major milestone.

Instructions

Each step in this stage of the process will provide the inputs used for deployment. Work through each part in succession. The hints and tips can guide you, but always add any elements based on the context of your 'thing'.

1. Assess and build

Collect the outputs of the previous exercises in this chapter and ensure that you have:

- assessed and agreed manageable chunks;
- designed and implemented a support framework;
- completed the communication canvas;
- identified transition measurements and created a transition report template.

2. Communication

Begin the communication canvas activities:

- Use any comments and feedback from the humans in the testing phase to support your communication – this helps build trust in what you are doing.
- The communication canvas includes tone suggestions to maximize the impact of your communications. Remember, you are supporting people through change, not ordering them to do something.

3. Early transition

Time to test the transition plan and support mechanisms:

- Activate and test the early life support mechanisms.
- Ensure the project team or deployment team are engaging the groups within this manageable chunk as part of the communications canvas.
- Prepare the transition report measurements and any associated activity (such as observational teams or on-site cameras).

Hint: If you are implementing something complex, consider starting the transition of a chunk with one or two individuals in each location who can act as on-the-ground support during the deeper transition.

4. Deeper transition

Now we know what works during transition, it is time to start deploying at scale:

- The project or deployment teams should now move on to the next manageable chunk and the created support mechanisms take over the support of this deployment chunk.
- Complete a transition report weekly (or more often if helpful).

Hint: If this is your first deployment chunk, then assess and identify possibilities to refine each element of your transition plan. Use previous transitions to support your communications for future deployments to highlight positive outcomes and be transparent about any opportunities for improvement and how you are responding.

5. End of transition

As we move towards the full transition and get ready for the embedding of your 'thing' as the new normal, the final transition tasks are needed:

- Complete your final transition report.
- Exit the early life support mechanisms and return to normal support operations.
- Hand over every element of the 'thing' to whoever the normal business operations owner should be.
- The project team should identify what to do with any use stories that were parked or put into a backlog – do not let them be forgotten! They either need to form a new project or be handed to the normal business owner of the 'thing' you have built.
- Conduct a final 'transition showcase'.

Embedding your 'thing' as the new normal

Embedding is never complete until all the support mechanisms that were due to be short term are removed and your 'thing' is standing on its own two legs. Don't be tied to the 90-day rule if it is not working. You may have to hold onto it longer than you would like as you refine your 'thing' or parachute out. This is all about how to make sure that the plan works, and the humans involved have no adverse impacts on their day-to-day actions.

Although it is a bold ambition, you should plan for the removing of early life support having zero impact. It is almost impossible to hit this, but in a perfectly executed change, you will end up with no one using the early life support within that 90 days. This is rarely going to happen, and you need to be prepared for that, but you need to prepare and plan for removing early life support so you can move those resources onto the next deployment 'chunk' or the next 'thing'.

Once you know why early life support is still being used, you can decide to do one of the following:

1 **Remove it because it is being misused:** Humans like the path of least resistance. Sometimes moving to new normal behaviours is challenging and the early life support will be used as a crutch long after it is necessary. Be careful, though. Do not just pull the plug on early life support without being convinced that it is no longer necessary.

2 **Adjust your 'thing':** Refine it so people can use it without early life support.

3 **Consider changes to your traditional business support mechanisms:** Allow them to support your 'thing'. Once you have chosen and enacted one of those choices, you can move on to your next 'chunk' of transition or your next 'thing'. You cannot move on without deciding on the above without risking your progress or your business.

Any situation that involves humans is going to be interesting and throw you some challenges. Feedback is a gift, and this gift is telling you how you can improve the 'thing' or your support of it. Moving on prematurely will just make the situation worse and create an environment hostile to future change.

Plan early! Think about early life support for your 'thing' and how it best works. Test your early life support system in your early transition chunks and make sure you make changes to it as you learn how it performs.

Hint: the less it is used, the better you have designed your 'thing', the communication plan and your engagement plan. Some self-reflection may be needed.

Moving on to the next 'thing' or the next transition chunk without disconnecting previous chunks from the early life support means that you are potentially risking performance. Be ready to make decisions, refine the 'thing', the communications and engagement plan, or the early life support as new information becomes available.

Conclusion

Humans are fickle. We each have our own versions of how we have evolved, with nuances in the way we perceive, interpret, behave and think. Therefore, getting a mass of humans to be logical and optimistic is incredibly challenging (see any example from world politics). Therefore, you need a plan to consider the 'thing' in the context of the humans and the system that it's impacting. You need to reduce the pain of change as much as possible, and to communicate how the design of the 'thing' has been considerate to them throughout its lifecycle. When you do this, you get faster adoption and better feedback for future improvements or other project ideas.

Humans do not like change, so embedding your 'thing' as the new normal is going to be challenging. By following the guidelines, we provide all you need to build a comprehensive transition plan that gives you the best chance of success. The three steps to the process are:

1 Building your transition plan and testing it.

2 The process of deploying your 'thing'.

3 Embedding your 'thing' as the new normal.

Retail is a people-intensive industry and it's tough to manage the human element of change. Our embedding process means you will be well prepared, have set up the right resources, and have a plan to take your 'thing' from innovation to the new normal. Don't forget, when your 'thing' is a raging success (which it will be, obviously, you've designed it so well!), you will be asked the question 'How can we get it out faster and bigger?' It is a good idea as you are going through this plan to be ready for that question. Maybe you can deploy faster with more money to spend on people supporting it, but if you can't or if you think it will negatively impact the performance of the 'thing' you're deploying, then say no. We humans are terrible at saying no, especially to our bosses, so be ready for it and practise for it. We do not want to jeopardise the incredible success of our 'thing'.

We have now demonstrated all six stages of our *ReFRAME* process, which we know will allow retailers to be quicker, more successful, and more efficient innovators. Sometimes the need for innovation is genuinely urgent and the process that works in normal times is simply not quick enough. In the next chapter we explain a process to apply to cases of urgent innovation.

Notes

1   Halvorson, HG (2012) Why we don't like change, Huffpost [Online] https://www.huffpost.com/entry/why-we-dont-like-change_b_1072702 (archived at https://perma.cc/L5ZB-GKDY)
2   Kotter, JP (1996) *Leading Change*, Harvard Business School Press, Boston, MA
3   Hughes, M (2011) Do 70 per cent of all organizational change initiatives really fail? *Journal of Change Management: Why does change fail, and what can we do about it?* 11 (4), pp 451–64
4   Tasler, N (2017) Stop using the excuse organizational change is hard, HBR [Online] https://hbr.org/2017/07/stop-using-the-excuse-organizational-change-is-hard (archived at https://perma.cc/CE43-NX9G)

PART THREE

The different paths of innovation

Sometimes the *ReFRAME* process needs to be adapted for a particular set of business circumstances. One of these is when the need to innovate is urgent and can't wait for 90–100 days for a prototype to be tested. Another is in small businesses where issues like management alignment, stakeholder management or multi-site deployment are much less relevant than acquiring the resources to innovate. In this Part, we show how *ReFRAME* can be adapted for both urgent innovation and small businesses and demonstrate why it is always better to drive innovation through a process than not.

Finally, we establish how *ReFRAME* can be extended from a process to manage innovation projects, to a way of doing business. We demonstrate that once innovation is woven into the operating fabric of a retail business, disruption in the operating environment can be viewed as an opportunity to be embraced rather than a threat to be feared.

10

Urgent innovation

Introduction

Sometimes, urgent innovation is required. Urgent innovation is required when your business faces an immediate and compelling opportunity or threat. Under these circumstances you cannot afford to spend 90–100 days or more from idea to test, you must implement change in a month, a week or even a day. Urgent innovation may be required due to immediate government mandated changes in the way you can trade, such as we have seen in the COVID-19 pandemic, or because of unexpected changes in the competitive environment. This can suddenly expose your business to a new and powerful competitor or an opportunity in the market that's time sensitive and only available to those who can move fast.

Situations requiring urgent innovation are rare, but when they arise the stakes are high. It may be that the situation you face threatens the existence of the business or offers a once-in-a-lifetime opportunity if you act now. In these circumstances it is more important than ever to choose the best ideas to support and to deploy them effectively. The paradox is that, although it is critical to get urgent innovation right, it comes with less time to get it right. Not to mention, as urgency increases the available time decreases even further. Normal processes must be skipped or compressed in the interests of making change quickly and that multiplies the chances that things will go wrong.

With so much at stake and so much at risk, it's important to be able to distinguish a situation that needs urgent innovation from one that can be dealt with using regular processes. Regular innovation will always be more efficient and less risky than urgent innovation. Sometimes management will demand urgent innovation when the opportunity or threat is not really immediate or compelling. They may simply be impatient with the rate of change in the business or feel they need to be seen to be responding decisively to activity in the market. Impatient innovation should be avoided at all costs (more on that later).

If the need for urgent innovation is genuine then process can help. Applying process in a critical situation facilitates objectivity, means more of the right decisions will be made and increases the chances of success. Reverting to gut feel or hierarchical decision-making increases the chances that the wrong ideas will be supported, risking project failure and thereby losing golden opportunities or putting the whole business at risk in extreme cases.

Retailers who have already deployed the *ReFRAME* process in their business will be at an advantage when the time comes to deploy urgent innovation. In stage 1 management and board will have become aligned around a culture of innovation and a clear business purpose. As we have seen, this is the launchpad for any programme of innovation. Other stages of the process will need to be compressed or skipped, depending on the time available. However, the fundamentals will remain familiar. Urgent innovation and a regular *ReFRAME* both require ruthless objectivity, discipline, cross-functional collaboration and a test-and-learn mindset. If your team is trained and experienced in these things, your programme of urgent innovation is off to a good start.

In this chapter we will explain what urgent innovation is, its advantages and disadvantages, when to use it and when not. Then we will show how the *ReFRAME* process can be adapted to one-month, one-week or even one-day innovation horizons.

What is urgent innovation and when should it be deployed?

Urgent innovation means adapting your business at a much faster pace than normal processes allow. It is an emergency response to critical incidents in the environment. Critical response frameworks often already exist for eventualities like industrial accidents, cyber-attacks, kidnapping and medical emergencies. We believe innovation should be considered the same because the consequences of not urgently innovating when circumstances demand it can be catastrophic.

There are two conditions to be satisfied before deploying urgent innovation. The need for action must be immediate and the threat or opportunity to the business must be compelling. Deploying urgent innovation is a bit like making the decision to dial emergency for the fire service. When you make an emergency call, they expect that you have a fire that needs to be dealt with now. They also expect that it's already grown beyond your capacity to deal with it using whatever fire-fighting resources you have available on your premises. Making an emergency call for a fire you could have put out yourself is an irresponsible waste of resources. Furthermore, the high-pressure hoses and axes used by a professional fire service may end up causing more damage than the fire itself. Deploying urgent innovation when it is not required comes with the same risks.

Urgent innovation is not to be confused with 'innovation at speed'. For many years, academics and consulting companies have extolled the benefits of innovating at speed (as do we). According to the Boston Consulting Group,[1] innovation at speed allows companies to react to trends as they emerge, leave competitors flatfooted and reduce the cost and improve the quality of innovation projects (we agree). Zara, famous for its ultra-fast design-to-rack processes, is used by BCG as an exemplar of innovation at speed.

Urgent innovation is a process that compresses and applies short cuts to regular innovation processes. Innovation at speed at Zara is their regular business process that has been ingrained in their business model for many years. Nevertheless, Zara does practise what we call urgent innovation when circumstances demand it. A small example is a programme called 'shot from home',[2] instituted during the COVID-19 pandemic. With regular studio photoshoots rendered impossible due to lockdowns and social distancing regulations, Zara instead sent product samples directly to models so that they could self-shoot the campaign from their homes. This urgent innovation allowed Zara to promote its new collection in a creative way on its website (over 3,000 stores were temporarily closed) and maximize the sales opportunity with buyers in lockdown.

Urgent innovation should never be confused with impatient innovation. Impatient innovation is when management decides to force the pace of projects without determining that the need for change is immediate and the opportunity or threat is compelling. This could be motivated by frustration with the speed of change, anxiousness to deliver a pet project or pressure to be seen to be doing something by the market or other stakeholders. Normally, management support for increasing the pace of innovation is a good thing, but not if it forces projects into urgent mode when it is not really necessary. Putting innovation projects into urgent mode means reducing regular checks and balances, increasing the risk of failure and potentially wasting resources. The risks of urgent innovation are always high, and these risks should not be taken for impatient innovation.

The circumstances that justify the deployment of urgent innovation in retail are rare. They may only arise once or twice in a career. In most cases, retailers have more than enough time to deploy innovation within the classic 90–100 day idea-to-test window practised by Amazon, Starbucks, Walmart and others. Digital technology and globalization have facilitated serious disruption in the industry since 2000, but retailers have had years, if not decades, to adjust. The arrival of a new, popular competitor can cause serious disruption for a retailer, but incumbents are usually alerted by advance announcements, real estate activity and tip-offs from suppliers that allow many months to make the necessary changes. It's when changes in the environment are immediate and unpredictable that the need for innovation can become urgent.

From 1990 to 2020 there were only a handful of major events that necessitated urgent innovation. Natural disasters like Hurricane Katrina and the Californian and Australian wildfires caused immediate and compelling reasons for retailers to innovate, however, the effects were usually localized and temporary. On the other hand, major economic crises like the global financial crisis of 2007–08 and epidemics like the SARS outbreak in China in 2003 and COVID-19 throughout the world in 2020 can cause deep retail crises and necessitate urgent innovation throughout the market. Sometimes the need to urgently innovate can be much more specific, like the sudden loss of a major supplier, licence agreement or change in government regulation specific to your sector. All these events are rare, so it is unlikely that when the time comes you will have a team of people experienced in urgent innovation.

Urgent innovation as a process

Urgent innovation events are rare and critical, which makes the need for a process to manage them doubly important. Having a process for urgent innovation provides a substitute for experience, which you are unlikely to have, helps create objectivity in decision-making and allows teams to concentrate on action.

Some would say there is no time for process when the need is urgent. While not every fire is an emergency, when your house is burning down in front of your eyes it needs to be put out immediately. While this is true, even in a critical situation, following a proper process using skilled and trained people will invariably deliver a better result than the alternative. That's why businesses have critical response processes for industrial accidents, cyber-attacks, terrorist attacks and other events that might threaten their future. Untrained and inexperienced amateurs, no matter how enthusiastic or how much water they have access to, are no match for a professional fire service when the threat is real. Your business is much more likely to get the result it needs in urgent innovation situations if you are guided by process more than enthusiasm.

If your business is already experienced in *ReFRAME* you are at an advantage in deploying urgent innovation. Stage 1 of the *ReFRAME* process means the management and board should be aligned around a culture of innovation and a clear purpose for being in business. It is possible to execute urgent innovation without an aligned management team (managers can agree to disagree and sort their differences out later[3]), but it's going to be easier and smoother if they are aligned.

The rest of the *ReFRAME* process will be compressed depending on the time available, but some underlying principles will be familiar. The team will know the golden rule. They will know that only ideas that benefit the customer and the business, and align with purpose, should be deployed. This will protect your business from pursuing ideas that don't work. They will know innovation is best fostered by process and doesn't rely on charismatic leaders or teams of special geniuses to be successful. That will ensure a methodical and objective approach despite the urgency of the situation. They will know not to become too attached to any idea and be conditioned to drop projects that clearly are not delivering on their brief. They will be used to working in cross-functional teams to speed and smooth the path to deployment.

It is no accident that some of the quickest and most effective pivots we saw in the COVID-19 pandemic came from retailers with well-established innovation processes. In Australia, Dominos introduced 'zero contact delivery'[4] in early March 2020 ahead of most of the competition. This was at a time when restaurants and bars were still open in Australia and strict social distancing rules and border closures were yet to come into effect.[5] At the end of March, with supermarket panic buying at its peak, McDonald's Australia added basic grocery items (bread, milk and later eggs) to its drive-through menu,[6] providing a benefit to its customers and extra revenue to McDonald's when dine-in restaurants had been forced to close.

Internationally, other well-known innovators were also quick out of the blocks. At the beginning of the pandemic Nike decided to make access to the premium workout section of its Nike Training Club app free, to encourage more downloads. In an interview with Modern Retail[7] Heidi O'Neill, President of Consumer and Marketplace for Nike, revealed that the year-on-year rate of downloads for the app tripled. In addition, Nike started weekly streaming of its Nike Training Club community workouts on YouTube,[8] each edition garnering hundreds of thousands of views.

Engaging customers online with video was a strategy also adopted by noted Chinese innovators Alibaba and JD.com in China.[9] In March 2020 Alibaba livestreamed Shanghai fashion week through its T Mall and Taobao platforms. JD.com partnered with Anheuser-Busch and Rémy Cointreau to stream live DJ sets promoting their products in a virtual club environment. During one of these live shows a partner brand increased its sales by 70 per cent and sales of whiskey products increased by a factor of eight compared with the day before.[10]

All the examples of urgent innovation presented so far are of relatively low risk to the businesses involved and could easily be wound back if required. Urgent innovation can also mean accelerating much more significant projects, already in development, that may carry much higher levels of risk. In the USA, Williams Sonoma is a noted innovator and had been transitioning the business towards digital for some time before the COVID-19 pandemic.[11] By the end of 2019 its e-commerce sales revenue had grown to be 55 per cent of sales. Williams Sonoma's strategy of pivoting to digital included plans to gradually close a significant number of physical stores, which is high risk for any retailer. The emergence of COVID-19 and the consequent changes in consumer behaviour accelerated this strategy. E-commerce grew 31 per cent in the first quarter of 2020 to represent 71 per cent of total sales. This meant that, in contrast to almost all of the industry, Williams Sonoma were able to report comparable store sales increases to the market in its earnings call on 3 May.[12] More importantly, the crisis created the opportunity to announce plans to accelerate its digital strategy, including increasing physical store closure from a planned in 32 in 2020 to double that number.

In businesses with no **ReFRAME** experience, adopting a process to address an urgent innovation situation will face more barriers. These businesses are much more likely to revert to gut feel and seniority or rank of leaders as the determining factors of what ideas to pursue and how to deploy them. Urgent threats or opportunities make management teams and boards anxious. They know the business must take decisive action and become very frustrated if it does not happen quickly. They need to be kept updated regularly and shown that following process can be just as quick as any other type of deployment and will increase the chance of success and reduce the cost of failure of the action.

BEING PREPARED

Brands from many industries who respond well to crises are often those who practise for it. Crisis management practices (sometimes referred to as war games or crisis simulations) are an important part of any business being ready to respond to a rapid change of the environment. Not always a pandemic or newsworthy event, crises come in many forms. The practice sessions will allow your teams to comprehend and be able to execute the simple mechanics of responding. This includes getting the right team in the room, assessing risk and opportunity, filtering the right ideas to pursue and swiftly allocating the space needed to respond. Use the tools in this chapter to set up a system of practice for your team. In our experience, best practice is at least one exercise per year with all areas of the business represented.

How to know when innovation is truly urgent

Genuine opportunities for urgent innovation are rare so it's important to be able to recognize them when they come. If you are in any doubt as to whether the situation you are faced with is genuinely urgent, is really just impatient innovation, or can be better handled using a regular *ReFRAME* process, then try this exercise. There are six questions and it should take less than ten minutes to complete.

EXERCISE
Checking if your urgent need for innovation is truly urgent

1 This project must be completed in less than:

   a. 7 days

   b. 30 days

   c. 90 days

   (If your answer is 'a' or 'b' proceed to question 2. If your answer is 'c' consider deploying the regular *ReFRAME* process.)

2 Our company is experienced in deploying process driven innovation (*ReFRAME* or similar):

   a. Yes

   b. No

(If your answer is 'Yes' proceed to question 3. If your answer is 'No' proceed straight to the compressed **ReFRAME** process described later in this chapter.)

3 The risks associated with this project are:

   a. Low

   b. Moderate

   c. High

(If your answer is 'a' or 'b' proceed to question 4. If your answer is 'c' is it possible to mitigate the risks? If 'Yes' proceed to question 4. If 'No' consider deploying the regular **ReFRAME** process.)

4 The opportunity/threat to the business associated with this project are relatively:

   a. Low

   b. Moderate

   c. High

(If your answer is 'b' or 'c' proceed to question 5. If your answer is 'a' is it possible to delay the project? If 'No' proceed to question 5. If 'Yes' consider deploying the regular **ReFRAME** process.)

5 The resources (space) required to complete this project are:

   a. Low

   b. Moderate

   c. High

(If your answer is 'a' or 'b' proceed to question 6. If your answer is 'c' then are the resources (space) you need available now? If 'Yes' proceed to question 6. If 'No' consider deploying the regular **ReFRAME** process.)

6 Complete the following two paragraphs:

   a. The case for acting now and bypassing regular innovation processes is...

   b. We could delay the deployment of this project by 90 days by taking the following actions...

Read your paragraphs back. Do you still think this project is truly urgent, or are you just being impatient? If you still think it is truly urgent then proceed to deploy one of the processes described later in this chapter. If this is just impatient innovation, consider deploying the regular **ReFRAME** process.

Choosing the right pace

Now you are clear that you legitimately need urgent innovation, the next step is selecting the pace. This is important as it considers your organizational capability and the risk if things go wrong to ascertain how fast you can move without causing consequences that outweigh the value of your innovation. Of course, the risk of doing nothing immediately might mean that the pace is dictated to you. When faced with a compelling, urgent need to respond, there will be a desire to skip process and proceed to deploying untested ideas to gain the sense of achievement. It is a natural human response, especially when under threat, to want to simply take some action. It might make you feel better, but it introduces risk and potentially negatively impacts the value you get from your work. Using the techniques discussed earlier, you have identified that urgent innovation is warranted and that a faster pace is appropriate.

Trust in that and focus on maximizing the outcomes achieved from your action, not just the immediate feeling of relief from action itself. We group speeds of urgent innovation into two separate versions of the **ReFRAME** process. The speedy but safe **ReFRAME** enables compression of the **ReFRAME** process into less than 30 days and is recommended for times when a project is high risk or complicated. The second version is the compressed **ReFRAME**, which reduces the time of the process down to a week, or even a day if required. To select your pace, complete the following exercise. It will help you ascertain whether your 'thing' or your organizational capability creates a high risk, which should then dictate the pace. This is like the manageable chunks risk assessment in stage 6 of the embed process. If the pace of urgency required is being dictated to you, such as a government instruction, then go straight to the speed of process that you need.

EXERCISE
Assessing urgent innovation risk

What this is

This exercise enables you to assess the risk of your urgent innovation 'thing' in order to select which pace of process to take.

Instructions

1   For each variable in Table 10.1, select a statement that most represents your project environment.

2   To calculate your totals, sum how many times your 'thing' fits into each column (high, medium, low) and multiply it by that column's risk multiplier. For example, high has a x3 risk multiplier, so if you have selected high for 2 of the 6 topics, you get a score of 2 x 3 = 6.

3   Plot your answer on the meter in Figure 10.1 to ascertain your urgent innovation risk.

4   The table in Figure 10 tells you what speed is appropriate for your urgent innovation project.

TABLE 10.1   Assessing urgent innovation risk

Variable	High	Medium	Low	N/A
Stability	Lots of moving parts, lots of skills needed or a technology deployment	A somewhat complex system but not a technology deployment	Few moving parts, people and is not a technology deployment	
Early life support	We don't have any capability to increase support	We have some capability to improve normal support	We can have a dedicated and responsive support team	
Customer experience	Customer experience will be directly impacted if things go wrong	Customer experience is somewhat impacted	There will be minimal impact to customer experience	
People experience	There is a large impact or new work is required by our people	The impact is minimal, and any work is not new to our people	There is no direct impact and workload doesn't change	
Reversion capability	We cannot revert or it is complicated to do so	We can revert and impact would be minimal	We can revert without delay	
Deployment support team	We have no experts available to support transition	We have some experts available to support all transitions	We have experts to support each transition chunk	
Scores	x3 =	x2 =	x1 =	=0pts

FIGURE 10.1   Urgent innovation speed meter

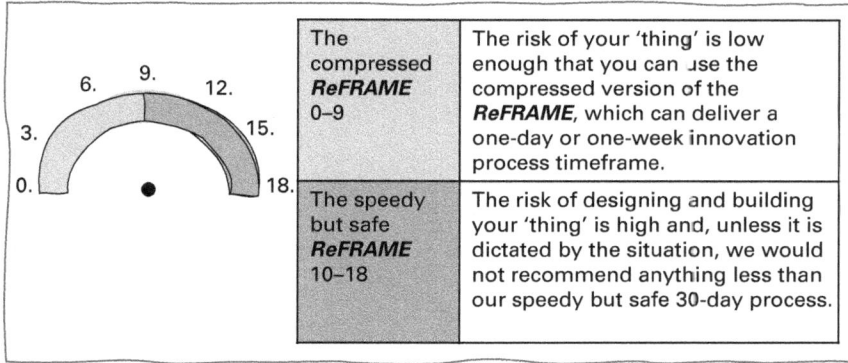

| The compressed **ReFRAME** 0–9 | The risk of your 'thing' is low enough that you can use the compressed version of the **ReFRAME**, which can deliver a one-day or one-week innovation process timeframe. |
| The speedy but safe **ReFRAME** 10–18 | The risk of designing and building your 'thing' is high and, unless it is dictated by the situation, we would not recommend anything less than our speedy but safe 30-day process. |

The speedy but safe *reframe*

The speedy but safe *ReFRAME* is a compressed version of the *ReFRAME* process that allows you to respond to an opportunity or threat that is high risk and high urgency.

The process

This process skips a number of the standard *ReFRAME* steps. Table 10.2 summarizes the steps of the process and refers to new exercises that show you how to support the faster pace where necessary. It also includes some guide timings to deliver an innovation in less than 30 days; however, timing will not be the same for everyone. Your particular project or organizational context may mean some areas need to have more focus and time allocated than we suggest. If your organization hasn't *ReFRAME*d before and you have not used evidence-led processes before, then we recommend you increase the amount of time spent on the 'Analyse and design the solution' and 'Make the design and scale it' stages of the process.

An urgent leadership alignment sprint

If you have *ReFRAME*d before, you should be able to skip this step. If you think it is helpful (and you have time) to run a refresh session with the management team to give them context on the urgency driver, then do it. It can help to minimize time spent on this later in the process.

TABLE 10.2 The speedy but safe process

Stage	Step	Keep	Compress	Skip	Activities and timing
	Clarity of purpose		1a. If not previously ReFRAMEd: use your organizational purpose to test innovation ideas against. If required, add characteristics and value traits to the purpose to help	1b. If previously ReFRAMEd: skip this step, but reaffirm in the Filter the ideas compressed step	2a. Leadership alignment sprint – half day | ***Chapter 10*** 3. Filter the ideas planning – half day| ***Chapter 10***
Reset the foundations (up to 1 day)	*Leadership alignment*	3. Plan and prepare for the filter the ideas session	2a. If not previously ReFRAMEd: run a half-day sprint session to align leadership team and agree roles	2b. If previously ReFRAMEd: skip this step, but reaffirm in the Filter the ideas compressed step	
	Culture			No time to engrain this into the organizational culture, this gap will be compensated for in the get innovation-ready stage	

Filter the ideas (up to 1 day)	*Business value*	4. Conduct virtual ideation sessions to align ideas with the golden rule Use the forced rapid disruption cards to disrupt thinking, ideas and to compress discussion		4. Filter ideas session with senior leaders – 2 hrs | ***Chapter 10*** Synthesize results by the project team – 4 hrs Report back and agree on ideas to pursue – 2 hrs
	Purpose alignment	Compressed ideation exercise (can be done virtually if required)		
	Customer value	Synthesize results, report back and agree on ideas to pursue (this can be done digitally if required or as a follow-up meeting that was pre-arranged)		
Get innovation-ready (up to 3 days)	*Sponsors*	5. Identify requirements of team and estimated resources (best estimate as this will be refined by the team later) 6. Have a coffee with yourself and assess your sponsorship style and complete your sponsorship plan		5. Complete team skills canvas – 1 day | **Fig 6.2** 6. Assess your sponsorship style and complete sponsorship plan – 30 mins | ***Chapter 6***

(continued)

TABLE 10.2 (Continued)

Stage	Step	Keep	Compress	Skip	Activities and timing
	Team		7. Compress the team recruitment and resource allocation phases. Remove external support/consulting options and focus on internal skills where possible. If going external, ensure that any consultants are able to come onboard quickly and are aware of the compressed timeframes		7. Recruitment and resource allocation – 1.5 days
	Resources		For resource allocation, ensure that any stakeholders with sign off processes in place are aware of the compressed timeframe and give you expedited access		

Analyse and design the solution (up to 5 days)	*Narrow*	8. Narrowing canvas still applicable and completed by project team within 1 day	8. Complete the narrowing canvas – 1 day	*Chapter 7*
	Collect evidence	9. Evidence collection compressed and focused on breadth of evidence rather than depth. Ie look at getting a broad range of evidence, but time constraints won't allow you to go deep into understanding and clarifying	9. Complete evidence collection cards – 2 days
	Analyse and test	10. Compressing this stage will require resource dedication to testing, process remains the same but in a reduced time frame	10. Complete evidence assessment – 2 days	*Fig 7.2*

(continued)

TABLE 10.2 (Continued)

Stage	Step	Keep	Compress	Skip	Activities and timing
Make the design and scale it (up to 12 days)	*Ideate/build*		11. Compress the initial prototype build to sticky tape and string 14. Compress build phase for minimum effort in real world 17. Compress build phase for real-world scale-ready		11. Complete sticky tape and string maturity blueprint build phase – 2 days	*Chapter 8* 14. Complete minimum effort real world maturity blueprint build phase – 2 days	*Chapter 8* 17. Complete real-world scale-ready maturity blueprint build phase – 2 days	*Chapter 8*
	Prototype/test		12 & 15. Compress test phases to within 1 day, focusing on breadth not depth	Skip real-world draft level of maturity and progress to real-world scale ready after minimum effort real-world test complete	12 & 15. Complete the testing card and plan refinements – 1 day each	*Chapter 8*
	Refine		13. Compress refine stage of sticky tape and string 16. Compress refine stage of minimum effort real-world		13 & 16 - Complete refinement worksheets – 1 day each	*Chapter 8*

Embed as the new normal (up to 5 days)	*Transition plan and test*	18. Complete the communications canvas 19. Complete the manageable chunks analysis 20. Complete a compressed transition test		18. Communication canvas – 1 day | **Fig 9.3** 19. Manageable chunks assessment – 1 day | **Fig 9.1** 20. Transition test – 1 day | **Chapter 9**
	Deploy	21a. For complex deployments, keep process as normal and deploy in chunks that are manageable. Complete regular transition reports	21b. For standard or low complexity deployments, increase size of chunks and compress refine stages. Complete regular transition reports	21. Complete regular transition reports – as required | **Chapter 9**
	Embed	Remove early life support as per normal ReFRAME process		Early life support assessment – when ready | **Chapter 9**

If you have not **ReFRAME**d before, then the next exercise will allow you to compress the first stage of the process. Use the process to help you prepare and facilitate the session. The forced disruption cards (online at www.koganpage.com/RIR) will also support faster ideation sessions – use them where they will add value.

EXERCISE
Urgent leadership alignment sprint

What this is

This is a quick reference guide to help prepare and run your leadership alignment sprint. This is a lot more pointed than a full leadership alignment strategy, obviously, as we have to get outcomes in hours, not weeks. Speed makes things feel messy and uncomfortable; that is normal and the more you and the team are prepared for that, the more likely you'll be objective in making decisions about the inclusions and clarity of your alignment outcomes at pace.

Preparation

1   Book in the session with all leadership stakeholders as early as possible. This should come from the CEO or most senior member to prevent delays in acceptance.

2   Prepare the answers to the questions posed in the session run sheet below.

3   Send out any questions or content as early as possible.

4   Find an appropriate space and prepare it, including any virtual elements. Ensure that all members can clearly see each other and the content, and can participate. This includes having physical or digital space visible to all participants where ideas can be shared and discussed as a group.

The session

1   Discuss the rules of engagement for the meeting. See Chapter 5 for more details.

2   Discuss the situation's context in detail. Here are some questions to help you frame this part of the discussion:

    o   What is the cause of the urgent innovation need?

    o   What will happen if we don't respond?

    o   What are competitors doing?

- o   How are customers reacting?
- o   What are the possible responses we want to investigate further?

3   Define the opportunity/threat area to narrow down your response options. Some questions to help:

- o   What are the options for our response? (Suggest a five-minute silent sprint of ideas individually, announce and group them, then discuss as a group.)
- o   What are the final two or three areas we want to synthesize with more time with the appropriate group? Use the online disruption cards at www.koganpage.com/RIR to finalize the selections.
- o   Discuss the pace and ensure there is alignment on the speed.

4   Facilitate a discussion about the role each person plays, the speed required and operating rhythm that will ensure the pace is maintained. Some questions to help:

- o   Who is sponsoring the work?
- o   What is required from each part of the business now?

Synthesizing

1   Write up the results and share them with the group.

2   Book in the filter the ideas session with the appropriate group (include experts from the area of the responses discussed).

3   Collect any evidence that will help the filter the ideas session.

Download the forced disruption cards at www.koganpage.com/RIR

Filter the ideas

Once you have identified your opportunity areas it is time to filter the ideas down to a select few for your team to act on. This is a compressed version of the process laid out in Chapter 5. The process flow is the same but the timeframes are compressed. The disruption cards will also help you get the best possible ideas in the shortest timeframe. The next exercise is a guide sheet to assist you in completing the compressed 'filter the ideas' session.

EXERCISE
The filter the ideas guide sheet

What this is

A session plan for a filter the ideas session at pace. To help with the compressed timeframes of this step, use this guide sheet and the disruption cards to generate and test ideas.

Instructions

Follow the exercise formula in order as it is designed to generate the best outcomes as quickly as possible. However, you may need to add some nuances in to ensure the full context of your ambition is incorporated. **Hint:** Film the session if possible, as the discussion will be helpful for the project team, but also have someone taking notes. Quotes, reasoning and context are all pivotal when you move on to 'get innovation-ready' and 'analyse and design the solution'.

Preparation

1 Invite the right humans. Remember, this is a team game, so ensure you get a breadth of representation, especially from the customer-facing team.
2 Find the right space. Face-to-face is always best, but if that's not possible use the information in Chapter 5 to help you prepare whatever space you can get.
3 Set your goals and define success.
4 Design your agenda, including scene setters and rules of engagement.
5 Have a plan to capture the plan! No actions from the meeting is the worst outcome – be clear on what types of actions and decisions you need agreed.

Step 1: Fast paced idea generation

If you have decided urgent innovation is needed, you will have a specific opportunity/threat area to focus on. Spend five minutes getting everyone to produce ways to solve it in silence. Don't be caught up on the time, let it flow until ideas are being written down at a much slower pace. Then get everyone to explain them to the group whilst you group them in themes.

Step 2: Test the problem statement

You need to spend most of your time on the problem, not the solution. Remember, humans have agendas; it is part of our design to think about things through our pre-frontal cortex filled with ambitions, experiences and prejudices As ideas flow, ensure that the problem is being discussed, not the solution. For example, if someone says, 'We should have an app that does X' stop them and get them to rephrase it in a more helpful way, such as 'Customers can't do X without ringing us or visiting the store.'

Step 3: Assess ideas against the golden rule

Once you have themes it is time to narrow down to your selected one or two ideas to pursue. Assess each of the grouped ideas against the golden rule from Chapter 5. The group discussion should lead to a natural conclusion of the top ideas; however, if needed, you can run a voting exercise to select the top few to be assessed with evidence. **Hint:** Continuously test any ideas based on feasibility for rapid implementation. For example, if an idea requires a major IT change that will require months, it can be eliminated immediately.

The compressed reframe

The compressed reframe allows you to respond to an opportunity or threat within a week, or even as fast as a day, by using a more heavily compressed version of the *ReFRAME* model.

If the urgency required means you have less than a week, then you need to compress or skip elements in the *ReFRAME* timelines even more than for the speedy but safe process, and this will introduce more risk.

As the process compresses it will feel rushed and more chaotic than the full process and you may question whether reverting to a more naturally intuitive traditional execution process (ie 'how we used to do things around here') will feel more comfortable. It is important that you prepare for that feeling of discomfort and are ready to overcome it. When I was learning to fly planes, as it is for any new pilot, the downwind checklist is the most stressful to learn. It is the main checklist before you enter your final approach to the runway and it feels so rushed that you never seem to have enough time to complete it. Without it, though, you risk landing a plane without its wheels down or hitting another aircraft. The process (in this instance a checklist) keeps you on track and as you keep practising it, you end up feeling comfortable with the rush. Even during a compressed, or rushed, focus on process, trust your retail instincts. Retailers are uniquely equipped to execute in a stressful environment because we live by processes. Trust in the process and stick to it and you will land your urgent innovation smoothly and intact.

TABLE 10.3 The compressed **ReFRAME** process

Stage	Step	Keep	Compress	Skip	Activities and timing
Reset the foundations (up to 1 day)	Clarity of purpose			1. Skip this step, but reaffirm in the filter the ideas compressed step	
	Leadership alignment		2. Complete the leadership alignment sprint and agree roles 3. Complete a compressed filter the ideas planning session		2. Urgent leadership alignment sprint – 2 hrs | Chapter 10 3. Filter the ideas guide sheet planning – 30 mins | Chapter 10
	Culture			No time to engrain this into the organizational culture, this gap will be compensated for in the get innovation ready stage	

Filter the ideas (up to 1 day)				
	Business value			
	Purpose alignment	4. Conduct virtual ideation sessions to align ideas with the golden rule and agree on ideas to pursue in the session NEW EXERCISE – Use the forced rapid disruption cards to disrupt thinking, ideas and to compress discussion		4. Filter the ideas session with senior leaders – 2 hrs	Chapter 10 Session preparation – 2 hrs
	Customer value	NEW EXERCISE – The filter the ideas guide sheet (can be done virtually if required)		

(continued)

TABLE 10.3 (Continued)

Stage	Step	Keep	Compress	Skip	Activities and timing
	Sponsors		5. Identify requirements of team and estimated resources (best estimate as this will be refined by the team later)	Skip the sponsorship style and mindset exercises and focus on building the right team and resource them adequately	5. Complete team skills canvas – 2 hrs	Figure 6.3
Get innovation-ready (up to 3 days)	Team		6. Compress the team recruitment and resource allocation phases. Remove external support/consulting options and focus on internal skills where possible. If going external, ensure that any consultants are able to come onboard quickly and are aware of the compressed timeframes.		
	Resources		For resource allocation, ensure that any stakeholders with sign off processes in place are aware of the compressed timeframe and give you expedited access		6. Recruitment and resource allocation – 4 hrs

		7. Compressed narrowing canvas sprint		8. Complete the narrowing canvas – 30 mins to 2 hrs | Chapter 7
Analyse and design the solution (up to 5 days)	*Narrow*			
	Collect evidence	8. Evidence collection to be conducted via a desktop exercise NEW EXERCISE: Desktop evidence collection		8. Complete evidence collection cards – 30 mins to 6 hrs | Available online (see Chapter 7)
	Analyse and test	9. Compressing this stage will require resource dedication to testing, process remains the same but in a reduced time frame		9. Complete evidence assessment – 30 mins to 2 hrs | Figure 7.2

(continued)

TABLE 10.3 (Continued)

Stage	Step	Keep	Compress	Skip	Activities and timing
Make the design and scale it (up to 12 days)	Ideate/build		10. Compress the initial prototype build to sticky tape and string 13. Compress build phase for minimum effort real-world 16. Compress build phase for real-world scale-ready	Skip real-world draft level of maturity and progress to real-world scale ready after minimum-effort real-world test complete	10. Complete sticky tape and string maturity blueprint build phase – 2 hrs | Chapter 8 13. Complete minimum effort real-world maturity blueprint build phase – up to 1 day | Chapter 8 16. Complete real-world scale-ready maturity blueprint build phase – up to 1 day | Chapter 8
	Prototype/test		11 and 14. Compress test phases to within 1 day, focusing on breadth not depth	If innovation is not complex and a faster turnaround is required, you can also skip real-world draft level of maturity and continue to embed after your initial sticky tape and string tests	11 and 14. Complete the testing card and plan refinements – up to a ½ day | Chapter 8
	Refine		12. Compress refine stage of sticky tape and string 15. Compress refine stage of minium effort real-world		12 and 15 – Complete refinement worksheets – up to 1 day | Chapter 8

Transition plan and test			17. Complete the communications canvas 18. Complete the manegable chunks analysis 19. Complete a compressed transition test		17. Communication canvas – 1 hr | Figure 9.3 18. Manageable chunks exercise – 1 hr | Chapter 9 19. Transition test – up to a ½ day | Chapter 9
Embed as the new normal (up to 5 days)	*Deploy*	20a. For complex deployments, keep process as normal and deploy in chunks that are manageable. Complete regular transition reports	20b. For standard or low complexity deployments, increase size of chunks and compress refine stages. Complete regular transition reports	Skip test of transition plan and refine after first deployment	20. Complete regular transition reports – as required | Chapter 9
	Embed	21. Remove early life support as per normal *ReFRAME* process		For simple whole of channel deployments, skip refine stages and increase initial investment in early life support	21. Early life support assessment – when ready | Chapter 9

Table 10.3 will guide you through which steps of the process are kept, which are compressed, and which can be skipped. Any new exercises to support this urgent *ReFRAME* are above in the speedy but safe process section. As per the speedy but safe process, if there is new information that comes to light that either reduces the urgency or increases it, then consider changing the pace to be more appropriate. The rapid disruption cards (available online at www.koganpage.com/RIR) will be referenced and helpful throughout this process.

Conclusion

Opportunities and threats present a major challenge to innovative organizations. They require the use of the same muscles but at different speeds and rhythms. Having a strong understanding of when you can compress or skip parts of the *ReFRAME* process to innovate at the required speed means you can not only react to these urgency drivers, but also capitalize on them when they arise.

In this chapter we have discussed what urgent innovation is, its advantages and disadvantages, when to use it and when not to use it. We went through how the *ReFRAME* process can be adapted to enable different innovation horizons, ranging from one day to one month. It is important that you are evidence-led and objective when assessing whether or not urgent innovation truly is required. We know many retailers who often convince themselves that their lack of patience is a legitimate reason for urgent innovation. It is never a substitute for the full process and never yields as strong a result as could have been achieved with the full process.

It is also important to remember that working at pace introduces tension, especially in creative innovation tasks such as design. This can impact team dynamics, cause distractions and waste time. Face these head-on and prepare the team for the reality of the pace of the project and explain how that differs from the standard *ReFRAME* process and how they may need to compromise on certain elements of their normal work methods.

Innovation impacts all retailers, big or small. Small retail business is different to large retail business and has different challenges when it comes to innovating. In the next chapter, we will discuss those differences and how *ReFRAME* can be adapted for smaller organizations.

Notes

1   Ringel, M, Taylor, A and Zablit, H (2015) *The Rising Need for Innovation Speed*, The Boston Consulting Group

2   Devlin, K (2020) Zara's shot-from-home campaign innovation, Stylus [Online] https://www.stylus.com/models-selfshot-zaras-new-campaign-from-home (archived at https://perma.cc/3SZF-B3KZ)

3   Li, F (2018) In business innovation, timing is of the essence, CEO Today [Online] https://www.ceotodaymagazine.com/2018/07/in-business-innovation-timing-is-of-the-essence/ (archived at https://perma.cc/56YW-HRQ3)

4   Domino's (2020) Domino's offers zero contact delivery [Online] https://newsroom.dominos.com.au/media/2020/3/12/dominos-offers-zero-contact-delivery (archived at https://perma.cc/NH3W-W33U)

5   ABC (2020) Australia's social distancing rules have been enhanced to slow coronavirus – here's how they work [Online] https://www.abc.net.au/news/2020-03-20/coronavirus-covid-19-scott-morrison-enhanced-social-distancing/12075532 (archived at https://perma.cc/K468-A8Q9)

6   Daoud, E (2020) McGrocery list grows: Macca's finds new ways to make money during COVID crisis, 7 News [Online] https://7news.com.au/lifestyle/mcgrocery-list-grows-maccas-finds-new-ways-to-make-money-during-covid-crisis-c-970522 (archived at https://perma.cc/4BXW-G3QV)

7   Hensel, A (2020) Nike's Heidi O'Neill on the brand's digital – and coronavirus – strategy, Modern Retail, 11 May [Online] https://www.modernretail.co/retailers/nikes-heidi-oneill-on-how-the-company-plans-to-turn-first-time-app-users-into-regular-customers/?utm_campaign=mrdis&utm_medium=email&utm_source=mrdaily&utm_content=051120 (archived at https://perma.cc/RSQ8-PZMM)

8   Nike (2020) NTC community workout, YouTube [Online] https://www.youtube.com/playlist?list=PLNqKTn4CuEXdcqbJINlNNsFmhMQRBFcsV (archived at https://perma.cc/XU8Q-N27H)

9   Cheung, MC (2020) How brands in China are responding to consumer expectations during the coronavirus, Emarketer, 28 April [Online] https://www.emarketer.com/content/how-brands-in-china-are-responding-to-consumer-expectations-during-the-coronavirus (archived at https://perma.cc/2KBQ-E2Z4)

10 Clements, A (2020) JD.com 'reinvents' clubbing – combining live-streaming and drinks ecommerce, 9 April [Online] https://www.retailconnections.co.uk/articles/jd-com-reinvents-clubbing-combining-live-streaming-and-drinks-ecommerce/ (archived at https://perma.cc/NXJ8-PKWZ)

11   Weissman, CG (2020) How Williams Sonoma's digital bets made it a coronavirus winner, Modern Retail, 1 June [Online] https://www.modernretail.co/retailers/how-williams-sonomas-digital-bets-made-it-a-coronavirus-winner/ (archived at https://perma.cc/2M4L-S73G)

12   The Motley Fool (2020) Williams-Sonoma Inc (WSM) Q1 2020 earnings call transcript (WSM earnings call for the period ending May 3, 2020), 28 May [Online] https://www.fool.com/earnings/call-transcripts/2020/05/29/williams-sonoma-inc-wsm-q1-2020-earnings-call-tran.aspx (archived at https://perma.cc/GQC7-FTEG)

11

Innovation in small retail businesses

Introduction

Small business retailers are different to medium and large business retailers and this affects the process of innovation. Their owners tend to work in the business and are therefore generally closer to their customers than managers in larger retail businesses. They have their whole lives and wealth invested and are emotionally connected to their businesses in a way other retailers are not. They are passionately committed, but sometimes have problems making detached and objective business decisions. They are not constrained by organizational barriers to innovation like larger retailers, but they have less access to the resources like finance, expertise, and time to make innovation happen.

Small retail businesses are an important part of the retail industry. They represent the largest number of entities and generate a large proportion of the turnover and employment opportunities in the retail sector. They are also an important engine of innovation because they are invariably founded on bringing new value to the market. That might mean offering new products or services, serving the customer in a better way, offering lower prices or entering new geographic markets that incumbents have ignored. All the large, successful retailers of today were once small retailers with an innovative idea.

Small retail businesses are different, but they operate in the same market as all retailers. They are therefore under the same obligation as everybody else to innovate when the environment changes. The consequences of failing to innovate when the environment demands it are much more severe for small business retailers than for managers in larger retail businesses. While managers in larger retail businesses may, at worst, lose their job if their business fails to innovate, small retail business owners stand to lose not only personal financial assets (like their house) but also the creation that they have personally built and put their heart and soul in to over a number of years.

In this chapter our focus is on small retail businesses that have relatively unrestricted capacity to innovate. They do not operate under a licence, like a franchise which puts most of the responsibility for innovation in the hands of the licensor or franchisor. The businesses we will discuss are owned and operated by entrepreneurial, spirited founders who got in to retail because they had a good idea.

In this chapter we will demonstrate: why small retail businesses are different to larger retailers, why they are a vitally important part of the industry and society as a whole, why innovation is different for them, how they can leverage their unique strengths to become successful innovators and how suppliers and governments can best support their aspirations. We then outline a customized **ReFRAME** process for small business.

Why are small business retailers different?

Official definitions of what constitutes a small business vary around the world. In the European Union (EU)[1] a small business is defined as one having fewer than 50 employees, less than 10 million euros in turnover and less than 10 million euros on the balance sheet. They separately define micro businesses as having fewer than 10 employees, less than 2 million euros in turnover and less than 2 million euros on the balance sheet. In the USA the definition of a small business varies by business sector. In retail about a third of retail categories are defined as 'small' by the Small Business Administration (SBA) if they have a turnover of less than US$ 7.5 million.[2] In Australia, the Australian Bureau of Statistics (ABS) definition of a small business is one that has an Australian Business Number (ABN), is registered for Goods and Services Tax (GST) and has a turnover of less than A$ 2 million per annum or employs fewer than 20 people.

Despite the differences in definition, all agree that the small business sector is big and important. Small business represents 99 per cent of all firms in the EU, 99.7 per cent in the USA and nearly 98 per cent in Australia. A report by the Australian Small Business and Family Enterprise Ombudsman (ASBFEO)[3] consolidating data from separate government agencies, shows

TABLE 11.1   Small business survival rate over four years (Australia)

	Businesses June 2014	Survived to June 2018	Survival %
Non-employing	1,273,769	758,922	60%
1–4 employees	571,206	395,953	69%
5–19 employees	199,965	155,270	78%
20–199 employees	51,619	42,408	82%
200+ employees	3,603	3,084	86%
Consolidated			
1–19 employees	771,171	551,223	71%
20–200+ employees	55,222	45,492	82%

SOURCE Based on ASBFEO data and author calculations

that small retail businesses account for 31.4 per cent of all retail employment and 34 per cent of all research and development spend in the sector.

Small businesses do have a lower survival rate than large businesses, but their rate of failure is not as high as you might expect. One of the myths of small business is that the vast majority fail in their first year or very soon after. In the USA, Fundera[4] cites 2017 government data showing that about 80 per cent of small businesses will survive their first year, 70 per cent their second year, 50 per cent their fifth year and 30 per cent their tenth year in business. In Australia the ASBFEO report shows that small business employing 1–19 people have a 71 per cent survival rate over four years versus 82 per cent for businesses employing 20 or more employees. As can be seen from Table 11.1, the gap gets smaller if only businesses of 5–19 employees (small retail business heartland) are compared with large businesses.

Small retail business and innovation

Small businesses all start with an innovative idea that disrupts the market, but they sometimes fail to innovate beyond that. The ASBFEO report found that small businesses lag larger businesses significantly when it comes to innovation. According to its research, 62 per cent of large businesses engaged in innovative activity (defined as the introduction of 'a new or significantly improved good or service, operational or organizational process or marketing method') but only 50 per cent of small businesses did the same. This is despite the clear performance benefits small businesses can derive from innovation. The ASBFEO research shows that innovative small businesses outperform non-innovative businesses in sales, profitability and productivity improvement.

According to the ASBFEO research, the main barriers to innovation in small businesses are lack of access to funds (23.3 per cent) and lack of skills to implement innovation (22.6 per cent). Whatever the reasons for not innovating, the result is the same as for large business. All retailers that don't change when the world changes enter the retail death spiral of losing customers, cutting prices and cutting costs. When this happens, a whole ecosystem of stakeholders becomes collateral damage. What is worse for small business is that owners often have the business secured against their personal assets.

To get an insight behind the numbers, we talked to Kelly Slessor. Kelly Slessor is the CEO of Shop You and has driven digital growth and innovation in retail and other industries since 2000. Kelly has worked with over 500 retailers and property groups globally to develop their digital marketing and technology strategy, build out technology platforms and ultimately drive higher conversions through connection. Having worked with businesses of all sizes, she is in a unique position to compare the challenges of innovation in small and large retail.

CASE STUDY
The differences between small and large retail innovation
by Kelly Slessor, CEO, Shop You

In technology, the difference between small business and large businesses is getting narrower. The access that small businesses have to technology is now comparable to that of larger businesses but there are differences in expertise, budgets, access to tech ideas and partnerships. If I look at corporate retailers, in every single department they have people who are up to date on trends and innovation. That does not happen in small business. Small businesses don't have the forums or the supplier ecosystems to make that possible.

Then there is the problem of time. A good example is a small Sydney-based business called Brooklyn Boy Bagels. Pre COVID-19 the business was set up to distribute through two small retail outlets and wholesale through similar small cafés. Just before the COIVD-19 pandemic hit, the owner lost his master baker, then when social distancing and lockdowns began to be implemented the business needed to pivot quickly. The owner re-trained himself as a baker and was up at 3am every morning baking for three weeks. But at the same time, he was also doing the website, social media, working out how to do delivery, pursuing the necessary HACCP accreditation for wholesale supermarket distribution, etc, so the business could pivot and survive. In large organizations they say they don't have time, but spend a lot of time in meetings and have more time to consider and develop opportunities than small businesses.

Another difference is the level of contact with customers. Sometimes you speak to a large retail executive and they tell you it's a long time since they spoke to a customer, but small retailers speak to customers every day, which makes them very attuned to their needs.

Small businesses are hands-on, which means they understand subjects in depth from all angles. This helps them make good decisions quickly. Big businesses often defer their decisions to other people and rely on consultants to help with the decision-making process.

The emotional connection to the business is greater for small retailers. When you set up a small business, you put huge psychological pressure on yourself. Your business is you. If the business fails, you fail, and sometimes that gets in the way of making smart decisions. Sometimes, small retailers do all the things that stop them failing rather than doing the things that would help them succeed.

Emotional attachment to the business can cloud objectivity, but the flipside is it makes small retailers really motivated to create a great experience for the customer. On digital strategy specifically, big corporates always talk about acquisition strategy and the cost of acquisition, whereas in small business they focus on retention, which is symptomatic of care for customers. Repeat visits to digital platforms are generally higher for small retailers than for larger retailers.

Small retailers' biggest advantage over larger retailers is that they can move quickly. If I have a mentoring session with a small retailer one day and say, 'Have you thought about... ?' by the next week they have already built it, tested it, implemented it and launched it. Whereas when I talk to the big retailers, even after they agree on a course of action there is a business case process, there are meetings there are budget sign-offs, etc. That's even with small investments.

One of the biggest disadvantages small retail businesses have is around resources, but more particularly resourcing to scale. Small retailers are very good at implementing quick technology, but scaling to something bigger can be a problem. It's an issue of confidence, skills, time and funding.

Small business retailers have nowhere to hide. The Brooklyn Boy Bagels story is a great example. The owner was going to fly or fail based on getting a master baker in and pivoting for the COVID-19 trading environment. He did everything himself for a few weeks. There are lots of places to hide if things fail in bigger businesses. Lots of people to blame. If it doesn't work, it's the system that's at fault or the policy or another department. You are not a single point of failure. There are big sign-off processes in large retail so that if it doesn't work there are a hundred people behind it. In small business there's only one.

Also, the small retailers have a lot of fun with it, and none of the fear of failure you can see in the corporate world that stops them making a decision. When promoting innovation in corporate, you need to find the unique individual who is prepared to take a risk and is respected enough in the organization to be supported.

There are innovation failures in small business. Some are due to idea testing. One owner I dealt with tried to do a wardrobe solution for women's lingerie. It failed because they hadn't tested out the customer appetite. It was a good idea that she had while at home with children and the problem was a genuine one for the business owner, but she didn't test to see if the solution solved the problem for others. Other failures are due to scaling costs. An example is a handbag solution that needed scale to make it viable but couldn't get the funding. Many small businesses can get to the point where they need $500,000 to make an idea successful and it just isn't available.

Fostering innovation in small retail businesses

When it comes to executing a programme of innovation, small business retailers have significant strengths when compared to larger retail businesses, but they also have challenges (Tables 11.2 and 11.3). To be successful innovators, small business retailers need to learn how to leverage their strengths and mitigate their challenges.

Small retail businesses represent a large section of the industry, can be an engine for innovation and employment, and serve markets that larger retailers ignore. Because of this, suppliers, partners and governments have a vested interest in them being successful. To foster innovation, they must recognize the strengths and challenges of small business retailers and support them in a different way.

TABLE 11.2 The strengths of small business retailers

Strengths	Implications for retailers	Implications for suppliers, partners and governments
Ability to move fast	This is the biggest strength that small retail businesses have when deploying a programme of innovation. It comes from being able to sense change quicker because they are closer to the customer, having no organizational barriers to implementing an idea and not having to worry about the problems of scale. It means small retailers can have innovation deployed in market while their larger business peers are still trying to organize a meeting with stakeholders or commission research.	Suppliers, partners and governments need to be able to move at the pace of small business if they want to foster innovation. This means lead times need to be re-thought. Any process that takes weeks must be reduced to days. This means abandoning customization for standardization and reducing complexity in favour of simplicity. Execution processes should be redesigned to be simple and quick. This means abandoning multiple sign-offs in favour of pre-approvals and reducing the time required from executed agreement to deployment.
Understanding of the business	Small retailers have a better understanding of their business than large retailers. This is because they, by necessity, fill the role of 'Chief Everything Officer' (or 'Chief Cook and Bottle Washer', as we used to say). While larger businesses have to be careful to get a cross functional team aligned to make innovation happen small business owners are cross-functional teams in one body. This gives small retailers the ability to make good quality, informed decisions, which is more difficult to achieve in larger businesses.	Small retailers are generalists not specialists. Teams who support them should also be generalists but with access to specialist skills when required. It is quite acceptable to lead a conversation with a large retailer with a deep domain specialist as it is likely they will have a peer in the organization. This is very unlikely in small businesses and may have negative consequences. If your representatives have experience of working in small retail, so much the better.

(continued)

TABLE 11.2 (Continued)

Strengths	Implications for retailers	Implications for suppliers, partners and governments
Financial and emotional commitment	Small retailers are committed to their business in a way that employees of larger businesses can never be. They are not only financially all in, but they are emotionally connected to their creation and driven by a strong sense of purpose of doing something special. This gives small retailers the energy and drive to overcome obstacles that is rare in larger businesses. It means small retailers are more likely to do whatever it takes to see change through than retailers in larger businesses.	Be prepared for small retailers to execute much quicker than their large retail peers. Project plans including times to follow up need to be shortened accordingly. A lot of work goes on in small retail businesses out of regular hours. Make sure support of some kind is available when it is needed.

TABLE 11.3 The challenges faced by small business retailers

Challenges	Implications for retailers	Implications for suppliers, partners and governments
Space	The lack of access to space is small retailers' most important challenge. We use the word 'space' to describe the resources retailers need to nurture innovation including money, time, physical space and expertise. Small retailers will never have more space than larger retailers. To mitigate this challenge, small retailers need to bootstrap wherever possible, parachute out of projects if the space is not available to execute them or look for external investors if the project is really vital to the development of the business. Above all, they need to dedicate time to innovation. This means trusting the team to step up while the owners step out and develop their plans.	Suppliers, partners and governments can help by providing some of the space that small retailers need to innovate. This may be in the form of financial grants, physical spaces where retailers can develop their ideas or providing access to a pool of expert help on particular topics of mutual interest. The problem of lack of time is one retailers have to solve for themselves.
Knowledge of industry trends	Small retailers are unlikely to have the knowledge of industry trends that their larger retail competitors have. They typically don't have time to attend conferences or be considered important enough by suppliers to have dedicated briefing sessions on trends in the industry. This means that they may be slow to learn of changes in the environment that represent either an opportunity or a threat. Small retailers can mitigate this weakness by dedicating 15 minutes per day to read about retail from overseas and local sites or listen to one the large range of quality podcasts on a commute or break. Webinars are plentiful but time-consuming; nevertheless, it is worthwhile dedicating one hour per month to attending or listening to the recording of a webinar. As always, we recommend writing down reflections on anything that's interesting to cement the learning and to file those reflections in a place where they can be found easily.	This is an area where suppliers, partners and governments can be of great assistance. Out of hours meetings exposing groups of small retail businesses to the latest thinking from around the world can be a great way to sow the seeds of innovation. To share the load, suppliers, partners and governments can collaborate on these events with, for example, governments or landlords providing venues and banks, consulting companies, tech companies or other service providers delivering the content. We argue face-to-face is always a better way to communicate but if there are geographical constraints then a good-quality webinar is a viable and cheaper alternative. These sessions run best when presenters speak with the voice of small businesses. For example, if the topic is cyber security bring a generalist not the leading world authority on the topic.

(continued)

TABLE 11.3 (Continued)

Challenges	Implications for retailers	Implications for suppliers, partners and governments
Financial and emotional commitment	The deep commitment small retailers have to their businesses is a strength but also a challenge. It sometimes causes them to hang on to their original idea when it has gone way past its use-by date. It also can cause lack of objectivity in decision-making. To mitigate this challenge, small retailers should seek external help. This can be often found free or relatively cheaply from local business organizations, local government or from suppliers like banks or Telcos. If there is a specific person's opinion that you would like to get, then many are willing to give it for the price of a coffee. Forming a board of advice can bring together a group of people with valuable external knowledge but a different perspective to investors. If there is something specific that needs looking at then there are plentiful retail advisors who specialize in small businesses that could be engaged for a fee.	Always treat small retail businesses with respect. Their businesses might not be as big as the one you work for but they have their whole existence invested in it. Suppliers, partners and governments can help by providing an objective voice and sounding board. Some local governments and business councils already provide programmes and mentoring sessions for small business innovators. Other organizations provide free 45-minute mentoring sessions contingent on small business owners coming to the meeting with a structured situation analysis and problem definition to consider. These sessions can be pathways to an innovation programme or to a series of paid sessions with a small retail business specialist.

Why size matters

Some say the small retail business sector may be large but it's not important. Proprietors get into the business for lifestyle reasons and stay small because they are not as good as larger retailers. Any systematic method of dealing with them is like herding cats. Suppliers, partners and governments are better off focusing their resources on larger retail businesses that are better organized and easier to deal with.

While some small business retailers do indeed get into the industry for lifestyle reasons, others are motivated to make a difference in the way customers and markets are served. History shows that these businesses can quickly become dangerous competitors for medium and large incumbents. In other cases, they can serve markets that medium and large retailers are unwilling or unable to serve, and as such provide a service to customers and society that governments should be interested in.

The exceptions are small retail businesses that operate under some sort of licence. They rely for their success on their ability to execute on somebody else's idea rather than developing their own concepts. They are also restricted by the licensor as to the amount of innovation they can bring to the concept and the markets they are able to serve. They have effectively been pre-herded by the licensor, which makes it easier for suppliers, partners and governments to deal primarily with the shepherd and not the sheep.

CASE STUDY
How Nutie leveraged the strengths of small businesses to innovate

Nutie (https://www.nutie.com.au/) is a Sydney-based retailer of vegan and gluten free cakes founded by Sina Klug and Jacques Dumont in 2017. They have two retail outlets and support a wholesale and events business from their inner-city kitchen. They have a team of twenty.

On Sunday 23 March 2020 the Government of New South Wales (NSW) announced from midday on Monday 23 March gatherings of more than two people would be banned, while restaurants and cafés would have to switch to takeaway only to help to curb the spread of the COVID-19 virus. This was a body blow to Nutie. Their events business and their eat-in business at their two retail outlets would be lost, while their wholesale business would be severely diminished. What's more, they knew their coeliac customers relied on them. This was especially true for those who had recently returned from overseas and were in lockdown. Non-coeliac customers can order take-away through Uber Eats or one of the other home delivery services but coeliac customers generally are cautious about doing that. It was time to innovate.

Nutie was able to achieve an extraordinary amount of innovation in a short amount of time. Home delivery began on the first day of the lockdown. Initially all the orders were being received by email as Nutie had no website, but the owners soon found a web developer friend who was able to create a simple online ordering tool to automate the process. The next innovation was delivery routing. Rather than disappointing customers who lived too far away to be economically viable to serve, they decided to bundle deliveries to a point and get customers in the surrounding area to come and pick up from their van. So popular was this with customers that the queue to the van at the pick-up points was often 50 to 60 metres long. The innovation continued with the menu. Sina and Jacques decided to productize some of the popular menu items from the eat-in café menu. That meant creating a packaged pancake mix and a drink mix called 'Mylie' (Australians might be able to guess the flavour). Additionally, they began partnering with other small businesses like Mae Thorani (https://www.maethorani.com/), who sells indoor plants. Mae Thorani plants were offered at checkout with the tag 'Add a plant friend – it's almost like going carbon neutral.' Hundreds of plants were sold.

Despite the fact that Nutie's events business was non-existent and the wholesale business severely diminished during the period of COVID-19 restrictions, revenue increased by 20 per cent. Rather than lose staff, three extra were hired to keep up with the increased volume of sales.

Sina and Jacques have both worked in a corporate environment. They feel that being small gave them a number of advantages in achieving so much innovation so quickly. First, they have no chain of command. They can enforce change within the same hour if they think it is the right thing to do. Second, they can both do all the jobs in the business. This means they are good judges of what innovation will work and what won't work, which in turn makes for quick, quality decision-making. Third, they have fostered a culture of innovation in their team, which has created a can-do attitude and creative approach to problem solving in the business that was needed during the period of trading restrictions. An example of this is the innovation day Nutie hold in their kitchen each week. All team members are encouraged to come up with new product ideas, they are made on the spot and there are prizes for the winners. At first the team were very cautious and worried about wasting ingredients, but now they get excited about the opportunity to be creative and contribute their ideas.

The small business *ReFRAME* model of innovation

For a small business, some of the steps of the *ReFRAME* process are less important (such as the deploy and embed transition steps), whilst others are more crucial (for example, the evidence collecting and analysis phases using objective methodology). We have adjusted the process based on research and discussion with small business retailers and industry advisors to small business retailers. We have also created some additional tools to help with the adjusted version of the process, which we will explain below.

EXERCISE

*The small business **ReFRAME** process*

What this is

The small business **ReFRAME** process (Table 11.4) has been designed based on our experience and that of many successfully innovating small business retailers we have either worked with or interviewed for this book. It will help you understand which parts of the **ReFRAME** process are most pertinent to the unique environment in small business retail.

Instructions

1   For each of the eighteen steps we have included a 'Check'. It will either simply tell you to skip this step or answer some questions to assess how you should proceed.

2   If you answer 'No' to any of the check questions in each step, then complete the actions in the 'Action' column. If you answer 'Yes' to all questions, then you can skip this step.

3   For some steps we do not suggest skipping and have listed that in the 'Check' column as 'Complete this step'.

4   If a step is listed as 'Skip this step' but there are actions in the 'Action' column, then we have provided these as optional support actions for those who want to focus on this area.

TABLE 11.4 The small business *ReFRAME* process

Stage	Step	Check	Action
Re-set the foundations	Clarify your purpose	1. Is your purpose clear and understood amongst your team and customers?	Have a coffee with yourself and complete the how to find your purpose exercise
		2. Is it referred to and used when making business decisions?	
		3. Have you checked on it with your team and customers in the last 12 mths?	
		4. Do all your business partners and/or investors understand and agree with the purpose?	
	Leadership alignment	Skip this step	
	Culture	Skip this step	To support you in fostering a strong innovation culture in small business we recommend that you: • Complete the how to find your purpose exercise • Complete the small business biases self-check exercises

(continued)

Filter the ideas	Customer value	1. Do you have a mechanism to capture ideas from the whole team, including frontline team members and customers?	Complete the small business biases self-check
	Business value	2. Do you find it easy to create disruptive innovative ideas that meet the golden rule?	Complete a filter the ideas session with key people, ensure this includes ideas or input from frontline people and customers – Chapter 5
	Aligned to purpose	3. Do you always assess new ideas by the golden rule?	Use the forced disruption cards to support this session
	Sponsors	Skip this step	
Get innovation-ready			Complete the team skills canvas to identify what skills you need for the 'thing' you are building
	Team	Complete this step	If these skills are not available in your team then ask yourself: • Can you bootstrap? If yes do so. If not, then... • Can you hire in at reasonable cost that fits the resource allocation estimates from the resources step? If yes do so. If not then... • Is this initiative so vital to the future of the business that you are willing to take on more debt or surrender equity? If yes do so. If no, parachute out of this idea and try something else.
	Resources	Complete this step	Estimate the resources for the project and ensure they are available

(continued)

TABLE 11.4 (Continued)

Stage	Step	Check	Action
			Provide seed funding for the project to begin
			Create the remaining space needed for the project
Analyse and design the solution	Narrow	1. Is the idea simple and are the specifics already obvious?	Complete the narrowing canvas exercise to get specific on your idea
	Collect evidence	Complete this step	Complete the evidence assessment tool
			Complete the evidence assessment in Figure 7.2
	Analyse and test	Complete this step	Use the small business biases self-check to support this work in Table 11.6
Make the design and scale it	Build	Complete a compressed version of this step	Complete the make the design – build exercise in Chapter 8
	Test	Complete this step. It is the most often skipped in small business but the most important to ensure the best possible outcomes for your time and money	Complete the testing card and assessment in Chapter 8
	Refine	Complete this step	Complete the make the design – refine exercise in Chapter 8

Embed as the new normal		If you have fewer than 5 stores, skip all 3 steps of this stage	Complete the support ecosystem exercise
	Transition plan and test	If you have more than 5 stores and your 'thing' is new or a significant change to an existing 'thing' (significant change is defined as a change that will require new knowledge, a new skill, or any training for humans)	Complete the transition report card creation exercises in Chapter 9
	Deploy	Complete the assessing manageable chunks assessment to ascertain whether your 'thing' is complex, standard, or simple. Is it simple?	Follow the deploying process exercise
	Embed	Is the thing working well?	Use the information on the transition report (complete one if you have not as yet) and identify how you can pivot, or parachute out of the deployment

Additional tools for the small business *ReFRAME*

For a small business owner, emotions are high. You are proud of the business you have created (for good reason) and want to see it succeed and grow. This increases the way we think about and react to perceive risk. Humans have spent millions of years analysing and preparing for obvious, visible risk. However, when it comes to uncertain and more abstract risk, we are still learning how to do that properly. Professor Daniel Gilbert posted an article that summed it up nicely:

> Our ability to duck that which is not yet coming is one of the brain's most stunning innovations, and we wouldn't have dental floss or 401(k) plans without it. But this innovation is in the early stages of development. The application that allows us to respond to visible baseballs is ancient and reliable, but the add-on utility that allows us to respond to threats that loom in an unseen future is still in beta testing.[5]

It is this not yet perfectly evolved sense of abstract risk that means we need to actively manage it. To help with that, in the following exercises you will find several additional tools for small business owners to manage that evolved sense of personal risk. As an introvert with anxiety, I can also attest to the fact that these work for those humans in corporate jobs too.

EXERCISE
Finding or checking on your purpose

What this is

Whether you have a purpose to test or want to create yours, this exercise will guide you through activities to get the right purpose to support your innovation agenda.

Instructions

1 Complete the action for each variable in Table 11.5.

2 If you are testing your current purpose, see whether the statement in the 'testing your purpose' column is correct. If it's correct, great! If not, then the actions in the 'what to do if there isn't alignment' column will help you.

3 If you are creating your purpose for the first time then after completing the action, follow the instructions in the 'creating your purpose' column.

TABLE 11.5 Finding or checking on your purpose

Variable	Action	Testing your purpose	What to do if there isn't alignment	Creating your purpose
	If you have a purpose already, follow the *testing* column, otherwise follow the *creating* column.	For each test, a great result will mean the statement in this column is correct.	If the statement wasn't correct, this is what to do next.	If the business has been just revolving around you and your ambitions, it's time to formalize your purpose.
What drives your team	Talk to some of your best performing team members. What is the purpose that drives them to produce excellence?	They all say similar things and it aligns with the company purpose.	Identify the differences between their drivers and yours. Bring some performers with different views together and discuss those differences and design a way to get greater consistency.	Capture the statements and group them into similar sentiments. Reflect on some of the reasons there may be differences between people and yourself. Proceed to collecting the 'the outside-in view'.
What the others are doing	Pick some brands that you respect and see as inspiring (in small or big ways) to your business ambition. What is their purpose?	You are as clear about your purpose as you are about theirs and find both inspiring.	Redo this exercise with your top performing people, did they agree with you? What are the characteristics of the other brand's purpose that was seen as most powerful? Use the formula below as a starter to rebuilding yours: We <do this> to <reason why you do it>. Keep evolving it until the testing statement is correct.	Break the statements down into parts. If it isn't clear, use our very basic formula We <do this> to <reason for why you do it>. Use these to help with the exercises in the workshops described in The outside-in view and What drives you.

(continued)

TABLE 11.5 (Continued)

Variable	Action	Testing your purpose	What to do if there isn't alignment	Creating your purpose
The outside-in view	Go out (yourself) and talk to as many people as you can about what your business means to the world now, and what it should mean in the future.	They were consistent with their answers and they aligned with your purpose.	Sort the answers into two groups: 1. Those that aligned with yours 2. Those that didn't. Eliminate those that aren't relevant (ie subjective or unhelpful, eg you should do it for free!). What are the key differences, what adjustments can you make to your purpose to get more alignment?	Collect the statements and group any that are similar. What are the patterns? If there were a lot of different views, why? Which had the strongest sentiment? Keep arguing for each group and either eliminate or combine the groups until you have the right parts. Form it into a sentence (one sentence). Once refined, proceed to What drives you.
What drives you	Have a coffee with yourself and write down your purpose in one short sentence. Share it with people from your business, customers, and friends and family and get them to explain it back to you.	It was easy and clear, it was authentic and everybody understood it in the same way and said positive things about it.	Get as many of the people you shared it with together in a room, get them to explain each of their answers in more detail and refine it as a group. Start by picking out key words or sentiments.	Complete the action in a room with the group. Capture key words from the group's replay of your purpose. Keep refining each part of the statement as a group.

EXERCISE

Small business biases self-check

What this is

When you have a strong emotional bond to your business and a house on the line, subjectivity is even more difficult to overcome. Use this self-check constantly throughout the process to help you maintain objectivity and maximize outcomes.

Instructions

1 Revisit the biases listed in Table 11.6.

2 Read through each bias's 'objective statement'.

3 If the statement is correct about you, you are good to go. If not, then have a look at the 'correction' column.

TABLE 11.6   Small business biases self-check

Bias	Statement	Correction
Egomania	You always ask and listen to your team or experts and trust them	1. Be more curious by asking more questions. 2. Always remind yourself that you might be wrong!
Group think	You look beyond your immediate team for feedback and ideas	As a group you need to: 1. Broaden evidence by collecting it from different sources (eg a new customer set, industry experts, etc). 2. Deepen evidence collection by spending more time collecting the reasons behind the behaviour or evidence. Use 5x why (ask why five times to get deeper evidence).
It's not fair	You seek out evidence regardless of whether it backs your point of view	You want to win, right? So listen to evidence when it tells you to stop, even if it doesn't align with your personal opinions. If you struggle still, then run more tests to collect more evidence before spending more money or time.

(continued)

TABLE 11.6 (Continued)

Bias	Statement	Correction
The doubter	You are aware of your prejudice and biases and act to overcome them	Use the heuristics and biases from Chapter 7 and reflect on your decisions and leadership behaviour. We all have most of these at times, so use examples of when you have overcome them. For any that you haven't got examples for, create a scenario and how you would overcome that bias in yourself. Constantly refresh the list with fresh examples and give yourself a score out of 10 on identifying and overcoming these biases.
Flight or fight	Fear of disruption doesn't stop you from acting or blind your objectivity	1. Do a contextual analysis of the situation. Drawing it is a good way to ensure that you can get a better picture of it. Put your business in the middle and all the things going on around it in circles. The bigger the circle, the bigger the impact on your business. Be honest, use numbers, behavioural evidence and data where possible to gauge the size of the circles. 2. Step back and think objectively about the way you're investing your and your company's energy and resources 3. Make changes as needed, but most importantly, act!
Headline seeking	Customers and business value are always the reasons behind decisions.	Every idea you pursue should use the golden rule to ensure that it is objectively the right thing to do. 1. Draw two circles on a page. I like to pretend that they are delicious cakes. 2. In circle one slice the cake up into pieces based on where your energy is being focused. Time is biggest part of energy, but as the business owner, you can spend the same amount of time on two things but bring much more energy to one of them. Make sure you account for energy.

(continued)

TABLE 11.6 (Continued)

Bias	Statement	Correction
		3. In circle two, using the golden rule of value to your customers, value to your business and alignment to your purpose, slice the cake up in sizes based on value. If you're struggling with this then I suggest finding the 'average' bit of work, the one that is somewhere in the middle. Give that a value of 1 then rank everything else compared to that. Eg if 'thing' 2 is three times the value then rank it 3, if 'thing' 3 is half the value then call it 0.5. Use these numbers to slice up that second delicious cake. 4. Compare the investment of your energy and value. This will help you define whether you're slicing your cake up in the most optimal way. 5. Eat some cake.
Fear of failure	You are willing to fail as you test new ideas to progress your business	1. Spend some time reflecting on how your business views failure and testing, and how common it is. 2. Ask your team why they think this is the situation and what could be done to improve it. 3. Assess the difference between your reflections and what you heard from your team. 4. Culture comes from the top, so if that's you then address the objections people have and create a positive conversation about testing and failure. Testing and finding failure stops you doing stupid things that waste time and money and put more risk in the business.

(continued)

TABLE 11.6 (Continued)

Bias	Statement	Correction
Blinkers on	You look outside your direct competitors for potential disruption	1. Create a table with three columns. 2. Fill the first column with who you currently think of as your competitors. 3. In the second column, list people who could potentially become your competitors. 4. In the third column, write down some brands who create experiences that your customers may start expecting from you (this is difficult, so don't worry if you initially find it challenging, an example to help you is how Uber changed the way customers expect transparency, simplicity and consistent updates of progress). 5. Highlight or circle anyone in any of the three columns that you look to in your competitor analysis. 6. Those you didn't highlight are those you should be looking at! If there are a lot there, or you expanded your list considerably, prioritize those who pose the greatest risk to you.
First serve bias	You explore and test options beyond the ones you may be enthralled by	This comes from getting excited by an idea that seems like it will solve the problem or opportunity perfectly, letting that distract you before you look beyond it for something that could be even better. Remember, by looking beyond the idea at other options you are essentially conducting a test of the initial idea you are enthralled by. This reduces risk and may uncover a better idea.
Seeking backup	You are always evidence led and constantly checking your ideas	Once enthralled by an idea you will naturally want to see if it exists or something similar so you can see if it works. Not to mention, if others are doing it, it will feel safer to you. Conduct objective evidence led testing like those set out in Chapter 7. This is what should make you feel safer proceeding with your idea.

(continued)

TABLE 11.6 (Continued)

Bias	Statement	Correction
But I know a guy?	Ideas come from everywhere, but you always collect broad and deep evidence	This is an easy one to overcome. Create a space where everyone tests anyone who uses a personal example as evidence. 'I was talking with someone the other day...' that's good, it is one singular piece of evidence. Back it up with more and from different sources to get the full picture.
Give me more data!	Evidence collection is important and you are decisive and driven for progress	When an idea is risky and your house is on the line, it is tempting to take it slow and keep collecting evidence. It is rarely the case that you have time, so: 1. You will never get a perfect set of evidence that proves unequivocally that something will work, so let go of that concept. 2. Build your version of the measured and driven mindset from Chapter 6. 3. Remember there are opportunities to parachute out or pivot your 'thing' at any point in the process, so if the evidence suggests to proceed, then you should proceed.
Choice blindness	If the evidence or testing suggests you need to pivot or parachute out, you do	1. Reflect on why you make the decisions to continue. 2. Talk to others about their opinion, make it a safe place, chances are that you are the reason! 3. Create a plan to intercept yourself when you make these choices and ensure you are acting objectively.
Myopic retailing	You have a balanced approach on short- and long-term ideas	1. Reflect on what percentage of your energy and resources is spent on ideas that are to deliver immediate metric improvements and have fast build times (short-term innovation). 2. Do the same for longer-term strategic innovation such as technology changes or new product or services development. 3. Finally, what about big disruptive ideas that sit outside your core business? 4. Assess those against a benchmark (we recommend 70/20/10).

(continued)

TABLE 11.6 (Continued)

Bias	Statement	Correction
		5. Write down some reasons as to why, risks and potential benefits of changing this investment to the benchmark. 6. Try some little nudges to your investment to get closer to the benchmark and assess the impact on your business.
Stereotyping	You challenge each other about how you group humans and their traits	Behavioural based groupings are much more helpful in making performance adjustments or building innovation. Humans make choices and behave in certain ways. To grow your business you need to think about intercepting those choices by reflecting on their behavioural traits and how you can add value to those. 1. Write down some examples of the stereotypes you apply now (common ones are age or location). 2. For each item, list out why you use them and what value they add to your work. 3. Try and produce behavioural based groupings that still account for all the same customers. 4. Introduce this thinking into a project or campaign and assess the differences in effectiveness and continue to refine your use of this style of grouping. A common example to help you could be 'young people are digitally native'. We know this isn't true in every case and isn't helpful in influencing our work. In other words, we can't do anything with it or if we try we risk not getting the outcomes we want. We are better off here removing the age definition and simply using 'all digitally native people'. With this segment definition, we can calculate the value of that group of people, how well we perform in that segment, and their behaviours and traits that we can intercept to improve our performance.
Engine stop	You are decisive when you need to be and always move at pace	Follow the same steps as 'give me more data'.

Conclusion

Small retail businesses are a substantial and important part of the retail industry. They are different in many ways to medium and large size retailers, but they compete in the same market and must be prepared to change when the market demands it.

Innovation is easier for small retail businesses in some respects but harder in others. Small retail businesses must leverage their strengths and mitigate the areas where they are challenged to be successful innovators. Suppliers, partners and governments have an important role to play in fostering innovation in small retail businesses; however, this must be done in a way that recognizes that small businesses are different.

All the stages of the *ReFRAME* process are relevant to small business retailers, but many of the steps of the *ReFRAME* can be skipped or compressed. Successful innovation will still be a product of process, even if parts of that process are sometimes implicit.

Small businesses face none of the organizational barriers to innovation faced by larger retailers, but they have equally compelling barriers to overcome. First is the emotional connection they have to their businesses, which can get in the way of making objective decisions based on evidence. Second is the lack of space (time and resources) to conceive and execute a programme of innovation. In both cases the modified *ReFRAME* process and the exercises in this chapter should be of assistance. In addition, small business retailers will sometimes need to consider enlisting external help either from the numerous free or low-cost programmes run by governments and service providers or from a specialized small retail business advisor.

If you are a small retail business operator:

- Block out an hour and complete our 'Finding or checking on your purpose' and 'Small business biases self-check' exercises (pages 252 and 255 respectively) to see how innovation-ready you are. What changes do you need to make to the way you operate before you start innovating?
- Join a small business group, lean on suppliers or simply go online to find out what is happening in the world of retail.
- Run a brainstorm with the team to develop a list of initiatives that would improve the business.
- Get some external opinions as to which of your ideas are the most viable and how they can be executed.
- Start the small business *ReFRAME* process.

We have now demonstrated how retail innovation can be executed in small, medium and large businesses and in situations where an urgent and compelling need presents itself. For all retailers, regardless of size, the job is still not done. Now the full innovation muscle is in place to make 'things' happen, we should use it more regularly. To do that, we need to make innovation not just a collection of projects but how you do business. In the next chapter we show how to weave innovation into the operating fabric of a retail business so that innovation becomes perpetual not episodic.

Notes

1 European Commission (undated) SME definition [Online] https://ec.europa.eu/growth/smes/business-friendly-environment/sme-definition_en (archived at https://perma.cc/EU4P-Q4T9)

2 McIntyre, G (2020) What is the SBA's definition of small business (and why)? Fundera, 27 May [Online] https://www.fundera.com/blog/sba-definition-of-small-business (archived at https://perma.cc/AZK4-V6AV)

3 ASBFEO (2019) Small Business Counts: Small business in the Australian economy, ASBFEO, Commonwealth of Australia [Online] https://www.asbfeo.gov.au/sites/default/files/Small_Business_Statistical_Report-Final.pdf (archived at https://perma.cc/G5HZ-FLRN)

4 McIntyre, G (2020) What percentage of small businesses fail? (And other need-to-know stats), Fundera, 25 April [Online] https://www.fundera.com/blog/what-percentage-of-small-businesses-fail (archived at https://perma.cc/VTF2-P9GA)

5 Gilbert, D (2016) If only gay sex caused global warming, LA Times, 2 July [Online] https://www.latimes.com/archives/la-xpm-2006-jul-02-op-gilbert2-story.html (archived at https://perma.cc/KS4K-PEJ2)

12

Weaving innovation into the operating fabric of your business

Introduction

Innovation is fragile. Sometimes it can disappear as quickly as it came. It's a bit like the sun disappearing behind the clouds on a summer's day. When the sun disappears it's a purely natural process – there are clouds in the sky and a wind is blowing. In contrast, when innovation disappears from a retail business it is because of the deliberate decisions of humans. It may be that a new CEO wants to do things differently, it may be that the management team sees innovation as a single idea rather than a new way of doing business, or it could be that hubris in the team created by great results convinces them that they don't need to change anymore. Whatever the reason, if innovation stops after one or two successful projects you have not finished the job. The business has not been reframed. Innovation is not a destination, it is a process that must be woven into the fabric of your business, so you are always ready to respond when changes in the environment create opportunities or threats.

THE IMPACT OF INNOVATION NOT BEING IN THE FABRIC
OF A BUSINESS
A story from Andrew

A few years ago, I was at the peak of delivery of innovation to a retail business and the sun was shining. Our numbers were good and what we were doing was getting global recognition. I was giving tours of our stores to people from all over the world as we showed what we had done and turned our retail experiences into products to sell. Whilst doing this I knew something that others did not. Our innovation pipeline was closed. Funding for innovation was being cut and instead we had been told to focus on taking cost from the business.

The result was predictable. As funding was reduced for innovation so were the outcomes from our remaining innovation pipeline. When our core KPI changed from innovation to reducing costs the team stopped work on projects that were in progress, cancelled others in planning and instead focused on how to reduce the cost footprint. Cutting costs caused increased wait times, negative impacts on customer and employee experience, and left our ability to respond to customer imperatives greatly diminished. Innovation that once thrived was suffocated and slowly those innovation-focused few that were holding the innovation ideal together left the ship. The sun had gone behind the clouds.

In this chapter we will learn how to overcome the fragility of retail innovation by weaving innovation into the operating fabric of your business. This can be achieved by focusing on *legacy*, not the short-term success of a project, linking innovation to *learning*, and creating structural *innovation co-dependency* in the management team.

Some will still say that innovation drains the resources of a business and argue that periods of rest from innovation are necessary so that profits can be replenished. They would say that innovation is better done in sprints rather than some sort of perpetual ultra-marathon with no end. The truth is that the biggest drain on resources is going into decline. History shows us that once innovation stops, competition catches up, customers defect and retailers are left to close stores, lay off staff and cut costs just to stay alive. It's the retail death spiral in which everybody loses except the surviving competitors. To illustrate, it's worth reflecting on a classic case where a dominant incumbent lost its innovation nerve and suffered terminal consequences.

CASE STUDY
Blockbuster vs Netflix 2000–10

In 2000 Blockbuster was the largest video store operator in the USA.[1] Under
relatively new CEO John Antioco, it had gained an edge over its rivals by introducing
an innovative revenue share scheme with the movie studios that allowed it to stock
up to support new releases. By the end of 2000 Blockbuster's sales had grown by
over 11 per cent from the previous year to almost $5 billion (Table 12.1).

In 1997 Reed Hastings and Marc Randolph founded Netflix. Netflix had no stores
and delivered movies by mail. This was made possible by the small form factor of the
then-new DVD discs. Netflix offered a much bigger range to its customers than the
average video store, while avoiding the expense of maintaining thousands of bricks
and mortar retail outlets. In 2000 Netflix introduced a monthly subscription service
and Cine Match, which suggested movies to customers based on their ordering
history. Netflix was still a tiny company in comparison to Blockbuster and was losing
more money than it was taking in revenue (Table 12.2).

In 2000 the founders of Netflix met with Antioco and his team to propose a deal
to run an online by-mail business for Blockbuster. Later in the same year Netflix was
offered for sale to Blockbuster for $50 million. Both deals were rejected and

TABLE 12.1 Blockbuster sales and income 1999–2010

	Sales ($'000)	Growth	EBITDA ($'000)	Net income ($'000)
1999	4,463,500		$1,189,100	−$69,200
2000	4,960,100	11.10%	$1,238,800	−$75,900
2001	5,156,700	4.00%	$1,079,800	−$240,300
2002	5,565,900	7.90%	$1,612,800	−$1,621,100
2003	5,911,700	6.20%	$2,996,300	−$978,700
2004	5,932,500	0.40%	$2,763,200	−$1,248,800
2005	5,721,800	−3.60%	$1,413,700	−$583,900
2006	5,522,200	−3.50%	$987,700	$50,500
2007	5,314,000	−3.80%	−$573,400	−$73,800
2008	5,065,400	−4.70%	$107,400	−$374,100
2009	4,051,100	−20.00%	$1,054,000	−$558,200
2010	3,240,700	−20.00%	$469,100	−$268,000

SOURCE ADVFN

TABLE 12.2 Netflix sales and income 2000–10

	Sales ($'000)	Growth	EBITDA ($'000)	Net income ($'000)
2000	35,894	N/A	−$37,725	−$57,363
2001	75,912	111.50%	−$7,994	−$39,182
2002	152,806	101.30%	$15,804	−$20,948
2003	270,410	77.00%	$55,463	$6,512
2004	500,611	85.10%	$107,558	$21,595
2005	682,213	36.30%	$109,991	$42,027
2006	996,660	46.10%	$223,026	$48,839
2007	1,205,340	20.90%	$317,431	$66,608
2008	1,364,661	13.20%	$364,342	$83,026
2009	1,670,269	22.40%	$449,473	$115,860
2010	2,162,625	29.50%	$622,336	$160,853

SOURCE ADVFN

Blockbuster instead pursued delivery of movies on demand with Enron Broadband Services.[2]

In 2001 Netflix began to turn the tables on Blockbuster. It struck its own revenue-sharing arrangements to help build range. It enjoyed a seven-fold increase in sales between 2000 and 2003. A successful initial public offering (IPO) in 2002 significantly eased Netflix's debt burden and in 2003 it announced its first profit. Blockbuster's growth was slowing and profit was replaced by large losses. Antioco's team began to innovate.

In 2004 Blockbuster launched its own DVD by-mail delivery service called Total Access. Total Access offered customers more benefits than a Netflix subscription. Every subscriber received bonus vouchers redeemable in-store and could also return movies in-store if they wished. Antioco announced a bold ambition to change the purpose of the video store. 'Our mission right now is to transform Blockbuster from a place you go to rent a movie to a place you go to rent or buy movies or games new or used, pay by the day, pay by the month, online or in store'.[3] In 2005 late fees were abolished.

The innovations worked. By the end of 2006 Blockbuster had two million Total Access subscribers and announced its first profit for some time.

Some Blockbuster stakeholders were not aligned with Antioco's vision.[4] Activist shareholder Carl Ichan thought more value could be extracted from the business by focusing on the stores and cost control than through innovation. Ichan launched a proxy fight to gain control of the board, and did so in 2005.

Antioco was replaced in 2007 by former 7-Eleven CEO Jim Keyes. Under Keyes the benefits of Total Access, which by then had grown to 3.6 million subscribers, were wound back. Half a million subscribers were lost in one quarter in 2007. Meanwhile, Netflix continued to innovate, finally introducing a video streaming service in the same year, five years after Blockbuster had originally planned to do so.

Over the next three years Blockbuster pursued a strategy of cost cutting, closing stores, doubling down on marketing tactics that had worked in the past and outwardly ignoring the threat posed by Netflix. By 2010 Blockbuster sales had fallen to almost half what they had been in 2004. On 23 September 2010 Blockbuster filed for Chapter 11 bankruptcy protection, declaring $930 million in secured and unsecured debt and a market capitalization of only $24 million.

Netflix kept innovating. In 2011, worried that its lack of focus on streaming had allowed new entrants to gain a foothold, Netflix split its by-mail business from the streaming business. In a blog post explaining the changes, Reed Hastings offered an insight into the challenges retailers face in weaving innovation into the operating fabric of their business, especially after becoming successful:

> In hindsight, I slid into arrogance based upon past success... My greatest fear at Netflix has been that we wouldn't make the leap from success in DVDs to success in streaming. Most companies that are great at something – like AOL dialup or Borders bookstores – do not become great at new things people want (streaming for us) because they are afraid to hurt their initial business. Eventually these companies realize their error of not focusing enough on the new thing, and then the company fights desperately and hopelessly to recover. Companies rarely die from moving too fast, and they frequently die from moving too slowly.[5]

Legacy

The New Zealand rugby team, the All Blacks, are famous for their team culture. One of the principles that guides the group is based on the Maori cultural principle of *Whakapapa*. It means to put yourself into the wider context of existence and to be a good ancestor by respecting what you have been given and give back something stronger. Every player knows the history of the number they wear and has an ambition to give it on to the next person having made it stronger, wanting that person to make it stronger still. This has inspired the team to an incredible level of success, including a record for the most consecutive test wins at home, a 47-match winning streak achieved between 2009 and 2017 that included going through all of 2013 without losing a match home or away.[6]

If you have run some successful innovation projects or been involved in a sustained period of innovation in a retail business, you will know how good that feels. I think you can probably equate it with going on a 47-match unbeaten run at home or being unbeaten home and away in a whole season. If we know our retail victories have been due to innovation what could be better than leaving behind a legacy of innovation through processes and culture embedded so deeply in the business that they cannot easily be dislodged?

Building a legacy may seem like a distraction from running your current innovation programme, but building that legacy will also deliver results in the short term. When you set out to build a legacy for the long term your team will see your current programme as part of a bigger picture. They will see your motives as doing good rather than looking good. This will help recruit more people to the cause, create better leadership and sponsorship styles within your project teams and ultimately deliver innovation outcomes faster. Pursuing a purpose-led quest to create a legacy of innovation will also foster higher levels of trust in the new systems and processes you develop from their intended internal customers.

Some will say that aspiring to build a legacy is all about ego and that is not as important as the welfare of the company. The problem is that the alternative (not leaving a legacy of innovation) is much less attractive both professionally and personally. Without a legacy of innovation, retailers will continue to innovate in fits and starts or be vulnerable to stopping innovation completely under the influence of new leadership or new strategies. If this happens you are likely to experience the pain that many of us have felt when businesses we helped become market-leading innovators fall back to the pack or, even worse, disappear completely. Creating a legacy of innovation not only gives the business a better chance of success, it will also make your CV a lot easier to write.

Learning

Disruption is a normal part of retail. Every disruption in the external environment creates an opportunity for retailers, which can become a threat if they do not respond. The bigger the disruption, the bigger the opportunity or threat and the greater the need to innovate. Heraclitus, the Greek philosopher, is attributed with the saying 'Change is the only constant in life.' Retailers cannot expect to ever reach a place where disruption in the external environment stops and they can take a break from innovation. More disruption of the retail environment in the future is not just likely, it is guaranteed.

To be prepared for the perpetual disruption of the retail environment, retailers need to commit to a culture of continuous learning. Continuous learning means challenging how things are being done and why they exist, questioning the customer, the product, the people, the processes to ensure that you are always aware of the environment surrounding your brand and are able to respond to changes in it. This ongoing focus on learning creates an organization that can respond faster and innovate better. In other words, learning and innovation go hand in hand.

Having the skill to take advantage of one disruption in the external environment does not mean you will recognize the next one unless you have a culture of continuous learning. Sears was founded in 1893. Until the 1980s it was one of the most innovative retailers in the world.[7] Sears' initial success was founded on leveraging the mail service to bring a large selection of goods to small-town America through its catalogue. In the 1930s it became renowned for innovative merchandising and cutting-edge wide aisle layouts. After the Second World War, Sears was one of the first to enter the suburban shopping mall (offering pick-up for mail order catalogue customers), which helped it become America's biggest retailer. But somewhere along the line Sears stopped learning. It missed the emergence of supply chain efficiency and collaboration that allowed Walmart to offer lower prices and eventually take Sears' number one sales crown in 1990. Sears also missed the emergence of ecommerce and omnichannel shopping and may not be in business at all by the time you read this.

Whether you think Sears' decline can be attributed to failures in analysing data, reading trends, strategic leadership, or negotiation tactics, the point is that no business, even one trying to innovate in their own way, can do so without constant learning. We define learning as the acquiring of knowledge that enables a greater understanding of your business, its context, and its performance that enables better choices. This means that it does not have to involve a change in behaviour but must include one if what you've learned dictates it.

EXERCISE
The innovation learning test

What this is

To ascertain how well your business learns, use the following test. You will need to find at least five examples of events that have occurred over the last six months that fit the following criteria:

1 **New information became available:** It does not matter whether you discovered it, it was given to you, or it was discovered outside of your organization from a source such as a news outlet.

2 **It had some impact to your business or its context:** A good example is how Uber changed people's expectations on transparency of a service delivery. This impacted many sectors of the economy, including retail.

This exercise follows the rules of five. Find at least five examples that fit the criteria and get at least five people to do the assessment. This will give you a good indication on your organization's ability to learn.

Instructions

Read the statements in Table 12.3 carefully and then use this scale to score each learning area:

1 This statement does not reflect our organization in any significant way.

2 There are parts of the business that do this, but it isn't consistently applied or impactful.

3 This is done in parts of the organization and does have some impact, but we aren't putting large amounts of organizational energy into improving it.

4 This statement reflects most of our organization and has a good impact, and we are working on improving the area.

5 This is a key strength and is consistently and impactfully used in our business.

TABLE 12.3   The innovation learning test

Learning area	Statement	Score
Knowledge	New information is received either passively (through sharing) or actively (through searching) consistently throughout the organization and we are learn-it-alls, not know-it-alls	
External curiosity	Our organization encourages people to read, learn through courses and content, attend conferences and events and share that back to the organization to ensure that we are learning from the best in the industry	
Historic curiosity	We know what has and hasn't worked in the past and pass on stories of past strategies to ensure that we always learn from organizational history	
Imperative management	We identify, define, select and solve the right imperatives (commercial or human drivers) using objective evidence-led decision-making processes	
When things go wrong	Failure is embraced as part of our innovation strategy, and we have organizational structures to learn from errors and share that learning openly in the business	
Organizational performance	We have objective structures in place that assess organizational performance and learning and put in place action plans to improve as required and is a shared responsibility across the organization	

Now plot your scores on the scale in Figure 12.1 and track over time.

FIGURE 12.1   Your innovation learning test results

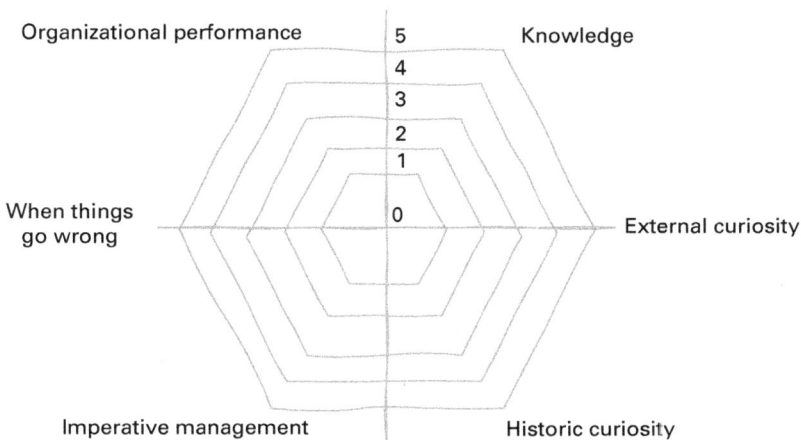

Once you have your score you have the blueprint to help you build stronger organizational learning. Good learning systems must incorporate organizational learning as well as constant individual learning. Most organizations have annual reviews of individuals, but rarely conduct annual reviews of business processes. We instead lump that in with the individual whose name is above the door. This creates a culture of defensiveness and subjectivity rather than one of insatiable curiosity.

Satya Nadella, CEO of Microsoft, embarked on a learning ambition as part of that business's innovation transformation he led. He asked, 'How can we build a business of learn-it-alls instead of know-it-alls?'[8] Having a business full of people who constantly want to learn promotes a creative culture, embraces failure as learning, and promotes a higher level of curiosity with each other and the world around them. The result is an organization that supports innovation episodes but also injects innovation behaviours into the business. When retailers become learn-it-alls they help weave innovation into the operating fabric of their business.

A common short-term fix to organizational learning gaps are consultants. This is not always a bad decision. Some consulting companies are dedicated to building long-lasting change rather than just short-term injections of results that seem appealing, particularly when the board or the market are breathing down your back waiting for something that resembles growth. Whoever you chose to help you, the changes must stick. A culture of learning must be embedded.

Innovation co-dependency

One of the most common times for a retailer to lose its innovation zeal is when it changes CEO. Another is when innovation is championed by one function of the business but is stopped when another function gains the ascendancy. We don't need to give examples – we're sure you can think of some from your own career. One company that has continued to innovate over the tenure of a number of CEOs and avoided functional competition in innovation is McDonald's Australia. McDonald's Australia has been recognized as one of Australia's most innovative retailers. International innovations like McCafé, packaging with nutritional information and the introduction of healthy menu choices have their origins in Australia. McDonald's Australia also pioneered the use of delivery via Uber and customer self-service.

According to former CIO Henry Shiner, one of the keys to consistently delivering innovation at McDonald's has been the structural co-dependence of the various functions of the business through a series of interlocking internal boards that provide direction for most of the operations of the business.[9] The 'franchise board' has the responsibility of reviewing franchisee performance, approving renewals and recruiting new franchisees. The 'menu board', which includes franchisee representatives, deals with any changes in food or processes. The 'IT board' deals with any IT development needed to support the business. All the boards contain members of the executive team and the CEO.

The IT board was instituted when Henry Shiner entered the business in 2007. The previous IT committee met infrequently and when they did they were limited to reviewing project progress and budgets. The result was slow delivery of new projects and a fragmented approach to innovation. Frustrated executives often tried to solve their own problems in isolation from the needs of the rest of the business by approaching technology vendors independently. Shiner recognized that IT was a key facilitator of innovation in the modern era of retailing and that he needed to create co-dependency with his peers if McDonald's was to move forward.

The new IT board consisted of Shiner, the CEO and all the CEO's direct reports. The first thing that was agreed was that, before any supplier could be considered, they must be approved by the IT board as being compliant. This solved the technical compatibility problems created by executives sourcing their own technology solutions, but it also eroded functional competition between executives. The next requirement was that every initiative to be considered supported the strategy of the business and its values. This helped further align the executive team.

A template was developed so that all the basic information needed to consider an initiative for approval could be reviewed by the board at its regular meeting. An executive manager had to sponsor an initiative for it to be considered. Each executive manager now had a stake in creating the overall programme either as a sponsor or an approver. This led to co-dependence within the IT board and shared accountability within the executive team for delivery of projects.

Shiner says, 'Overall, the introduction of the IT board accelerated innovation at McDonald's and forced a culture change in the executive management team from "We solve our own problems" to "We solve the businesses problems together by supporting the strategy and vision".'

EXERCISE
Identifying innovation barriers

List all the innovation projects your company has attempted over the last three years. What were the barriers to implementing the project three years ago? What have been the barriers to implementing your most recent project? Are there any differences? Over the three-year period, is your success rate improving? Is it getting easier or is each project just as hard?

Results

If the barriers to innovation in your business are the same as three years ago you are still at the start of your innovation journey. Use the **ReFRAME** process to diagnose where the problems lie. Is it, for instance, ongoing lack of alignment in the executive team, poor process in the selection of projects to pursue, old-school approval processes that demand too much and take too long, or poorly formed innovation teams with poor resourcing and sponsorship? Whatever the reasons, your organization needs to go back to innovation basics and **ReFRAME**.

If the barriers to innovation have changed, that may mean you have made progress. Perhaps the management team are now aligned and the process of selecting projects is better, but design or scalability are the problem. Use the **ReFRAME** process to isolate the issues and keep the improvement going.

If it is getting harder to get innovation projects up and your success rate is getting worse, it would suggest your business is going backward as an innovator. This is the beginning of a disaster. While in the short term your results may be good, should the environment change, or another crisis hit, you will be less equipped to respond to it than you were three years ago. It is time to shock the team into action or look for a new place to work.

If you have been able to get more projects up and running, it is getting easier and your success rate is better now it is time to weave innovation into the operating fabric of your business.

Conclusion

Innovation is fragile but enthralling. Sometimes it shines for a few brief episodes then disappears behind the clouds as organizations revert to pursuing other agendas like efficiency. A successful episode or two of innovation is not enough. Retailers need to weave innovation into the operating fabric of their business to have any chance of being able to adapt to disruption and crises in the external environment. Disruption and crises have occurred throughout retail history and will inevitably occur again. Winning retailers learn to see disruption and crises as opportunities not threats.

The three key threads to be woven into the fabric of the business are *legacy*, *learning* and *innovation co-dependency*. These three things ensure retail organizations focus on the long term as well as the success of individual projects, continue to be curious and ask the questions 'What can we improve?' and 'What have we learned?', and replace the ebb and flow of functional dominance in innovation with collaboration and mutual obligation. Retail leaders and boards must take responsibility for weaving these threads to ensure their organizations remain resilient, whatever challenges the environment presents.

The challenge for the weavers of innovation is to ensure that the natural equilibrium of organizations is operating efficiently. Innovation represents variation and is therefore incorrectly perceived as the enemy of efficiency. Organizations will naturally revert to their natural operating rhythm when an innovation project is deployed successfully. There will be moments when, as leader, you will need to push through the natural tendency of the organization to take a rest, enjoy the applause that a very successful project creates and keep weaving. To be successful, retailers must become comfortable with the discomfort associated with constant change. Successful teams need to share the limelight and leaders need to be vigilant not only to protect the present but also to protect the future by keeping the organization grounded.

When it comes to the innovation imperative facing retailers, there is plenty of advice flying around. Sometimes it is important to reflect on what some great retailers have learned on their respective journeys in the past. Whether they were fighting for their brands or aggressively growing them, every generation sees disruption and faces challenges. In his book *Onward: How Starbucks fought for its life without losing its soul*, Howard Schultz put together this simile on how a plan for survival grew into a legacy of innovation culture and learning:

> Grow with discipline. Balance intuition with rigor. Innovate around the core. Don't embrace the status quo. Find new ways to see. Never expect a silver bullet. Get your hands dirty. Listen with empathy and overcommunicate with transparency. Tell your story, refusing to let others define you. Use authentic experiences to inspire. Stick to your values, they are your foundation. Hold people accountable,

but give them the tools to succeed. Make the tough choices; it's how you execute that counts. Be decisive in times of crisis. Be nimble. Find truth in trials and lessons in mistakes. Be responsible for what you see, hear, and do. Believe.[10]

That is the *outcome* you can achieve when you **ReFRAME** your retail business. The best way to do that is to follow the advice on leadership from Sam Walton:

> My role has been to pick good people and give them the maximum authority and responsibility.[11]

Now it is time to turn inspiration into action as we conclude this book and get on with making retail innovation happen. We wish you all the best as you **ReFRAME** your version of retail, and we are here to help however we can.

Notes

1   Antioco, J (2011) Blockbuster's former CEO on sparring with an activist shareholder (how I did it), *Harvard Business Review*, **89** (4), p 39

2   Carr, A (2010) Blockbuster bankruptcy: A decade of decline, Fast Company [Online] https://www.fastcompany.com/1690654/blockbuster-bankruptcy-decade-decline (archived at https://perma.cc/T4XV-6BB2)

3   Gopal, B, Gothandapani, B and Chattergee, C (2008) *The Price War: Netflix vs Blockbuster*, IBS Research Centre, Hyderabad

4   Antioco, J (2011) Blockbuster's former CEO on sparring with an activist shareholder (how I did it), *Harvard Business Review*, **89** (4), p 39

5   Kaplan, S (2012) Don't get Netflixed: Your current business model isn't going to last much longer, in *The Business Model Innovation Factory*, Wiley, Hoboken, NJ, pp 1–16

6   EPSN (undated) Most consecutive wins at home [Online] http://stats.espnscrum.com/scrum/rugby/records/team/most_consecutive_wins_home.html?id=1;type=class (archived at https://perma.cc/ZN9F-Z6QS)

7   Lansner, J (2018) Death of Sears: Early innovator of shopping from home is now bankrupt of fresh ideas, *Los Angeles Daily News*

8   Walsh, S (2018) 10 tips for continuous learning, Learning Teams [Online] https://blog.anderspink.com/2018/04/10-tips-continous-learning/ (archived at https://perma.cc/KEU3-3GQR)

9   Personal communication with author 11 October 2019.

10 Schultz, H (2011) *Onward: How Starbucks fought for its life without losing its soul*, Wiley, Hoboken, NJ, p 309

11 Walton, S (1993) *Made in America: My story*, Bantam Books, New York, p 147

Conclusion

Throughout history retail has been defined by disruption and crises. Those retailers that adapt prosper, while those that cannot or will not die. Which retailer do you want to be? It is a choice. One choice is to see change as a threat, double down on what has always worked for you, cut costs, complain to the market about the economy, taxes, rents, wages or unfair competition and do nothing to adapt to the new trading environment. It is a choice many retailers have made, including many well-known brand names that no longer exist.

The other choice is to see disruption as an opportunity, create the culture and processes in your business to facilitate innovation and *ReFRAME*. Innovation is not about charismatic leaders, great technology, or new store design (although they can be great facilitators). It is not even about knowing what is going on in the world and what the winning trends are (although constant learning should be ingrained in an innovation culture). It is about implementing processes that weave innovation into the operating fabric of your business. Processes that allow you to bring ideas to market that benefit your business, your customers and align with your purpose as quickly as disruption presents the opportunity. Retail innovation is not about knowing 'what', it is about knowing 'how'.

It's easy to feel powerless, frustrated and a victim when well-known retail brands fail, when disruption and crises are relentless, when the media presents a perpetually negative narrative about the industry, when your own organization just doesn't seem to get it, when inaction leads to round after round of expense cutting and job losses or when a project you have sponsored fails. But if you want to be in the vanguard of retail innovation you must *ReFRAME*.

When you *ReFRAME*, instead of feeling powerless you feel empowered, instead of feeling frustrated you feel fulfilled, instead of feeling like the victim you feel like the victor. You will soon stop losing customers and start winning them again, stop making excuses for daily sales results and start celebrating growth, stop the cycle of expense cuts and start increasing opportunities for your team and suppliers. Success is never guaranteed in life but applying a *ReFRAME* puts you, not the environment, in control of your destiny.

By definition, a disrupted business environment means navigating through a set of conditions that you have never experienced before. What the industry has lacked is a guide to help navigate disrupted environments and the *ReFRAME* process is it. There are six stages. They are sequential and none can be missed. One break in the chain can end your innovation quest.

1 *Re*-set the foundations of your business to become a launchpad for the quest. That means aligning the executive team and board around a clearly defined business purpose and culture of innovation.

2 Create a process for *f*iltering the right ideas to invest in. To be considered for investment an idea must deliver something positive for customers, a return to the business and align with your purpose. (This is the Golden Rule.)

3 Get innovation-*r*eady. That means forming a cross-functional implementation team with all the space they need and the right sponsorship to become successful.

4 *A*nalyse and design the actual 'thing'. This involves taking the innovation idea, narrowing down on the specifics, collecting evidence and assessing whether it will work in its intended environment. You can parachute out at any point from here onwards if the 'thing' does not look like delivering on the objectives you have set for it. Better to fail fast than slow.

5 *M*ake the design and scale it. This is an iterative process of ideate/build, test and refine over a multiple of levels of maturity.

6 *E*mbed your 'thing' as the new normal. This requires that a transition plan, a deployment process, and your 'thing' becomes business as usual.

All these steps may seem straightforward, but it is, with some very notable exceptions, uncommon to find retailers who are successfully innovating or following a structured process of innovation.

When that is all done, there is no time to bask in the glory of a successfully deployed project because the work is not finished. Innovation processes need to be embedded into the operating fabric of your business so that innovation becomes perpetual, not episodic. Once that is done you will have achieved your quest and left a lasting legacy of innovation in your business.

You will encounter many obstacles on your innovation quest but always remember that the risks of not innovating are much higher than those of innovating. Innovation is hard for individuals and organizations. Some say that innovation is particularly hard for retailers because of the short-term thinking and focus on execution baked into our DNA. On top of that you'll encounter resistance from members of the team who believe the solution to every problem is what has worked in the past, who want to deploy their pet project, who want to skip steps and just get on with deployment or want to slow down, take a rest and replenish profits.

You can overcome all these difficulties by demonstrating that innovation is not a dark art but an identifiable and repeatable process. Nobody does process better than a retailer and if innovation is a process, retailers can become the best innovators in the world. Remind your colleagues of examples of brands that didn't innovate and faced the consequences as well as brands that did **ReFRAME** and thrived in the same market. There are plenty of examples in this book. When you have a day filled with disappointment or disagreement, go home and relax. Do what you need to do to recuperate. You have a plan, and you will get to your destination. Some days are hard, but others will be joyous. And the results will soon speak for themselves.

As leaders in retail, we are in an incredible position as we steer brands that play big roles in the lives of our customers, and the decisions we make are having ever-increasingly visible impacts to the way people perceive us. Retail is an industry that has long been incredibly important, but often does not get the recognition for the duty it plays in society every day. The importance of the retail industry and the resilience of those in it was demonstrated in 2020 when billions of people were forced to stay at home in isolation in the midst of a global pandemic. The retail industry, its workers and delivery drivers at risk to their own health, got on with their job and ensured society was fed, watered and had everything else it needed to keep functioning.

We have spent most of our careers in the retail industry because we love it. We wrote this book to change the conversation around retail and create a movement for change. Retail is not dying (it's growing), online isn't killing the industry (it's growing the industry) but nevertheless the gloom created by the procession of well-known brands faltering or going out of business is palpable. This is not helpful. It stops talented young people choosing retail as a career and it stymies investment. Retail needs a positive narrative that change is possible. Once we become capable of change, we can shift the conversation about the industry from failure and loss toward opportunity and hope.

We would love you to join us and create a worldwide network of retailers who **ReFRAME**. We call ourselves *Uncommonists*. You might have questions, ideas, challenges to our thoughts and process, and if so then you should contact us directly or set up a time for us to have a chat. We promise we are friendly, have a good sense of humour and are always happy to talk shop. Our opinions are always strong, but loosely held. As yours should be now that you have got that measured and driven mindset from Chapter 8!

When we set out to write this book, we did it because we wanted to play a bigger role in making the industry we love better, stronger and more successful. Spending time researching and engaging with retailers from all over the world to help create this process and write this book has been a privilege. However, none of that will come close to the feeling we will get when we see retailers everywhere aligning behind their strong core purpose and building an innovation engine around it. Retail is a gift of a place to work. Let's make it better.

INDEX

Note: Numbers within main headings are filed as spelt out; acronyms and 'Mc' are filed as presented; '@' is ignored for filing purposes. Page locators in *italics* denote information contained within Figures or Tables.

From 4 December 2025 the EU Responsible Person (GPSR) is:
eucomply oÜ, Pärnu mnt. 139b – 14, 11317 Tallinn, Estonia
www.eucompliancepartner.com

www.ingramcontent.com/pod-product-compliance
Lightning Source LLC
Chambersburg PA
CBHW041207220326
41597CB00030BA/5081